Working With the Problem Drinker

A Solution-Focused Approach

INSOO KIM BERG

SCOTT D. MILLER

Brief Family Therapy Center
Milwaukee, Wisconsin

W. W. Norton & Company
New York   London

A NORTON PROFESSIONAL BOOK

The text of this book was composed in California. Composition by Bytheway Typesetting Services, Inc. Manufacturing by Haddon Craftsmen, Inc.

Library of Congress Cataloging-in-Publication Data

Berg, Insoo Kim.
    Working with the problem drinker : a solution-focused approach /
Insoo Kim Berg and Scott D. Miller.
        p.   cm.
    Includes bibliographical references and index.
    ISBN 0-393-70134-4
    1. Alcoholism — Treatment.   2. Solution-focused therapy.
I. Miller, Scott D.   II. Title.
    [DNLM: 1. Alcoholism — rehabilitation.   2. Physician-Patient
Relations.   WM 274 B493w]
RC565.B465   1992
616.86'106 — dc20
DNLM/DLC   92-12746   CIP

W.W. Norton & Company, Inc., 500 Fifth Avenue, New York, N.Y. 10110
W.W. Norton & Company, Ltd., 10 Coptic Street, London WC1A 1PU

        5   6   7   8   9   0

To Steve de Shazer, my husband and colleague

IKB

To my parents, Paul and Darlene Miller

SDM

Foreword

If this book had been written twenty years ago, it could only have been viewed as pure heresy. Today, however, many individuals are seeking and entering alcohol treatment at a much earlier stage of their drinking careers. This shift has somewhat changed the alcohol-related clinical profile from one almost exclusively dominated by the 'alcoholic' to one in which the 'alcohol abuser' or 'problem drinker' is growing in prominence. Consequently, new and innovative treatment approaches that reflect this change have been called for.

In response, Berg and Miller have developed a set of useful step-by-step techniques that are commonsensical and deceptively simple to apply. The 'miracle question' alone is an elegant and powerful tool.

More importantly, however, the application of the techniques outlined in this book requires an alteration in a mind set that has traditionally held a pessimistic view of this population. In this regard, the authors draw heavily on the influence of the late Milton H. Erickson, who viewed all patients as being fundamentally healthy and eschewed therapeutic approaches based on notions of psychopathology.

This book is significant in that it makes an important contribution to the growing body of clinical knowledge on the treatment of alcohol-related problems.

— *Fulton Caldwell, Ph.D., C.A.C.*

Health Scientist Administrator
Treatment Research Branch
National Institute on Alcohol Abuse and Alcoholism

Contents

A Personal Preface

WHEN I LOOK OVER THE IDEAS PRESENTED in this book, it occurs to me that I have been writing this book for several decades. Indeed, this book is the product of a personal evolution that most likely started as I was growing up in Korea during the war. The personal experience of surviving the havoc and devastation of that war led me to volunteer to work with returning Vietnam veterans in the late 1970s. In looking back, these are the roots of this book and this way of working.

The veterans with whom I worked suffered from what is now known as post-traumatic stress disorder (PTSD). At the time of my work, however, this label had not been invented. Rather, these young soldiers were known by other diagnostic labels popular at the time. The most frequent labels were "alcoholic" or "drug addict." Admittedly, one of the many ways that these young men coped with the aftermath of their "trip to Hell" was by abusing alcohol and/or drugs. However, there were many other ways that these soldiers coped. In spite of nights tormented by the images of fellow soldiers with limbs and bodies shattered, of Vietnamese women and children hurt and maimed, these young men often kept going to school, held on to their jobs, and worked on their relationships. I often marveled at the strength of their spirit in the face of overwhelming problems and wondered what kept them going.

Despite the passage of many years, I have kept the images of many of the young men vivid in my mind — in particular, their unceasing drive to heal themselves and their vigilant efforts to put the shattered pieces of their lives together into a whole. More than any of my many training courses or degrees, these vivid images remind me of what is most important and essential in the context of therapy: the human spirit.

On one of my many trips conducting workshops, I happened to meet my co-author, Scott Miller. He had been using brief therapeutic approaches with problem drinkers in inpatient and outpatient settings and had presented his ideas at an international conference. We soon discovered that we shared similar clinical and theoretical views about working with this difficult population. Coincidentally, we also shared a similar dream for articulating these views in a book about alcohol treatment. Following a couple of years of correspondence and exchanges of ideas, the opportunity arose for us to work together at the Brief Family Therapy Center. This book is a result of our collaboration.

The book describes in detail the solution-focused approach for working with the problem drinking client. The solution-focused approach is situated within the tradition of brief therapy, which, in turn, fits within the broad category of problem-solving orientations in psychotherapy in general. Our view is that it is best for our clients to live their lives in the real world instead of in a therapy room. We firmly believe that the sooner the client gets on with the business of living, the better.

As will become obvious, the book is based on our faith that all clients have the resources and strengths necessary to solve their own problems, that they know and want what is good for them, and that they are doing the best they can.

My hope is that this book will give readers who share similar views some guidance on what to do and how to say things in such a way that their own faith in the client is expressed in their daily work.

Insoo Kim Berg, 1992

Brief Family Therapy Center
Milwaukee, Wisconsin

Acknowledgments

THIS BOOK HAS TAKEN MANY YEARS TO BECOME a reality. For both of us, it has been a long journey, painful at times, delightful at others. In retrospect, it is difficult to assess with any degree of certainty how indebted we are to those who guided and nurtured us along the way to this point of personal and clinical maturity. Nonetheless, it can be stated unequivocally that the debt feels great.

First and foremost, we owe a great deal of gratitude to the clients with whom we have worked. The strength, resourcefulness, courage, and creativity with which our clients faced oftentimes insurmountable obstacles taught us to have faith in the human spirit and formed the basis of the solution-focused model.

We are also indebted to our professional colleagues around the world who listened to us, challenged our thinking, told us we were wrong, and stuck by us as our thinking evolved. We must also thank all those who participated in our workshops, training seminars, and supervision hours. To thank you all personally is not possible. However, pieces from our interactions with all of these professionals have been incorporated into the book and model.

We certainly must thank our current team members at the Brief Family Therapy Center: Steve de Shazer, Larry Hopwood, and Jane Kashnig. Without their seemingly limitless patience, generous support, creativity, and clarity of thought this book would not have been possible. In addition, we wish to thank former BFTC team members, associates, and colleagues who have both mentored and expanded our clinical work and professional lives: Wallace Gingerich, Eve Lipchik, James

Derks, Elam Nunnally, Lynn D. Johnson, William Hudson O'Hanlon, Ron Kral, and Gale Miller.

Finally, we wish to thank our editor, Margaret Farley, who with patience and gentle nudges shaped this book into a readable and coherent text. Thank you also to Sarah Berg and Doreen Munson who gave us invaluable technical support and assistance up to the last minute.

Thank you all.

Introduction:
A Sobering Dilemma

It is not the things themselves that worry us, but the opinions we have about those things.

— Epictetus, *Zen to Go* (Winnokur, 1989)

Nan-in, a Japanese master, received a university professor who came to inquire about Zen. Nan-in served tea. He poured his visitor's cup full, and then kept on pouring. The professor watched the overflow until he no longer could restrain himself. "It is overfull. No more will go in!" "Like this cup," Nan-in said, "you are full of your own opinions and speculations. How can I show you Zen unless you first empty your cup?"

— *Zen Flesh, Zen Bones* (Reps, 1957)

THE DECISION TO WRITE THIS BOOK was an easy one. Together, we have been successfully treating clients with problems related to their own or others use of alcohol for more years than we wish to count. Because of our experience, we have for some time believed that we had something valuable to say with regard to the treatment of this population. However, this belief eventually led us to a second, and much more difficult decision — that is, *how* to write this book. To be sure, this was not a decision regarding the mechanics of writing the book (i.e., do we use a typewriter or word processor, who writes what chapters, etc.). Like our decision to write the book, those decisions were made with little effort. Rather, the dilemma we faced was how to express our ideas regarding the necessary ingredients of "good" treatment when the complaint involves alcohol.

The reason for our apprehension was that the model we had developed for treating individual problem drinkers and/or families with problem drinking members stood, in many ways, in stark contrast to "traditional" ideas regarding treatment — no small problem given both the current and the historical level of polemics surrounding alcohol treatment. We debated the relative merits of what appeared to be the only two possible ways of dealing with this problem. The first was to present the model within the guise of traditional alcohol treatment philosophy. By so doing, the book could then be viewed as merely an attempt to supplement rather than supplant the dominant treatment ideology. This, we thought, would have the dual advantage of avoiding controversy and guaranteeing that at least some people would read the book.

The other alternative was to simply present our ideas and see what happened. The advantage here was that the model would be presented as an effective alternative to traditional treatment. However, because of the unorthodox and, in some aspects, blatantly heretical notions, the entire model might be rejected out-of-hand, viewed as more evidence that mental health professionals did not understand *the disease* of alcoholism and were, in fact, "in denial" about the severity of the problem.

HINTS OF A SOLUTION: INSIGHTS FROM THE HISTORY OF PSYCHOTHERAPY

While debating the risks and advantages of these options, we recalled a time in the history of the field of psychotherapy that seemed to parallel the present atmosphere surrounding alcohol treatment. Specifically, we observed that our position vis-à-vis alcohol was not unlike that of brief therapists in general during the heyday of psychoanalysis. At that time, the prevailing ideology held that any effective therapy was of necessity intense, comprehensive, and therefore, long-term. Indeed, Freud once commented on the length of the treatment he pioneered, noting that "It would be magic if it worked rather quicker. . . . But analytic treatments take months and even years" (DeAngelis, 1987, p. 34). Several notable attempts have been made by psychoanalytically oriented thinkers to shorten the length of time required for treatment (Garfield, 1989). However, these briefer, less intensive treatment approaches were considered little better than "hand holding" and thought to be applicable only in those instances where, for some reason, long-term treatment was either not possible or not in the best interest of the patient (e.g., in crisis situations or when working with severely disturbed patients).

Various explanations were asserted for the *a priori* rejection of brief therapy as a plausible, as well as needed, alternative to long-term treatment. For example, it was argued that problems, which were believed to develop over a period of many years and/or to reside in "deep" unconscious intrapsychic conflicts, could only be ameliorated by correspondingly long and "deep" therapeutic work. Based on this hypothesis, theoreticians reasoned that any treatment concentrating solely on the removal of symptoms and failing to get to the source(s) of the problems would ultimately result in the reemergence of neurotic symptoms. As if that were not enough, treatment professionals were also warned that any efforts to expedite the process risked, at least, premature termination, and at most, total decompensation of the patient.

Cases that were treated successfully in shorter periods of time were similarly discounted. One common explanation was that these people had not really experienced a "true" cure, but rather a "flight into health." In other words, positive outcomes were interpreted as defensive maneuvers aimed at helping the patient escape or flee the treatment process. So prevalent was this phenomenon that analytic practitioners began warning their patients not to trust any changes that occurred early in the treatment process. Another way that such cases were discounted was by attributing success to the lack of any "real" maladjustment or psychopathology — the existence of which, it was argued, would have necessitated long-term treatment (Watzlawick, 1988).

As is now obvious, however, brief treatment has become the norm of psychotherapy practice (Budman & Gurman, 1988; Garfield, 1989; Garfield & Bergin, 1986). Indeed, research indicates that the mean number of sessions attended by clients is somewhere between five and six (Garfield, 1971, 1986, 1989; Garfield & Kurtz, 1952) — an astonishingly low number when contrasted with the number of sessions that were historically thought necessary for therapy to be effective. Moreover, research on treatment outcome has consistently demonstrated that such short-term treatment is as effective as traditional, long-term therapy — in spite of all of the predictions to the contrary (Howard, Kopta, Krause, & Orlinsky, 1986; Koss & Butcher, 1986; Smith, Glass, & Miller, 1980). In fact, the results of a 12-year study recently published by the Menninger Clinic, a psychoanalytically oriented treatment and training facility, showed that clients who received brief, supportive treatment profited as much as from that experience as those who had undergone extensive, long-term, psychoanalytically oriented treatment (Wallerstein, 1986, 1989).

The change from long-term to short-term treatment did not, however, occur overnight. Rather, over the last 40 years numerous events have gradually shaped treatment toward briefer forms. For example, in his review of the history of the field, Garfield (1989) points to the significant impact of the post World War II period on both the practice and philosophy of therapy. In particular, the return of a large number of military personnel resulted in a dramatic increase in demand for mental health services that could not be met by a system dominated by the long-term treatment ethos. Eventually, this led the Joint Commission on Mental Illness and Health (1961) to conclude that styles of therapy, both lengthy in terms of preparation of practitioners and time required for treatment, were not useful in meeting the majority of needs for mental health services.

Perhaps the most profound impact on the delivery of treatment services, however, has resulted from recent changes in the environment in which mental health service providers practice. Specifically, the practice of psychotherapy has become increasingly governed by the economic forces of the competitive "marketplace" atmosphere in which clinicians work (Cummings, 1977, 1986, 1988; Cummings & VandenBos, 1979). For example, in response to the high inflation rate in mental health service delivery, insurance companies, third party payers, employers, health provider organizations, and government funding agencies have implemented cost containment measures including the placement of limits on the numbers of sessions and/or the amount of financial compensation for services offered (Cummings, 1986, 1988; Frank & Kamlet, 1985; Shulman, 1988). In addition, there has been a dramatic increase in the number of individuals and corporations offering treatment services thereby increasing the competition for each mental health dollar available in the marketplace. These powerful economic changes have combined to force treatment, and therefore practitioners, to be more effective and *efficient* than ever before (Cummings, 1986).

STARK SIMILARITIES: ON THE VERGE OF A SOLUTION TO OUR DILEMMA

We took heart from our observation that the current status of the field of alcohol treatment is very similar to that of brief therapy only 40 short years ago. Indeed, much like the historical dominance of psychoanalysis in psychotherapy, the field of alcohol treatment is today almost exclusively dominated by the "disease model of alcoholism" and treatment precepts of the Twelve Steps. This prevailing ideology holds that "alcoholism" results from a primary, progressive, irreversible, and fatal *unitary* disease process that affects all alcoholics similarly. Indeed, in the opening statement of his book, *I'll Quit Tomorrow*, Vernon E. Johnson

(1973), one of the leading proponents of this approach, boldly asserts that "all alcoholics are ultimately alike. The disease itself swallows up all differences and creates a *universal alcoholic profile*" (p. 4).

Within the traditional model, problem drinking clients are most often viewed as resistant to treatment and "in denial" (Beattie, 1986; Johnson, 1973). Treatment is seen as an "all for one, and one for all" approach to which clients must simply adhere if they ever hope to "recover" (Alcoholics Anonymous, 1976; Johnson, 1973). Not surprisingly, the same model accepts only *one* outcome as indicative of successful treatment—that is, abstinence and/or sobriety. For these reasons, traditional alcohol treatment is most often considered a long-term process that in the best of circumstances begins with some form of intensive inpatient or residential treatment and continues with years of outpatient follow-up and a lifelong commitment to "recovery" in a self-help aftercare group (cf. Johnson, 1973). Family members, viewed within the traditional model as "enablers" and co-conspirators in the promotion and maintenance of problem drinking, have traditionally been considered a liability and, therefore, excluded from direct involvement in the treatment of the problem drinking member (Zweben, Perlman, & Li, 1988).

Many alternatives to this traditional conceptualization of alcohol and treatment have been developed and implemented with success, but most, like their predecessors in brief therapy, have been rejected out of hand. Moreover, no alternative conceptualization or treatment approach has gained the same widespread support and popularity among both practicing professionals and the lay public as the traditional model (Annis & Davis, 1989; Bratter & Forrest, 1985; Hester & Miller, 1989; Peele, 1989). Various explanations have been given for the *a priori* rejection of plausible alternative approaches. In some instances, the same type of circular argument that was used to discount positive responses to brief treatment by the psychoanalytic school has been applied to positive outcomes from these alternative approaches to alcohol abuse treatment. For example, since the popular conceptualization holds that the problem is caused by an irreversible, fatal disease requiring a lifelong commitment to recovery, any individual who experiences a positive response to briefer, less intensive treatments is simply dismissed as not having been a "real alcoholic" (Alcoholics Anonymous, 1939, 1976; Heather & Robinson, 1985). In other instances, a kind of phobic argument has been made. This argument asserts that the promulgation of alternative views threatens the sobriety of thousands that have been helped by the traditional model (Armor, Polich, & Stambul, 1978; Black, 1987; Peele, 1989). Finally, as mentioned earlier, some have suggested that the alternative models are further evidence that mental health professionals, especially those not "recovering" from alcoholism, do not understand *the disease* and are, in fact, in "denial" about the severity of the alcohol problem.

The field of alcohol treatment is now encountering some of the same powerful forces that eventually led to change in the field of psychotherapy in general some 40 years ago. Perhaps the most powerful of these forces is economic. The cost of the traditional treatment approach is high and increasingly on the rise. For example, one study (Kamerow, Pincus, & Macdonald, 1986) traced the rise in the cost of alcohol treatment services and support from 10.5 billion dollars in 1980 to 14.9 billion only three years later in 1983. More recent estimates indicate that the costs for such treatment are approaching 15% of the entire national health bill (Holden, 1987). Already, insurance companies, third party payers, employers, health provider organizations, and government funding agencies are implementing cost containment measures similar to those now in place for mental health services. One can safely assume that such economic changes will serve as an impetus for the creation of more efficient alcohol treatment models.

In addition, there has been a sharp increase in the demand for alcohol treatment services, much like the increase in demand for mental health services accompanying the return of veterans from World War II (Holden, 1987). Indeed, one study found that the number of individuals seeking treatment in for-profit residential treatment centers increased by 400% in the six-year period between 1978 and 1984 (Weisner & Room, 1984). Several factors have likely contributed to this increase, chief among them the heightened national awareness of problems related to the misuse of alcohol. This new consciousness about alcohol on the part of individuals, educators, mental health practitioners, and the justice system is, in many instances, leading to *earlier* identification of problem drinking (Institute of Medicine, 1990). Such cases would seem to us to warrant less intensive treatment approaches than are presently available (Sanchez-Craig, Annis, Bornet, & McDonald, 1984). This seems especially true in the case of children and adolescents who, with drug and alcohol education now a required part of most school curricula, are being identified and referred for treatment with increasing frequency. In fact, in the four-year period between 1980 and 1984, hospitalization of adolescents and children increased 350%, due largely to alcohol and drug related referrals (Peele, 1986, 1989). These treatment programs are generally based on the ideology of Alcoholics Anonymous and the principles of the Twelve Steps. Not surprisingly, membership growth in Alcoholics Anonymous has been highest among this age group (Alcoholics Anonymous, 1987). However, using the A.A. guidelines to teach *this* population that their problems are the result of an inherited "disease" over which they have no control — meaning that their only hope is to abstain from all use and attend self-help support groups for the rest of their lives — seems, at the least, to encourage a lack of individual responsibility and, at most, to risk self-fulfilling prophecy. For this reason, the early identification of children and adolescents demands the development of less intensive treatment alternatives.

Further, outcome research has demonstrated that briefer and more efficient treatment alternatives are as effective as traditional, long-term, recovery oriented approaches — again, in spite of all the predictions to the contrary. While various measures have been employed in outcome studies (e.g., abstinence, decreased number of problem drinking days, decreased number of relapses, decreased medical utilization, decreased social consequences of drinking), length of treatment is of particular relevance to the model presented in this book. With regard to the length of treatment for the problem drinker, numerous studies have found no appreciable difference in treatment outcome between short- and long-term treatment (Fingarette, 1988; Hester & Miller, 1989; Holden, 1986, 1987; Miller & Hester, 1986; Mosher, Davis, Mulligan, & Iber, 1975; Zweben et al., 1988). Similar studies have shown no difference in outcome between the traditional, expensive inpatient or residential programs and the less costly outpatient treatment option (Miller & Hester, 1986). Moreover, some recent research in the area of brief therapy indicates that alcohol abusing clients can experience positive change *rapidly* with only minimal or brief intervention when treatment is targeted, individualized, and focused (Berg & Gallagher, 1991; Hester & Miller, 1989; Institute of Medicine, 1990). Indeed, in one recent study of over 16,000 Medicaid patients, Cummings, Dorken, Pallack, and Henke (1990) found that treatment lasting an average of only six sessions produced a significant impact on the problem drinker. Overall, the weight of the evidence is such that in their landmark study on the treatment of alcohol problems the Institute of Medicine recently "urged a significant shift of resources from intensive hospital and residential care to less costly brief interventions and outpatient care" (Institute of Medicine, 1990).

LETTING THE CHIPS FALL WHERE THEY MAY

Eventually we came to the conclusion that the field of alcohol treatment is on the verge of some rather dramatic changes. Economic pressures and the changing treatment population are leading the field in the direction of diversifying in order to meet the demands of the changing marketplace and clientele. From this, we decided to present our ideas as they were and "let the chips fall where they may." In doing so, we had to accept the possibility that the model might suffer the same fate as the other alternatives to the traditional approach that have preceded us.

A number of considerations eventually led us to assume the risk associated with presenting our ideas in a straightforward manner. First and foremost, perhaps, is our experience in observing that many of even the most serious cases of problem drinking undergo rapid and enduring changes in response to minimal or brief therapeutic interventions. Indeed, treatment professionals are often shocked and surprised to hear us talk about how our clients willingly making changes in their problematic drinking within only a few outpatient sessions (average number of sessions is 4.6; de Shazer, 1988; Kiser, 1988, 1990; Kiser & Nunnally, 1988; Zweben, Perlman, & Li, 1988). Contrary to the traditional view of these clients as "resistant" to treatment, we found this population pleasant and willing to work with us in solving their unique problems.

The second reason for choosing to present our approach "as is" has to do with the toll of problem drinking on a growing number of individuals and families. The "traditional" treatment approach simply cannot accommodate the increasingly diverse population now in need of and seeking services. If alternatives exist that use scarce treatment resources more efficiently, then we have a responsibility to make them available to those in need.

Third, we have noted a gradual but significant *shift* in the attitudes of professionals toward the treatment of alcohol-related problems. Part of the reason for this shift is that more practitioners outside of the professional alcohol treatment community have finally recognized the significance of the problems related to alcohol and are treating problem drinkers in their own practices. This makes sense given that some experts estimate that alcohol may figure in as many as 50% of the cases seen by therapists (Treadway, 1987). For the most part, these clinicians have little allegiance to any one treatment model and are primarily interested in learning whatever they can about working effectively with such problems. We have also noticed a shift in the attitudes of those in attendance at workshops who have been trained in traditional models of alcohol treatment. Here again, the movement seems to be toward expanding the available treatment options and tailoring treatment approaches to the individual problem drinker.

Lastly, we are excited by recent developments that have opened the door to new and innovative ideas in the treatment of alcohol problems: for example, the relapse prevention work of Alan Marlatt, the informed eclecticism of William Miller and his colleagues at the University of New Mexico, and the recent research of the Institute of Medicine. When the contributions made by these and other innovative thinkers are considered, the field does appear to be gathering a *momentum* which promises to provide new insights into this complex problem, as well as dramatic improvement in delivery of treatment services.

The treatment model developed at Brief Family Therapy Center (hereafter BFTC) is a good example of one of the many creative approaches now being applied to alcohol problems. Certainly, we do not presume to have discovered the one and only true way to treat clients who experience problems resulting from their own or others' problematic use of alcohol — to do so would be to repeat the mistakes of the past. Neither do we believe that the model is applicable to all cases of problem drinking. In fact, we do not believe that any one model is or will ever be applicable in all cases. In contrast to the traditional model, we do not believe in *alcoholism* per se and, for this reason, do not feel that the pursuit of a single treatment strategy for all cases of problem drinking is either logical or useful. Instead, we have come to believe that there are many alcoholisms — perhaps as many as there are problem drinkers. Because of this, we feel that the multifaceted and complex nature of the problem calls for an equally complex and varied package of strategies that can be applied in an individualized, eclectic fashion to those seeking treatment. The model presented here represents only one of the many possible strategies.

LOOKING FORWARD: A SOLUTION-FOCUSED APPROACH TO PROBLEM DRINKING

The approach developed by Steve de Shazer and his colleagues at BFTC has come to be known as "solution-focused" therapy. While a great deal has been written about the application of the solution-focused therapy model to a variety of problems and complaints (Amatea, 1989; Berg, 1991; Berg & Gallagher, 1991; Cox, Chilman, & Nunnally, 1989; de Shazer, 1985, 1988; de Shazer, Berg, Lipchik, Nunnally, Molnar, Gingerich, & Weiner-Davis, 1986; Kral, 1988; Kral & Schaffer, 1989;

Molnar & de Shazer, 1987; Molnar & Lindquist, 1990), this book is, as far as we know, the first to apply the model specifically to the treatment of alcohol-related problems.

From the outset, our intention has been to write a practical, step-by-step, "how to" book that can be used both by those unfamiliar with the treatment of the problem drinker and by those already expert in the area. The order and presentation of the book evolved over the last five years, as we have given presentations and workshops both at BFTC and on location around the world. With a few exceptions, the book parallels the manner in which we present the model in those workshops and seminars.

The book presents the actual model in five parts (Chapters 2 through 7). We refer to this format, somewhat tongue-in-cheek, as our "five step" approach to problem drinking. Chapter 1 covers the principles and assumptions of the solution-focused approach to problem drinking, while Chapters 8 and 9 contain entire case examples.

Working With the
Problem Drinker

1

Principles and Assumptions

Man has such a predilection for systems and abstract deductions
that he is ready to distort the truth intentionally, he is ready to
deny the evidence of his senses only to justify his logic.

—Dostoyevsky, *Zen to Go* (Winnokur, 1989)

Clay is molded to make a vessel, but the utility of the vessel lies in
the space where there is nothing. . . . Thus, taking advantage of
what is, we recognize the utility of what is not.

—Lao Tzu, *Tao Te Ching* (1963)

THE TRADITION FOR MOST OF THE TWENTY years that the Brief Family
Therapy Center has been in existence has been to eschew discussions
about theory and principles in favor of practical, step-by-step, "how to"
type descriptions of the solution-focused approach. Including a theoretical discussion on principles and assumptions in this book represented a
significant departure from our usual pragmatic emphasis.

We worried that this chapter might give the reader the mistaken
impression that one needed to first understand these principles and
assumptions in order to successfully practice the approach described in
the book. Our experience has always been the opposite: those students
least burdened with abstract theoretical notions are usually the *most*
capable of learning solution-focused therapy and, for that matter, therapy skills in general.

The strong emphasis on the pragmatic to the exclusion of the theoretical stands in stark contrast to the training experience that most professionals receive. Graduate school is largely devoted to learning various
theories of human behavior, problem development, and psychotherapy.
Precious little time is devoted to practical, step-by-step descriptions of
what one is actually supposed to *do* in therapy. This, unfortunately, is

1

either relegated to internships or, as is more often the case, omitted altogether (Efran, Lukens, & Lukens, 1990). Frequently, the real training on how to *do* therapy occurs on the job while "flying by the seat of the pants."

It is no wonder that this same pattern of focusing on abstract and theoretical discussions is so often repeated in describing cases to colleagues, once students have entered the field. Indeed, so pronounced is the tendency that Efran, Lukens, and Lukens (1990) observed:

> . . . it is revealing to sit back and observe professionals interacting at clinic case conferences. There is typically a disproportionate amount of time and energy devoted to describing the client—his or her foibles, history, complaints, and characteristics—as contrasted with the time and attention devoted to developing a specific treatment plan or evaluating the therapist's activities. The client's behavior is explored with great relish, but the therapist's behavior and the treatment plan are often disposed of in a few brief comments. (p. 2)

True to our initial training, we were both, at one time, expert in problem detection and description. So expert were we that we could detect mental health problems at a distance. While creeping along the interstate during rush hour, we were able to diagnose those drivers suffering from "low self-esteem" from their slumped posture and sagging shoulders. The supermarket provided an even greater opportunity to observe complex and varied human problems ranging all the way from parents lacking adequate child-rearing skills to shoppers with serious eating disorders. Alas, it seemed that we were therapists in search of problems and, not surprisingly, we found them everywhere we looked.

Over the years, we have been successful in turning down the volume on and eventually eliminating our "problemometers." Consequently, we rarely spend time uncovering, describing, and then cataloging the mental health problems of our clients or, for that matter, our fellow shoppers and rush hour compatriots. The majority of our time is now focused on describing and cataloging those therapist activities that lead clients toward solutions.

We do not believe that the following principles or assumptions are "true" in any empirical or objective sense of the word. Rather, the following material is only a description of the general values and philosophical underpinnings that simultaneously guide and inform our therapeutic work. The ideas presented here stem from what we have come to believe about our clients and the nature of change. The model will change and evolve as we continue to learn from and adapt to our clients.

Broken Promises: An Illustrative Case Example

A woman and her "alcoholic" husband came to BFTC for treatment (de Shazer, 1988). At the beginning of the first session, Mrs. Z reported that her husband had a serious and chronic problem with alcohol. She recounted the many times that Mr. Z had promised to stop drinking, each time breaking that promise with more drinking episodes. Mr. Z maintained that he did not have a problem with alcohol and, further, that he did not want to stop drinking. When asked, he freely admitted having made the many promises to stop drinking that he had subsequently failed to keep. According to Mr. Z, however, he really had never wanted to make such promises in the first place. He reported that most often after making such promises he would visit his parents who owned a local tavern. While there, he would decide to have "just one drink." Then, feeling guilty for having broken his promise, he would stay at the tavern and drink even more.

After listening to the clients' brief descriptions of the complaint, the therapist immediately began to explore what was different about those times when Mr. Z did *not* drink. Perhaps for the first time in the session, both Mr. And Mrs. Z agreed that there were times when drinking was not a problem and that such times had a beneficial impact on them individually and as a couple.

Utilizing those periods when drinking was not a problem, the "healthy" periods already in existence but unrecognized by the couple, became the overall theme for successful treatment in this case. This is the first of eight principles or assumptions of the solution-focused approach — an emphasis on mental health as opposed to mental illness.

EMPHASIS ON MENTAL HEALTH

This first principle translates into therapy sessions in which the primary focus is on the successes of clients in dealing with their problems. Client strengths, resources, and abilities are highlighted rather than their deficits and disabilities. In a solution-focused approach, rather than looking for what is wrong and how to fix it, we tend to look for what is right and how to use it. In the "Broken Promises" example, the therapist focused the conversation on those times when the healthy pattern — not drinking — occurred and then merely helped to increase the frequency of that pattern. Though ample evidence existed that pointed to pathology (e.g., chronic alcohol use, out-of-control drinking behavior, alcohol-related marital difficulties, etc.), the therapist skillfully redirected the focus away from such pathology and toward hygiology.

If one accepts the premise that healthy patterns already exist but have simply gone unrecognized, then capitalizing on such patterns should lead to solutions without having to go through the traditional process of discovering the problem and *then* developing a solution. As de Shazer (1988) has pointed out, successfully solving the problems that clients bring to therapy, "does not mean that the client's problem needs to be explored in great detail or defined exactly or even talked about at great length" (p. 52). In fact, "solutions need not be directly related to the problems they are meant to solve" (de Shazer, 1988, p. 51). A shocking notion to say the least.

Another, less obvious effect of this principle is that treatment sessions are devoted to discovering the *client's* answer to the problem. Focusing on healthy patterns leads us to believe that clients, rather than therapists, have the answers to their problems. In the solution-focused approach, this idea is much more than a pop psychology cliché. It is the very basis upon which the model is built and leads us to a view and style of interaction with clients that is different from that observed in more traditional approaches. We rarely have "difficult" or "resistant" clients because we believe they possess the skills and resources necessary to bring about a solution and, thus, we avoid having to "sell" them our answer to their problem.

At one time in the field of mental health, the key to helping others *was* the study of health, as opposed to illness (Maslow, 1976; Super, 1980; Whiteley, 1980). In 1908, Charles Beers published his autobiographical account, *A Mind That Found Itself*, which raised public awareness about the treatment of the mentally ill and sparked the "mental hygiene" movement — a movement dedicated to promoting psychological health rather than treating mental illness. So powerful was this movement that it subsequently influenced the development of an entire subspecialty in the field of psychology known as counseling psychology. Unfortunately, that specialty, along with the entire mental health field, gradually returned to the previous focus on illness and pathology. Only recently, concurrent with developments in brief therapy, has the focus returned to mental health (de Shazer, 1982, 1985, 1988, 1991; de Shazer, Berg, Lipchik, Nunnally, Molnar, Gingerich, & Weiner-Davis, 1986; Fisch, Weakland, & Segal, 1982; Miller, in press; Watzlawick, Weakland, & Fisch, 1974).

UTILIZATION

Richard Rabkin, a strong proponent of strategic therapy, draws a parallel between the old Russian story of the cook who is preparing stone soup and the therapeutic interaction. The following directions are offered:

> To make this remarkably nutritious and filling food you [the therapist] boil the stone in a pot of water. Then you suggest to your guests [the client(s)] that, although it would taste fine as it is, it would be even better if they happened to have an onion they could donate, as well as some parsley, tomatoes, meat, and so on. (Rabkin, 1983, p. 15)

The point is that quality treatment involves eliciting from the client those strengths, resources, and healthy attributes that are needed to solve the presenting problem. This is known as *utilization* and is the second principle of the solution-focused approach.

Brief therapists O'Hanlon and Wilk (1987) summarize the principle of utilization succinctly:

> The principle is one of utilizing the clients' existing resources, skills, knowledge, beliefs, motivation, behavior, symptoms, social network, circumstances, and personal idiosyncracies to lead them to their desired outcomes. (p. 132)

The therapist merely acts to elicit from the client those characteristics that give the solution a unique personal flavor.

Case Example: The Zen of Alcoholics Anonymous

Beth had read a large amount of literature published by Alcoholics Anonymous and regularly attended their meetings. From the outset, she expressed a strong desire to integrate the Twelve Steps into her personal program of sobriety. Beth believed that following the "Twelve Step" philosophy was the only way for her to become sober. Despite her strong conviction, she had so far been unable to make even the first step "fit" with her Buddhist background. The problem was solved when the client's religious beliefs were *utilized* by translating each of the Twelve Steps into Zen Buddhist Koans — mental puzzles used by practicing Buddhists to obtain enlightenment. For example, the first of the Twelve Steps, in which clients admit that they are powerless over alcohol was translated into a koan that read, "Giving in is the greatest form of control" and then given to the client to consider while meditating. The difficulty was resolved in this single session and thereafter she was able to continue with her own personalized sobriety program!

The term utilization was first used by Milton H. Erickson (Erickson, 1959; Erickson & Rossi, 1979) to describe his method of "exploring a patient's individuality to ascertain what life learnings, experiences, and mental skills are available to deal with the problem . . . [and] then utiliz[ing] these uniquely personal internal responses to achieve therapeutic goals" (Erickson & Rossi, 1979, p. 1). A particularly relevant example is the case of a medically retired police officer (Gordon & Myers-Anderson, 1981; Rosen, 1982) who sought treatment because of his excessive consumption of alcohol, tobacco, and food. The man suffered from both emphysema and high blood pressure, and was 80 pounds overweight. While he enjoyed jogging, he indicated that, because of his poor physical health, the best he could do was walk. Erickson quickly began to make a detailed inquiry into the ex-police officer's daily routine. Erickson learned that the man cooked all of his own food, purchased from a "handy little grocery store" located just around the corner. He purchased his cigarettes from the same store, three cartons at a time, and his alcohol from a nearby liquor store.

When he finished his inquiry, Erickson told the retired police officer that correcting his problems was not "going to require very much" (Gordon & Myers-Anderson, 1981, p. 111). He then continued:

> You can do all the smoking you want . . . buy your cigarettes one package at a time by walking to the other side of town to get the package. As for your own cooking, well you haven't much to do so shop three times a day. Buy only enough for one meal but no left-overs. . . . As for your drinking . . . I see no objection to your drinking. There are some excellent bars a mile away. Get your first drink in one bar, your second drink in a bar a mile away. And you'll be in excellent shape before very long. (p. 112)

The man left the office swearing at Erickson. A month later, however, a new patient, who had been referred by the retired police officer, came to see Erickson. According to this patient, the man had since changed his unhealthy habits and considered Erickson, "the only psychiatrist who knows what he is talking about" (Gordon & Myers-Anderson, 1981, p. 112; O'Hanlon & Hexum, 1990.

In this case, Erickson employed the principle of utilization by integrating one of the only healthy actions that the client indicated he could do — walking — into the overall solution. In addition, he accepted and then utilized the eating, drinking, and smoking as an incentive to promote the more healthful physical activity of walking. Equally important, Erickson utilized the man's background as a police officer to insure that he would follow through with the treatment recommendations. Erickson explains:

Now why would I treat him [this] way? He was a retired police man . . . he *knew* what discipline was and it was entirely a matter of discipline. And there would be no way for him to refuse from any other way.

The principle of utilization implies that the treatment professional should accept and work within the *client's* frame of reference. As in the example of the Buddhist woman, the difficulty rested largely in the inability or unwillingness of those treatment professionals involved to adapt to and utilize her unique background. Once her religious orientation was utilized in the treatment the problem was solved very quickly!

This view stands in stark contrast to that of traditional alcohol treatment approaches, which have been based largely on the client's accepting and then working within the frame of reference of the *therapist* and/or treatment model. In traditional models, clients are expected to learn and adapt to the frame of reference of the treatment model or be considered difficult, resistant, or "in denial"; until very recently, there have been no viable alternatives (Miller, in press; Zweben et al., 1988).

We should point out that solution-focused therapists are not immune to the problem of not accepting and working within the client's frame of reference. We have consulted with and supervised many solution-focused therapists who have experienced difficulty in their work with problem drinkers owing primarily to the therapists' unwillingness to work within the frame of reference of those clients who believe in the Twelve Steps and Alcoholics Anonymous. It must be stressed that traditional approaches *do* work for many, but not all clients.

AN ATHEORETICAL/NONNORMATIVE/ CLIENT-DETERMINED VIEW

The solution-focused approach makes no assumptions about the "true" nature of the problems that clients experience as a result of alcohol. Instead, it looks to the individual's particular complaint about her own or others' use of alcohol and attempts to find a solution for that *individual*. In this regard, Milton Erickson once said that he invented, "a new treatment in accord with the individual" (Zeig, 1980). Rather than treating *one* alcoholism, the solution-focused therapist treats many different alcoholisms — a different type for each client that is treated.

Assuming an atheoretical, nonnormative, client-determined posture toward alcohol problems allows the mental health professional to relinquish the role of expert or teacher in favor of the role of student or apprentice. As such, the therapist serves the client by learning his unique way of conceptualizing the complaint that brings him into treatment. Only after taking the time to learn from the client can the therapist expect to be of any assistance. Again, in the words of Milton Erickson (Zeig, 1985):

> Each person is a unique individual. Hence psychotherapy should be formulated to meet the uniqueness of the individual's needs rather than tailoring the person to fit the Procrustean bed of a hypothetical theory of human behavior. (p. viii)

This philosophical orientation toward treatment is responsible for the two very diverse solutions developed in the case examples presented thus far. It is likely that neither solution would have been possible if the therapist were bound by a strong allegiance to any particular theoretical, normative, or model-determined view of alcohol problems. This was the problem in the treatment of the Buddhist client. The loyalty of the treatment professionals to the theoretical dogma of their treatment model prevented them from being flexible enough to accommodate the needs of that client — a client, by the way, who wanted desperately to be helped! Thus, the atheoretical, nonnormative, client-determined view of alcohol problems encourages flexibility on the part of treatment professionals.

Because the solution-focused approach is atheoretical and client-determined, little time is devoted, either in treatment sessions with clients or in discussions with colleagues, to figuring out or *explaining* why problems exist. The client's view is simply accepted at face value! For this reason, no time has to be expended trying to convince clients that they must accept a particular theoretical orientation in order to be helped or dealing with the resistance or denial when they disagree. Instead, solution-focused therapy, as the name implies, immediately takes up the task of developing solutions. As communications theorist Robert Norton (1982) concludes:

> Psychiatry and psychology spend time trying to unravel the correct, clear cause of the problem . . . [whereas] the brief therapist will settle for any dirty little solution that works. (p. 307)

In the words of de Shazer (1986):

> Traditionally, therapy focused on problems and problem solving . . . when solution-focused, the therapist talks about changes, differences that make a difference and solutions, rather than talking about difficulties, complaints, and problems. (pp. 48–49)

PARSIMONY

An apocryphal story about Steve de Shazer illustrates the principle of parsimony. A visitor once presented de Shazer with the Henry David Thoreau quotation, "Simplify, simplify, simplify," believing that the quotation exemplified the parsimonious nature of de Shazer's work. Upon reading Thoreau's dictum, de Shazer picked up a pencil and, directly underneath the quotation by Thoreau, quickly scribbled, "simplify." After considering his own edited version of the quotation for a few moments, he then said, "Ah, much better!"

As the story implies, de Shazer prefers the simplest and most straightforward means to an end, and this view permeates the solution-focused approach he developed. In fact, he regularly quotes the 14th century philosopher, William of Ockham, "What can be done in fewer means is done in vain with many" (de Shazer, 1985). The solution-focused model strives for economy in the therapeutic means used to obtain desired therapeutic ends. This is accomplished by conducting treatment from the bottom up rather than from the top down. The therapy proceeds with the most straightforward assumptions and strategies and adds complexity only as needed. One hears this same idea expressed in many of the slogans used by regular attenders of Alcoholics Anonymous, such as "Keep it simple, stupid!"

Working from the bottom up diverges sharply from more traditional approaches to both alcohol and mental health counseling, which so often work from the top down. That is, these approaches often *start* with the most complex and difficult assumptions and treatment strategies and then add simplicity only as an afterthought, if at all. Efran, Lukens, and Lukens (1988) refer to this tendency as an "obscurity complex," noting that, when faced with the ordinary problems clients present, many therapists often develop "convoluted formulations and elaborate interventions . . . [that] complicate, rather than clarify, the practitioner's work" (p. 17). A good example of this is the common assumption that the complaints clients bring to treatment are simply the "tip of the iceberg," the superficial manifestations of deeper, more pathological underlying problems that of necessity will require correspondingly deep and prolonged treatment if there is to be any hope for success. Given this orientation, it is not difficult to see how problem drinking so often becomes transformed into something more pathological. Such drinking quickly becomes a chronic and progressive primary disease process or the manifestation of unresolved intergenerational issues that require long-term, intensive treatment. For that matter, when working from the top down, any complex formulation of the problem and elaborate intervention strategy may be substituted for the more parsimonious approach of accepting the client's complaint at face value, and then choosing the simplest, least invasive treatment option.

A story related by O'Hanlon and Hudson (personal communication, 1989) about a case treated by marriage and family therapy pioneer R. Lofton Hudson is a prime example of the benefits of working from the bottom up. Hudson, while providing a training workshop in marriage and family therapy, was asked to meet privately with a young man who was in training for the clergy. Hudson was told that the young man had a problem with cross-dressing, a rather serious problem for someone being trained for the ministry, that had been resistant to treatment. Hudson agreed to meet with the young man and conducted a single session of "therapy." Following the workshop, Hudson did not hear anything about the outcome of that single session until he happened to return for another workshop engagement many years later. Upon Hudson's return, he was met with many questions about the "technique" he had employed in the case of the young cross-dresser. Hudson soon learned that following the session the young man had stopped cross-dressing altogether. Somewhat embarrassed, Hudson initially declined to reveal the technique that had resulted in the miracle cure. When the questions persisted, however, Hudson finally confessed that he had merely asked the young man, "Son, why don't you stop this foolishness of dressing in women's clothes?" to which the young man responded, "All right."

One can only speculate about the various treatment strategies that were employed in this case without success, as well as the multifarious theoretical assumptions that likely guided the choice of such strategies. Obviously, however, they did not include the idea that the young man could control his behavior, and it is likely that no one ever considered simply asking him to stop. With all of the current interest in the so-called "sexual addictions," one wonders if the situation would be treated any differently nowadays.

Aside from simplifying matters tremendously, as in the case of the young cross-dresser, another benefit of working parsimoniously is that therapy often becomes, as Erickson once said, a simple matter of "tipping the first domino" (Rossi, 1973, p. 14). In other words, a small change in one area can ultimately result in profound differences in many other areas. Spiegel and Linn (1969) refer to this as the "ripple effect" and note that frequently only minimal changes are needed to initiate solving complaints and, once the change is initiated further changes will be generated by the client. For this reason, we rarely find the need for the elaborate and/or invasive treatment approaches so often employed in the treatment of problem drinkers. Most often, all that is needed to bring about dramatic changes are minimal interventions designed primarily to get the patient going in the direction of the desired change.

Case Example: Getting the Hell out of the Way!

A 54-year-old self-described "alcoholic" male entered treatment a few days following a two-month long "relapse" (Miller, in press). The man described a lifelong history of problems with alcohol and multiple treatment failures. Discouraged by his relapse, he thought he needed to stay in a 28 day inpatient treatment facility in which he had been placed. He responded to an inquiry about those times when he had successfully managed his problems with alcohol, noting lengthy periods (e.g., months, years) during which he had successfully managed his problems with alcohol. When queried in more detail, he was able to specify what he had done differently during those times that contributed to his success. Among a host of other things, he indicated that he attended at least a few A.A. meetings a week. Thereafter, the man was asked what it would take to begin doing more of what had previously worked. He expressed relatively high confidence that he could at least begin doing some of those things (e.g., attending a few A.A. meetings). The man was released from the hospital the day after the initial meeting. Over the course of two subsequent treatment sessions, this simple strategy was employed to create the opportunity for a solution to develop. Just recently, the man sent a copy of his one-year sobriety token from Alcoholics Anonymous to the therapist. When asked during a congratulatory phone call about what had been helpful about his treatment, he replied, "You got me started and then you got the hell out of my way!"

CHANGE IS INEVITABLE

The previous example not only illustrates the "ripple effect" but also demonstrates the inevitability of change. The man had already started to change by stopping the relapse a "few days" prior to entering treatment. These changes inevitably resulted in one year of sobriety. The solution-focused approach is based on the assumption that change is so much a part of living that clients cannot prevent themselves from changing (de Shazer, 1985). Oftentimes then, therapy becomes a matter of simply identifying those naturally occurring changes and then utilizing them in bringing about a solution.

The idea that change is inevitable is related to the observation that "nothing always happens" (de Shazer, 1988; Kral, 1988). In any problematic situation there are bound to be times when the problem does not happen or when the problem is not considered a problem by the client. This is true even in the most difficult cases. However, because clients typically view the complaints that they bring into treatment as being constant in nature, any and all such exceptions go unnoticed (de Shazer, 1985, 1988; Miller, in press). In order to correct this, the solution-focused therapist searches for those times when the problem is not a problem. By discovering what is different about those occasions the therapist hopes to increase the frequency of their occurrence. For example, in the case of "Broken Promises," the therapist focused the discussion on those times when drinking was *not* a problem.

The idea that change is inevitable is certainly not a new one. However, in the alcohol and mental health fields, theory and methodology are most often based on an assumption of *constancy* or lack of change. When clinicians ask, "When did you first notice this problem?" or "How long has this been a problem for you?" or even, "How often do you feel this way?" their questions are based on the implicit assumption that the problem under consideration is constant in nature or, at least, that the occurrence of the problem is more informative as regards potential change than the non-occurrence of the problem. Whatever the case, the operative underlying question is usually "When *does* the problem happen?"

The assumption of constancy, and the related belief that change not only is *not* inevitable, but in most cases unlikely, is often espoused with considerable zeal in the field of alcohol treatment. In most cases, the only inevitable change ever referred to is one for the worst. Consider, for example, the viewpoint of Johnson (1986) a leading expert in the field of alcohol treatment:

> Unless the chemically dependent person gets help, he or she *will* die prematurely. . . . chemical dependency is . . . progressive . . . [and] this means that it *always* gets worse if left untreated . . . once a person becomes chemically dependent, he or she remains so forever. (pp. 6–7)

In our work with problem drinkers, however, we have found such pessimism totally unwarranted. Indeed, our observation is that changes for the better are at least equally, if not more likely to occur with our problem drinking clients. One can only wonder how much of what traditional alcohol counselors say they observe is attributable to self-fulfilling prophecy. More importantly, the traditional view does not take into account a growing body of literature conducted across a number of diverse settings that has found anywhere from 10 to 42% of problem drinkers alter their problematic drinking without benefit of formal treatment (Bailey & Stewart, 1966; Barcha, Stewart, & Guze, 1968; Goodwin, Crane, & Guze, 1971; Kendall & Stanton, 1966; Kissin, Rosenblatt, & Machover, 1968; Smart, 1975/1976; Vaillant, 1983; Vaillant & Milofsky, 1982). Given these findings, the traditional assumption that treatment is an absolute necessity if clients are to have any hope of avoiding death is presumptuous if not arrogant.

PRESENT AND FUTURE ORIENTATION

The sixth principle of the solution-focused approach is a strong orientation toward the present and future. In this respect, the present and future adjustment of clients is given precedence over that of the past. This is not to say, however, that what people communicate about their past *in the present* is considered unimportant in the solution-focused model; rather, such information is considered a reflection of how clients are currently living their lives. For this reason, rather than delving into the past, the primary focus of treatment is on helping clients in their present and future adjustment. In the words of Milton Erickson:

> Emphasis should be placed more on what the patient does in the present and will do in the future than on a mere understanding of why some long-past event occurred. The sine qua non of psychotherapy should be the present and future adjustment of the patient. (p. 406, Haley, 1967)

While the present and future orientation permeates all aspects of the solution-focused model, it is perhaps most obvious in the unique way that clients are interviewed. This specially designed interview process orients the client away from the past and the problem and toward the future and a solution (see Chapter 5). For example, the following question is a routine part of the solution-focused interview process and is known as the "miracle question":

> Suppose that one night, while you are asleep, there is a miracle and the problem that brought you into therapy is solved. However, because you are asleep you don't know that the miracle has already happened. When you wake up in the morning, what will be different that will tell you that this miracle has taken place? What else?

The miracle question directs the client to imagine a time *in the future* when the problem no longer exists. Continuing with the question,

"What else?" further directs the client to develop a highly detailed and vivid description that serves to make a future time of change and health all the more real. Thereafter, asking clients to describe when even small parts of the miracle happen serves to make the description salient to the present.

Case Example: Food-oholic

A woman sought treatment following years of failed attempts to control a weight problem. At the very beginning of the first session, the woman attributed her many failures to being "addicted" to food and quickly began to present evidence to support her belief. She then talked about a number of painful experiences from her childhood that she believed had caused her to become what she called a "food-oholic." The therapist listened thoughtfully and attentively and could easily agree that the woman had suffered a great deal. However, at one point during the discussion the opportunity arose for the therapist to ask the woman the miracle question. As the woman thoughtfully considered the question, a smile slowly began to creep onto what had been a very serious and, at times, tear-stained face. The woman then began to describe the many ways that her life would be different following this "miracle." Her outlook quickly changed from one of discouragement about the past to one of hopefulness about the future. Moreover, this hopefulness carried over into subsequent sessions and served to provide the momentum that was needed for her to eventually achieve and maintain her treatment goals.

COOPERATION

While this principle has not been mentioned directly, it is obvious that an overall attitude of cooperation permeates the solution-focused approach. Cooperation was included as a central organizing principle of the solution-focused approach in the first systematic explication of the model and, despite considerable evolution of the method, remains in the present version (cf. Berg, 1989; de Shazer, 1982, 1985, 1988, 1991).

Almost all treatment models have at least some specific strategies for securing the client's cooperation with the recommended treatment. For example, in traditional alcohol treatment the cooperation of the client is often obtained through a confrontational process known as an "intervention" (Anderson, 1987; Forman, 1987; Johnson, 1973). Viewing such clients as delusional and suffering from poor judgment that prevents them from cooperating with the very treatment that could save their lives, treatment professionals rally family, friends, and other influential people together for a meeting with the problem drinker. According to experts in this approach, the purpose of this aggressive intervention technique is "to have him see and accept enough reality so that, however grudgingly, he can accept in turn his need for help" (Johnson, 1973, p. 51).

The traditional emphasis on obtaining the cooperation of the client is, however, hopelessly one-sided and, therefore, does not constitute cooperation at all. In fact, cooperation, as routinely described by treatment professionals, is analogous to a therapeutic *Animal Farm*, in which the rule is that all participants in therapy must cooperate equally, but some participants must cooperate more equally than others — the latter referring chiefly to the client. In the "intervention" process described above no attempt is made to see the problem from the client's perspective, to speak his or her language, to work within his or her unique frame of reference, to negotiate a mutually agreeable treatment goal, or to utilize existing strengths and resources in an effort to solve the problem. The entire process is based on the idea that the client is "delusional" and "out of touch with reality" and must be forced to "cooperate" with the treatment as recommended.

Cooperation, as Sesame Street's Big Bird is so fond of pointing out, means working together *with* one another. Therefore, in a truly cooperative therapeutic relationship, not only must the client cooperate by working *with* the therapist, but the therapist must also work *with* the client. At BFTC, a consistent, conscious effort is made to cooperate with clients seeking treatment services. In return, we fully expect, and most often find, that our clients make a deliberate and conscious effort to cooperate with us. That cooperation promotes cooperation should not be all that surprising but that is exactly the response of other treatment professionals when we tell them that the majority of our clients are eager and willing — cooperative — participants in the treatment process.

Case Example: Just a Glue Head

A young man was ordered into treatment following his arrest for "sniffing glue" and public intoxication; the order for treatment followed a four-year history of arrests for the same offense. On each occasion, Elmer was arrested by the local police who, while on patrol, found him sitting on the front porch of his parents' home sniffing glue out of a plastic bag. Of the 50-plus arrests, Elmer had been referred to treatment on at least ten separate occasions. This included seven referrals for outpatient treatment, two for inpatient programs, and a single referral to a long-term residential treatment facility. When asked about what he wanted to accomplish with this referral, Elmer answered that he was "just a glue head" who wanted to stop getting arrested. He added that he did not want to stop sniffing glue and that no one, present therapist included, could make him stop.

The therapist agreed that no one could force him to stop sniffing glue — Elmer's treatment history was certainly proof of that. The therapist then *cooperated* with Elmer by focusing the discussion on how he might prevent future arrests and referrals for treatment. The therapist first inquired about how Elmer had managed to get arrested and ordered into treatment so many times. With a puzzled look on his face, he said, "I don't know! I sure don't like gettin' arrested, . . . maybe it's that the police is just good at their job." After some additional thought, he continued, "They do come 'round and patrol my neighborhood a lot!" Elmer and the therapist jointly, and cooperatively, wondered what might need to happen in order to decrease the chances of any future arrests. Again, Elmer made it very clear that discontinuing glue sniffing was not one of the options. The therapist then wondered whether or not sniffing glue on the back porch might be an acceptable alternative to getting high on the front porch — a place, the therapist pointed out, where the police could see him easily. Elmer told the therapist that he had never considered this option. He readily agreed to try out the idea as "an experiment" and to return in a week to report his findings.

When Elmer returned the following week, he reported that the police never even bothered to check the back porch, even though they had driven by his home on several occasions. Moreover, much to his great amusement, the only time the police had stopped was late one afternoon as he sat relaxing on the front porch, "enjoying the sunset" — straight. After this experience, Elmer began sitting out on the front porch straight just for the fun of it! The result, of course, was that he did not get arrested again or referred for any more treatment. In the end, owing perhaps to the "ripple effect" discussed earlier, contact with this client established that once the arrests and referrals had stopped, Elmer began to curtail his use of inhalants on his own. In reality, Elmer had already started to decrease his use while he was in treatment. At last report, he had enrolled in a rehabilitation and training program.

CENTRAL PHILOSOPHY

The previous case example contains all three of the components of what we call the "central philosophy" of solution-focused therapy. The three rules are:

1. If it ain't broke, DON'T FIX IT!
2. Once you know what works, DO MORE OF IT!
3. If it doesn't work, then don't do it again, DO SOMETHING DIFFERENT!

By following these three rules, the therapist was able to help Elmer stop getting arrested and referred for treatment, which eventually resulted in his curtailing his use of inhalants. The therapist followed rule number three by shifting the focus of treatment away from the substance abuse and toward the multiple arrests and referrals for treatment. In doing so, the therapist avoided repeating the same strategies that had failed in the past and chose instead to "do something different." Once some progress had been made, the therapist followed rule number two by continuing to do more of what had worked with Elmer. And finally, the therapist followed rule number one throughout by skillfully avoiding a plethora of issues that might have been considered problems by the therapist but were not identified as such by Elmer.

2

Developing Cooperative Client-Therapist Relationships

> Merely to make a correct diagnosis of the illness and to know the correct method of treatment is not enough. Fully as important is that the patient be receptive of the therapy and cooperative in regard to it. *Without the patient's full cooperativeness, therapeutic results are delayed, distorted, limited, or even prevented.* (emphasis added)
>
> — Milton H. Erickson (1965)

> What is of all things most yielding, can overcome that which is most hard. . . . That the yielding conquers the resistant and the soft conquers the hard is a fact known by all men, yet utilized by none. . . .
>
> — Lao Tzu, *Tao Te Ching* (1963)

STUDIES (HESTER & MILLER, 1989; MILLER, 1985) demonstrate that compliance with treatment increases dramatically when the therapist cooperates with the client by allowing her to set and work toward her own treatment goals. These findings are robust whether a client chooses to follow the traditional model emphasizing abstinence or to simply modify/control her drinking. These same findings are echoed by the Institute of Medicine in its landmark study on the treatment of alcohol problems (Institute of Medicine, 1990).

Our own experience in applying the solution-focused model to cases of problem drinking also demonstrates the value of cooperation. In contrast to popular opinion, we have found this population enjoyable to work with and, more importantly, willing to work with us in developing solutions to their problems. In considering the possible reasons for this, we have come to the conclusion that the cooperative nature of the solution-focused model is, in large part, responsible for the positive results. In particular, the quality of cooperation is inherent in the ways that treatment becomes individualized in the solution-focused model.

Individualization begins with the identification of the type of relationship that exists between the client and therapist. It continues as treatment interventions are tailored to the unique qualities of that relationship. We have found that identifying the type of client-therapist relationship helps to determine the therapeutic intervention most likely to result in increased client cooperation and participation in the therapeutic process, and consequently, in a decrease in the length of treatment. We consider this process the "first step" of the solution-focused approach to working *with* the problem drinker.

CONCEPTUALIZATION OF THE CLIENT-THERAPIST RELATIONSHIP

The solution-focused treatment model distinguishes among three different types of client-therapist *relationships*: (1) customer type, (2) complainant type, and (3) visitor type (Berg, 1989; de Shazer, 1988; Miller & Berg, 1991). These three relationship distinctions describe and categorize the nature of the interaction *between* the client and the therapist. When reading the descriptions, it is easy to mistakenly conclude that they refer only to the client. And indeed, for the sake of convenience, we ourselves sometimes refer to clients as "visitors," "complainants," or "customers." However, as the word "interaction" implies, these labels are meant to describe the type of *relationship* between the client and therapist and *not* the individual characteristics, attributes, or traits of the client.

There are several reasons for emphasizing the relationship and interaction between the client and the therapist. The most important is that this emphasis serves as a reminder to the therapist that treatment outcome is dependent on both the client *and* the therapist. This interactional view contrasts sharply with the traditional model where, because the treatment approach is mostly the same from person to person, outcome is thought to derive largely from client characteristics. Indeed, the so-called "Big Book" of Alcoholics Anonymous (1976) states: "Rarely have we seen a person fail who has thoroughly followed our path. Those who do not recover are people who cannot or will not completely give themselves to this simple program . . . " (p. 58). The book goes on to explain that the reason some do not benefit from the treatment is that they "are constitutionally incapable of being honest with themselves, . . . [they are] born that way [and are] naturally incapable of grasping and developing a manner of living which demands rigorous honesty" (p. 58). The usual result of such a view is that clients are *told* what they must do if they ever hope to "recover." Those clients who are either unwilling or unable to accept the treatment are considered "resistant" and "in denial" of their problem (Johnson, 1973; Metzger, 1988). In the end, the result of such views and approaches is often that valuable opportunities to reach out to those who are actually in desperate need of treatment are lost (Miller & Hester, 1986).

Outside of the widespread, but clinically unsubstantiated, belief that treatment counselors who are themselves recovering problem drinkers achieve superior results, therapist contribution to treatment outcome has been ignored by the field (Aiken, LoSciuto, & Ausetts, 1984; Cartwright, 1981; Lawson, 1982). This is entirely consistent with a model in which the method is considered "infallible" (Alcoholics Anonymous, 1976). When such a view of treatment is held, the only variable in the equation is the client and, therefore, he becomes the only part worth investigating! In its comprehensive review of the literature, the Institute of Medicine (1990) concluded that "Although therapist skills and characteristics have long been regarded as important factors in treatment outcome, these variables have remained largely unexamined within the alcohol treatment field" (p. 532).

While some may argue that the exclusive focus on client characteristics has been necessary because research on problem drinking is only in its infancy, we believe that the consequences have been far from benign. Perhaps the most obvious and problematic of these consequences has been the field-wide bias toward attributing poor treatment outcome to the client (Fingarette, 1988; Peele, 1989). This bias is most obvious in the frequent use of terms such as "resistant," "difficult," "defensive," "codependent," and "in denial" as concepts that are uniformly descriptive of problem drinking clients who either experience difficulties or do not improve in traditional treatment. While such labels may be based on the most benevolent of treatment intentions, the actual effect they have is to subtly shift the burden of responsibility for treatment failure away from treatment programs and professionals and onto the problem drinker. Alcohol treatment professionals are able to use the labels to fix "blame" for treatment failure solely on the client. In addition, the labels have the effect of validating the treatment model both when it succeeds and when it fails. If a problem drinker improves as a result of confronting "denial," then this obviously proves the correctness of pushing problem drinkers to admit that they have a serious problem. If, however, the problem drinker does not improve, then this only proves that the confrontation has not been strong enough or that the drinker is not yet ready for treatment — in traditional alcohol treatment terminology this is known as "hitting bottom." Watzlawick (1976) calls this a "self-sealing proposition" and notes that "only too often we find that the limitations inherent in a given hypothesis are attributed to the phenomena which that hypothesis is supposed to elucidate" (p. 92). This point was demonstrated in a recent study that found that alcohol treatment programs that identified total abstinence from alcohol as the only acceptable treatment goal routinely attributed poor treatment outcome either to negative client characteristics or client unreadiness for treatment (Rush & Ogborne, 1986).

Very few in the alcohol treatment community have considered that the behaviors, which labels such as "resistant" and "in denial" are intended to describe, are at least as descriptive of the traditional alcohol treatment procedures as they are of the problem drinking population. This is precisely because of the lack of attention given to therapist variables, as well as to the interaction between the therapist and client. With the strong emphasis on the relationship and interaction in the solution-focused approach, we hope to remind treatment professionals that they are at least equally responsible for the results of treatment. Any labels used to describe this process, therefore, must in part be considered descriptive of the professional as well.

One additional reason for emphasizing the therapeutic relationship and interaction in the solution-focused model is our belief that the client and the therapist *together* determine the type of working relationship that develops. This belief further implies that the relationship between a client and a therapist is subject to change whenever one member of the dyad changes. Because the therapist is considered the treatment expert, this view actually requires the therapist to assume more responsibility for the type of relationship that develops. In the solution-focused model, this translates into a strong emphasis on the therapist cooperating with the problem drinking client in forming the best possible working relationship.

Now, we turn our attention to the three types of client-therapist relationships. These relationships should be considered dynamic, fluid, and in a state of constant change in response to changing input from both the client and the therapist. Because the type of relationship is not static, it is best to consider the evaluation of the type of relationship as more or less a continuous process. This process of evaluating the type of relationship becomes even more complex in cases involving multiple clients, such as couples and families. In such instances, a different type of relationship may be found to exist between each of the various clients and the therapist.

The Customer-Type Relationship

A "customer type" of relationship exists when, either during or at the end of a treatment session, a complaint or goal for treatment has been identified *jointly* by the client and therapist. In addition, the client indicates that he sees himself as part of the solution and is willing to do something about the problem. The therapist agrees to work together with the client on the identified complaint or goal and believes she has the ability to *direct* the client toward finding a solution or achieving his goal.

In a case seen recently at BFTC, a 35-year-old factory worker presented for treatment of problems associated with his use of alcohol. During the course of the first interview, the client and therapist agreed that alcohol represented a significant problem and should, for that reason, become the initial focus of treatment. At the end of the session, when the client was asked how willing he was to do something about the problem, he said, "I am willing to crawl on my belly on broken glass!" This statement, in combination with other statements made during the course of the first interview, indicated that the man saw himself as part of the solution to his problem and was willing to take action to solve his problem. While most clients in customer-type relationships do not make such dramatic statements, they do indicate that they see themselves as part of the solution and as willing to take purposeful action.

The following interchange is a further illustration of the customer-type relationship. The case involved a man in his early 40s who had developed a serious drinking problem while he was in the military service.

Client: I just decided that I've got to stop.
Therapist: Sounds like you have really made up your mind.
Cl: I have!
Th: So, what are you doing different that tells you that you have really made up your mind?
Cl: Well . . . I have already stopped drinking.
Th: (incredulous) Is that right?

Cl: Yeah, I haven't had a drink for over a week now.

Th: That's incredible! How did you do that?

Cl: I'll tell you . . . it wasn't easy . . . you know, all my friends drink . . . and so, well . . . it's been hard, but this is what I want to do.

In this exchange, the client and therapist jointly identify the alcohol problem as the focus for treatment. In addition, the statements of the client clearly indicate that he views himself as part of the solution and is willing to do something about the problem. This type of client-therapist dialogue is typical in customer-type relationships.

Curiously, the customer-type relationship is one that most alcohol and substance abuse counselors/therapists report experiencing the least with their clients. Indeed, most describe their cases in a manner that suggests that the majority of their client-therapist relationships fall into one of the other two remaining categories — the most frequent being the visitor type. The customer-type relationship is, however, the type of relationship that most counselors and therapists desire to have, as it is one in which clients appear receptive and motivated for treatment. Indeed, we have found that the desire to have such a relationship is often so strong that treatment professionals act as if all of their client-therapist relationships are of the customer-type and then become angry when the clients are not receptive and motivated.

The Complainant-Type Relationship

This type of relationship exists when, over the course of the session, the therapist and client are jointly able to identify a goal or complaint for treatment but have not been able to identify the concrete steps that the client needs to take to bring about a solution. Clients in complainant-type relationships are typically able to describe their complaint or goal in great detail. However, they may not readily see themselves as part of the solution and, in fact, may believe that the only solution is for someone other than themselves to change. In the complainant-type relationship, the therapist agrees to explore the complaint or goal further *with* the client and to do so in a way that is intended to facilitate a new perspective that might lead to a solution.

Excerpts from a case involving the parents of a 15-year-old illustrate the kind of dialogue that often occurs in complainant-type relationships. In the first session of family therapy, the parents described in detail their son's history of shoplifting, truancy, and most recently, drug

use. Among other things, they speculated that hormonal changes resulting from puberty might be responsible for some of the problems. When
the parents were asked about times when the teenager did better, they
responded:

Mother: I don't know. Sometimes he just gets it in his mind . . . and,
    then, uh, he is okay for a while . . .
Therapist: So, what do you suppose is different on those occasions
    when he is okay?
M: I have no idea . . . he just, I guess, he just decides for once to do it
    . . . I mean I know he can do it, but he just decides, or something,
    that he is not going to . . . maybe just to hurt me . . .
Th: What do you suppose he might say you or John [husband] are doing
    differently on those times when he is okay?
Father: I don't think he . . . it doesn't matter what we do, it's still the
    same . . . I mean, the only thing is if he decides to do it . . . then
    he will. If he doesn't want to . . . (laugh) then he won't.
M: He needs therapy!
Th: And, he doesn't want to come in right now? Is that right?
M: Yeah . . . it's hopeless . . . and how do we parent somebody who
    doesn't want parents?
Th: What do you suppose needs to happen for things to improve?
F: Well, uh . . . I don't know how this [coming to therapy] will help
    him . . . he really needs to be here.
M: He'll never come in . . . if he could get away from those . . . he is
    really influenced . . . by his friends.

Over the course of the interview, both parents continued to complain
about the teenager while simultaneously insisting that only he could
make the necessary changes. This type of client-therapist dialogue is
typical in complainant-type relationships.

The complainant-type relationship can also be seen in the following
interchange between a husband and a wife. Initially, only the husband
had presented for treatment. During that session, he had complained
bitterly about a recent ultimatum from his wife that he either enter
drug treatment or be faced with divorce. When the client consistently
maintained that his wife was the problem, the session ended with a
request that the man bring her to the next session. The following dialogue took place between the clients and therapist a few minutes into
the session:

Wife: (To the therapist) Well, you probably should know that I have recently become born again . . . you know, a Christian. I have turned my life over to Jesus and because of this, I am not going to have the evil influence of drugs or alcohol in my home . . . especially around the kids . . .

Therapist: Oh, uh huh.

W: . . . . and if he doesn't stop, well, then, uh . . . I want *him* out!

Husband: I hardly use any drugs or alcohol at all. She is so stuck on this. Maybe . . . maybe, I'll smoke a joint or two on the weekend . . . maybe! And I don't ever get drunk . . . maybe, maybe, I'll have a beer once or twice a week . . .

W: (To the therapist) If he doesn't stop, . . . (to her husband) if you don't stop, and I mean stop, no drugs, no liquor . . . then I want you out!

H: (To his wife) You know I don't have a problem . . . I hardly use . . . you know, the real problem is you. This time it's the church thing. It was something else before. You've gotta stop this church thing . . .

In this brief excerpt, both the husband and the wife have a complaint — and in each case, the complaint is about the other. At the same time, they each believe that the only solution is for the other person to take some action. Such dialogue is typical of a complaint-type relationship.

Another example of the complainant-type relationship is what, in popular terms, is called "codependency" (Beattie, 1987, 1989). It is not uncommon for a complainant-type relationship to initially exist when a non-problem drinking significant other (e.g., spouse, child, parent, etc.) is the client for treatment. In such cases, the client can usually be observed giving an accurate and highly detailed description of the origin, evolution, pattern, and reason for the problem. In addition, they often indicate that they know what *should* be done. At the same time, it is usually clear that they are not yet willing to *do* anything or not quite sure about what they should *do* first.

The Visitor-Type Relationship

This relationship exists when, at the end of the session, the therapist and client have not *jointly* identified a complaint or goal on which to work in treatment. In addition, the client may indicate that either no problem requiring treatment exists or that the problem belongs to somebody else. Because of this, the client in a visitor-type relationship is not likely to see any reason to change or, much less, to be in therapy. The therapist agrees that there may not be a problem that requires therapy but remains willing to help the client determine if, in fact, there is something else on which she would like to work.

The following interview illustrates how the therapist and client have difficulty in jointly identifying a goal or complaint for treatment. The session involved a 34-year-old man who was referred to us by a Capuchin Brother who operates an inner-city food and shelter program for the homeless. At the time of the referral, "Herbert" had been living on the streets for over four years. He reported a long history of alcohol, cocaine, and cannabis use as well as "unwavering ambivalence" about making any changes. Prior to the following excerpt, the therapist had spent a considerable amount of time trying unsuccessfully to determine what the client wanted from therapy.

Therapist: Do you have any idea why Brother Joel recommended that you, uh . . . come and see me?

Herbert: Yeah, well, uh, I guess? . . . to get off of . . . well, to get on some type of program.

Th: You want to get on some type of program?

H: (shaking head) Yeah. It's . . .

Th: For? (pause) What kind of problem?

H: Well, I *suppose* . . . for drugs and alcohol.

Th: So, you have been talking to Brother Joel about your drug and alcohol use . . .

H: Well, yeah . . .

Th: (continuing) And you want to . . .

H: Mostly, it's like I want to do something . . . but what I want to do, it's hard for me to say because I really . . . I really don't know myself.

Th: You don't know what you want to do . . .

H: (Nods affirmatively)

Th: You mean whether you should quit or whether you should continue to use? Is that what you mean?

H: Yeah, yeah . . . that's what I mean. Now, I know sometime ago, I wanted to stop . . . at least that's what I was telling myself that I wanted to do . . . to just quit.

Th: Quit? Quit altogether?

H: Yeah, but I don't know, I can't decide what to do.

Th: And so, um, your talking with Brother Joel has to do with whether you really want to quit or whether you want to continue and still get along doing what you have been doing?

H: Well, they have been telling me what *they* think I should do, and I imagine that I would like to get into something, some kind of program that is . . . at least, I think I want to but I am not sure. Mostly, I don't really know what kind or, uh, what I want to do.

The client and therapist were not able to jointly identify a goal or complaint for treatment. Following this segment, the interviewer inquired about the "special program" to which the client referred. Again, however, the resulting dialogue was vague and ambivalent. Despite continued attempts by the therapist and client to clarify a goal for treatment the session ended without a joint agreement. Such discourse is typical of a visitor-type relationship.

The visitor-type relationship may also develop with those problem drinking clients who have been referred for individual treatment by someone else (e.g., spouse, parent, family, employer, or judge). In these cases, it is typical for the client's view of the problem to be very different from the person who referred him. Indeed, it is not uncommon for a client to indicate that there is no problem except perhaps figuring out how to get the referring agent "off my back."

In a case treated recently at our Center, a police officer in his mid-thirties was referred by his captain for treatment of an alcohol problem and domestic violence. Before coming in for treatment, the officer had been evaluated by a psychologist who described a recurring pattern of alcohol abuse followed by domestic violence. At the time the officer was seen, charges had been filed by the District Attorney for the most recent episode of violence. In response to a question about why he had come in for treatment, he responded:

Client: . . . . it was recommended to me that it would be helpful to, uh, do it . . . to come in for counseling.

Therapist: So, are you in agreement with that recommendation?

Cl: Well, uh . . .

Th: Who recommended . . . ?

Cl: (interrupting) I, uh, basically got the recommendation from the police captain.

Th: Uh, huh. So, he heard about . . .

Cl: (interrupting) Yeah! From the District Attorney and psychologist. So . . . in order for them not to release me from the force, they

want me to . . . they just want to make sure that, uh . . . things
are in order.

Th: And, so, do you think it is a good idea for you to be here then?
(Pause) Do you think it's a good idea to go along with the captain's
orders?

Cl: Well . . . I think it is from the point of view of making sure that he
is happy . . . and when he is happy, it makes the district attorney
happy, so . . .

Th: That makes your job easier?

Cl: It makes my job easier so I don't have to put up with the heat from
the police captain.

Th: (Pause) Okay, so, uh . . . any idea what he is looking for then?

The client does not identify his drinking or violent episodes as a
problem requiring treatment even though this is the problem for which
he was referred. The therapist works with the client's perspective and
attempts to find out if there is some other complaint or goal on which to
work. As the interview proceeds, the only problem jointly identified by
the client and therapist is that the police captain is hassling him. This
may, at some later point in the interview, become a complaint or goal on
which the client and therapist can work together.

A case reported by Milton H. Erickson is a good example of another
visitor-type relationship (O'Hanlon & Hexum, 1990; Rosen, 1982). In
the case, a very wealthy man asked Erickson to help him quit drinking.
Little is known about the extent or duration of the drinking problem
with the exception that the man claimed to be "an alcoholic" who
wanted very much to quit. When, during the initial phase of the interview, Erickson asked the man if he was married, he replied, "Yes, very
much married." The client went on to tell Erickson that he and his wife
owned a beautiful, secluded summer cottage ten miles from civilization
where each summer they would spend two or three weeks drinking and
lounging around in the nude. Upon hearing this, Erickson told the man
that it would be very easy for him to cease having problems with alcohol
if he would follow a few simple instructions. The man was to drive to
the summer cottage with his wife. Once there, they were to pack any
liquor and all of their clothing, including what the man was wearing,
into the car. Then, his wife was to drive back into town where a friend
would be scheduled to meet her and drive her back to the cabin. After
arriving back at the cabin, she would hand over her clothing to the
friend and the two of them could then "have a delightful two, three
weeks, . . . free of booze." Erickson then added "I know you won't walk

over the desert for ten miles [in the nude] to get a bottle of booze" (Rosen, 1982, p. 129). The man then told Erickson, "Doctor, I think I'm mistaken about wanting to quit drinking" and terminated treatment (O'Hanlon & Hexum, 1990, p. 129).

THE DIFFICULT, RESISTANT, OR "IN DENIAL" CLIENT

In supervising the problem drinking cases of other therapists, we have found that the majority of cases where clients have been labeled "difficult," "resistant," and/or "in denial" are those in which the treatment professional has misclassified the type of client-therapist relationship. In the prototypical case, the therapist complains of having attempted numerous therapeutic interventions to which the client has neither complied nor responded. Usually, the therapist has reacted to this situation by working even harder at "helping" the client. The most common result of this is a series of increasingly complicated, creative, and/or aggressive-confrontational intervention tactics. Most often, continued failure has served to reinforce a vicious cycle in which the view of these clients as being difficult leads to increasingly aggressive treatment strategies, which in turn, are resisted, leading to more treatment approaches, etc.

Our experience suggests that the problem with such cases rests in large measure on the failure of the therapist to recognize and adequately cooperate with the type of relationship that exists between herself and the client. The most common of these errors is to mistake a visitor-type relationship for a complainant or customer-type relationship. In general, our suggestion in such cases is that the therapist reconsider the type of relationship and then treat the client accordingly. This solves the majority of problems we encounter. However, there are two other strategies that the therapist may also find useful.

Finding the "Hidden" Customer

The idea of the "hidden" customer is that while clients may not initially be customers for dealing with the problem for which they were referred (e.g., alcohol), they may be customers for dealing with something else. The therapeutic rationale is that cooperation with the client's view of the problem and/or what he would like to achieve in therapy promotes cooperation, thereby facilitating progress toward treatment goals.

An example of this approach occurred in the case of the policeman. This client, it will be recalled, came to counseling only after being threatened with termination from the police force. A typical strategy in such a case might be to "set limits" and/or aggressively confront the man in an effort to break through his resistance and denial. However, as has been pointed out, such a strategy usually acts only to increase and solidify defensiveness. Instead, the therapist found a "hidden customer" by accepting the client's view that he was only there to please the captain.

Therapist: And, so, do you think it's a good idea for you to be here then? (Pause) Do you think it's a good idea to go along with the captain's orders?

Client: Well . . . I think it is from the point of view of making sure that he is happy . . . and when he is happy, it makes the district attorney happy, so . . .

Th: What does he think you'll get out of it by coming here?

Cl: Uh, he just doesn't want to hear about any more problems.

Th: So . . . what will make him happy is if you don't get in trouble again?

Cl: Right! . . . Right.

Th: What do you have to do so that you don't have to be told what to do by the captain?

Cl: (Pause) Well, um, not use alcohol or have any kind of problems with my wife is what I have to do.

The interchange demonstrates that while the client was not initially a customer for the alcohol problem and the domestic violence, he was a customer for staying on the police force and decreasing the "heat" from the captain. By accepting, rather than confronting, the client's view of the situation, "resistance" and "denial" were bypassed. The question then became a simple matter of what he needed to do in order to achieve his goals (i.e., abstain from alcohol and domestic violence).

In another "hidden" customer case, a woman had worked for a number of years as a clerk in the children's section of a public library and was now being considered for promotion to head librarian of that section. The only problem was that a drug test was required as part of the interview process, and the woman had a serious cocaine problem. In addition to the drug use, she complained of serious bouts of depression. Over the course of the interview, it became clear that a visitor-type relationship existed on the issue of drug use. However, by interviewing for a "hidden" customer, it was determined that the woman was ready and willing to *do* something about the depression. Thus, a customer-type relationship existed on the issue of depression. At the end of the first session, compliments were given to the woman for recognizing her drug problem, the need for treatment, and her honesty. Thereafter, an intervention was delivered designed to deal with the depression. Over the course of three sessions, the woman reported gradual but steady improvement in the depression. At the beginning of the fourth session, the status of the relationship regarding the drug use changed and the drug problem became the central focus of treatment.

Finding the "Other" Customer

One final strategy that we find useful is to look for what we sometimes call the "other customer." Frequently, the person sitting in our office has been referred for or forced into treatment by another person or agency; for example, a spouse, an employer, the judicial system, etc. In such cases, it can be very useful to contact the referral source to find out what they would like to see happen as a result of treatment. Such contact can be helpful in fostering cooperation and engaging the referral source in the treatment process. Indeed, on many occasions, referral sources have agreed to participate in the actual treatment process at BFTC.

The benefits of such involvement are many. First and foremost, however, is that by finding out the goal or complaint of the referral source, the treatment professional is better able to tailor treatment to address that goal or complaint. In doing so, the therapist increases the probability that the "real" customer (e.g., the referral source) will obtain the results she desires and will, consequently, be satisfied with treatment. Moreover, we have observed that satisfied referral sources are much more likely to act to reinforce such changes in the persons they referred. On the other hand, without such contact, chances are great that, no matter how hard the therapist has worked or how great the therapeutic outcome, the results of the treatment will not be in line with what the referral source had hoped. In turn, we have found that dissatisfied referral sources are less likely to notice or reinforce other treatment gains regardless of how positive they may be.

3

"Well-Formed" Treatment Goals

If therapy is to end properly, it must begin properly — by negotiating a solvable problem.

— Jay Haley (1987)

The Cat only grinned when it saw Alice. It looked good natured, she thought. Still it had very *good* claws and a great many teeth, so she felt it ought to be treated with respect. "Cheshire Puss," she began, rather timidly, "Would you tell me, please, which way I ought to go from here?"

"That depends a good deal," said the Cat, "on where you want to get to."

Alice-in-Wonderland, Lewis Carroll

CLIENTS COME TO THERAPY FOR A REASON, and the professional relationship between client and therapist is a purposeful one. One of the most important aspects of the solution-focused approach to working *with* the problem drinker is knowing when this purposeful relationship can be terminated. Both the client and the therapist must establish criteria that will tell them that they have succeeded and can end therapy. Without such criteria, it will be difficult, if not impossible, to evaluate whether progress has been made or whether the treatment goals have been reached. Often, therapy continues for longer than necessary because neither the client nor the therapist realizes that the original goals for treatment have been met.

We find that the need to develop criteria for success is particularly important when working with the problem drinker. Very often, the problem drinker feels that she has not been successful in her life and often has daily reminders of how she has failed as a person, wife, employee, and so on. Such a client desperately needs to experience success and the feeling of moving ahead. Without explicit goals, it is difficult for the client to evaluate her successes.

32

Traditionally, one way that alcohol treatment professionals have identified the accomplishment of therapeutic goals is by the completion of formalized treatment programs (i.e., completion of a 28-day inpatient alcohol treatment program, five days of inpatient detoxification, 90 A.A. meetings in 90 days, six months of weekly therapy sessions). A similar approach, commonly employed by insurance companies, EAPs, and HMOs, is to establish a predetermined number of treatment sessions. Insurance policies often establish preset limits on the number of outpatient sessions or on the length of inpatient hospitalization. The advantage to using the completion of formal treatment programs and preset limits as treatment goals is that it is very easy for the therapist and the client to determine when the goal has been met. In addition, knowing at the outset that the length of treatment is limited is likely to motivate both the client and the therapist to accomplish what they need to by the predetermined deadline.

As we have indicated previously, however, not all clients are the same, nor do they all respond similarly to the programs or guidelines established by well-intentioned treatment professionals or insurance companies. Therefore, when treatment goals are determined in this manner, it is difficult to determine whether the end of therapy is simply a response to the external limit or really an indicator of successful treatment outcome; this is presently a source of frustration for many professionals.

There are numerous debates on the positive and negative aspects of determining the treatment goal by use of a time limit. At BFTC, however, we find it more useful to determine treatment goals by specifying the *qualities* of goals that lead to effective and efficient treatment.

Our strong emphasis on goals has led others to refer to the model we describe here as a "goal-driven" model. Over time, we have come to identify seven qualities of useful treatment goals. We find that when treatment goals reflect these qualities, the therapist and client are better able to determine whether progress is being made, thereby making therapy more efficient and effective. Therapy is considered finished when these goals are accomplished, regardless of how many or how few sessions it takes. Contrary to what one might expect, however, working in this way most often acts to shorten the length of treatment.

THE SEVEN QUALITIES OF WELL-FORMED GOALS

1. Saliency to the Client

The treatment goal must be *important to the client*, and the client must view the achievement of that goal as personally beneficial. When the treatment goal is important to the client, he is much more likely to be invested in the achievement of that goal. Some examples of goals that have been salient to our clients include: saving a job, saving a marriage, getting parents "off [their] back," complying with the conditions of probation or parole, and regaining a driver's license.

The suggestion that the therapist and client work together to identify treatment goals that are important to *the client* is based on the principle of cooperation presented in Chapter 1. In line with this principle, we believe it is more helpful to accept and work with the client's goal than to insist that the client have the "proper" goal for treatment (e.g, the therapist's goal, the program goal, etc.). And indeed, we find that when the professional reaches out and cooperates with the client, it is much easier for the client, in return, to "cooperate" with the therapist. Our clinical experience in working with problem drinking clients is that they are more likely to be motivated for treatment and have positive treatment outcomes when they choose their own goals for treatment. This is clearly the result of the studies reported in Chapter 2, which demonstrated that allowing the problem drinking client to set and work toward her own goal enhanced client motivation for treatment and had a beneficial impact on treatment outcome.

If the initial goal of the client is to "cut down" on his use of alcohol, and he is not willing to accept a goal of complete abstinence from alcohol, we find it more productive to agree with that goal, than to insist that the client remain abstinent. In such instances, the client will either be successful in managing his use of alcohol, or discover that he is not able to "cut down" on his drinking and will, perhaps, be more willing to renegotiate his original goal. The important point is that when the client chooses a goal that is salient to him — be it abstinence, moderation, or something else entirely — he is more likely to be invested in achieving that goal thereby making the therapist's job easier. The client, rather than the therapist, ends up doing the majority of the work needed to achieve the identified goal.

While identifying, and then accepting, the client's goals for treatment sounds simple enough, in practice it is sometimes very difficult to implement. For example, clients often have difficulty articulating in clear and precise language what is important to them or what they hope to achieve from being in treatment. The interviewing techniques presented in Chapter 5 were developed, in part, to help the client and therapist clarify what is important to the client and what she would like to achieve while in treatment.

Another difficulty encountered in implementing this idea occurs in the context of negotiating treatment goals when there are multiple clients, treatment professionals, or service agencies involved in the treatment of a problem drinker (e.g., couples or families, allied health care providers, the justice system, or insurance companies). In such instances, each person, provider, and/or agency involved in the treatment process may have a different goal for treatment. This is typically the case, for example, when a non-problem drinking spouse brings his problem drinking partner in for therapy or an employer insists that an employee get "help" for her problem drinking. In such instances, it is useful to elicit and acknowledge the viewpoint of each person and then to look for an area of agreement between the two individuals.

A recent case involving a husband and wife who had different goals for treatment illustrates how it is possible to generate agreement regarding the treatment goal.

Therapist: What do you think will have to change as a result of your coming here today that will tell you that it's been worthwhile for you to come here together?

Husband: If I can finally convince my wife that she needs to get help with her drinking.

Th: Okay. (To wife) So, what will have to change for you to say to yourself that it's been a good thing that you came here together?

Wife: My husband will stop being a policeman about my drinking and leave me alone.

Th: So, when that happens what will be going on between the two of you that will tell you that coming to therapy has been worthwhile?

W: Well, we . . . will get along better.

Th: And, what will be happening that will tell you both that you are "getting along better?"

W: Well, for one thing he will stop watching me . . . and I suppose that I will, you know, keep my drinking down to one or two beers . . .

Th: I see, uh huh.

W: (continuing) . . . and we will have more of a social life. We are so isolated now!

Th: (To husband) And for you? What will be different?

H: Well, I could certainly stand getting along better!

Th: Right, and so, when that happens what will be different?

H: Well, I won't be checking up on her . . . you know, I don't like being the "booze police."

Th: What else?

H: We would talk more, uh, and go out more often . . . even have
some friends . . . we don't have friends.

2. Small

The goals that the client sets must be small enough so that they can be
achieved. This quality is reflected in the old A.A. slogan, "one day at a
time." Clients are much more likely to be successful when the goals for
treatment are small. Additionally, accomplishing such goals gives the
problem drinker the feeling that he is succeeding, thereby instilling hope
and increasing his motivation for future work.

Some examples of goals that our clients have found manageable include: decreasing their consumption of mixed drinks from five drinks to
two, going one more day without a drink, taking a route home that does
not pass their favorite bar, and going for a walk after work. On the other
hand, some goals that our clients have found difficult to achieve include: attending 90 A.A. meetings in 90 days, the idea of not being able
to drink for the rest of their lives, changing their friends and acquain-
tances, not nagging their problem drinking spouses, never missing work,
and so on.

Dialogue from a session with a 42-year-old, unemployed problem
drinker named Jim can be used to highlight the process of negotiating a
small treatment goal. The segment begins as Jim is explaining what he
hopes to accomplish in therapy:

J: I have to get my life together.

Th: What will be the first sign that you are "getting your life together?"

J: I'll just be more happy and be able to accomplish more. I'll get what
I deserve in life.

The therapist and client have jointly identified a goal for treatment.
Initially, the client's goal is stated in vague terms. He notes for example,
that he will be "happy" and "be able to accomplish more." However,
such goals are not only too vague but also far too large to be considered
"well-formed." The therapist must then work with the client to identify
a smaller goal. One useful way to accomplish this is to ask the client
what the first small signs of success will be.

Th: I am still wondering about this, Jim, what will be the first step that
will tell you that you are on your way to getting those things you
deserve?

J: If I kick myself in the rear end and say, "Come on, let's get going."
Th: Let me understand this more clearly, Jim. What would be the first
    small step that you will be doing that will tell you that you are
    "kicking yourself in the rear?"
J: I will be a lot more eager to get out of the house, go for a walk, call
    someone else, go visit them. I will feel better physically.

For the first time in the session, the therapist and client jointly identify some goals that are small enough to be considered "well-formed." In
this instance, the goals are for the client to get out of the house, go for a
walk, call and visit a friend, and feel better physically. Such goals are
smaller and, therefore, easier to accomplish than the goals first stated by
the client. These smaller goals are described in very specific terms,
making it easier for both the therapist and the client to determine when
the goals have been achieved. Having the treatment goals stated in
precise and quantifiable terms is the next quality of "well-formed"
goals.

3. Concrete, Specific, and Behavioral

Goals such as "getting my life together" and "being happy" are not
considered "well-formed" because they are stated in imprecise terms;
they are too vague. The problem with goals stated in such vague terms is
that it is impossible for the therapist and client to determine whether or
not progress is being made. Furthermore, when such elusive goals are
allowed to be the focus of treatment, we find that the usual result is that
therapy ends up taking much longer than necessary. The advantage of
defining goals in precise terms is that it becomes easier for the therapist
and client to evaluate exactly what progress is being made, as well as to
determine what else remains to be accomplished. In the process, we find
that therapy becomes more effective and efficient.
    Some examples of goals that our clients have stated in specific, con-
crete, and behavioral terms include: making an arrangement for a des-
ignated driver or ride home before going out on the weekend, getting to
work on time Monday morning, drinking two beers instead of five, not
drinking on Friday night when out with friends, announcing to friends
and/or family that they (the problem drinker) will not be drinking,
talking calmly with concerned family members about alcohol use, and
so on. Some vague and imprecise goals that our clients have found it
difficult to achieve include: having more self-esteem, dealing with issues
related to being an adult child of an alcoholic, living a sober life-style,
getting in touch with feelings.

In addition to helping the client and therapist assess progress, we find that when goals are stated in precise terms the opportunity develops for the client to immediately take credit for his successes. Conversely, when the goal has not been reached, having precisely stated goals helps the client figure out what else he needs to do in order to accomplish his goal. In this way, either the client is given all of the credit for achieving his goal or they are protected from feeling overwhelmed in the event that he has not been able to reach his goal.

4. The Presence Rather Than the Absence of Something

When we ask clients what they hope to accomplish by being in treatment, they often answer that they want to eliminate or be rid of a problem. The problem drinking client may say that she no longer wants to be a problem drinker, or that she does *not* want to come home drunk or become intoxicated in front of her children. Similarly, the partner of the problem drinking client may state that she *doesn't* want her husband to ever drink again, or that she *never* wants him to drive again while intoxicated. In other words, we find that the client's idea of a successful therapeutic outcome is often stated as the absence of the problem. Such goals, when verbalized, usually contain negative words such as no, never, not, can't, shouldn't, don't, won't, etc.

In our experience, we find that goals that do not contain negative words, and that instead state the presence of something rather than the absence of something, lead to more efficient and effective treatment. Goals must be stated in positive, proactive language about what the client *will* do instead of about what she will *not* do.

There are several reasons for defining treatment goals in positive terms. First, in contrast to goals stated as the absence of something, it is much easier for the therapist and client to determine when a positive goal has been met. Knowing when the client and therapist have met the goal is essential to practicing efficient and effective therapy. When the goal for treatment is stated as the absence of something, the client and therapist can never be sure that the goal has been met as there is always a chance that the problem might occur again. For this reason, it can be very difficult for the client and the therapist to know whether treatment can be ended when the goal is stated in such negative terms. Treatment becomes, out of necessity, long-term.

A second reason for preferring that goals be stated positively is the observation that it is not possible to *not* do something. As humans, we are always in a state of doing something—even when we say that the something we are doing is "nothing." In such instances, we may be less active (e.g., sitting or meditating) but we are still doing *something*. Because it is not possible for the client to not do something, we find it more useful to help the client identify exactly what he *will* be doing when he is no longer engaging in the problem behavior. In the case of a problem drinker, rather than agreeing to work on a goal of remaining abstinent from alcohol, we attempt to negotiate goals that tell us and the client what he will be doing when he is no longer drinking (e.g., hobbies, family activities, exercising, attending meetings, etc.).

A third, and final, reason for preferring positive goals involves a paradox that results whenever we try to tell ourselves *not* to do something. That is, whenever we tell ourselves to *not* do something we are forced to think about the very activity that we are supposed to avoid. We must first conjure up the image of the forbidden activity in our mind and then attempt to ignore the image. The result, of course, is that we end up thinking about the forbidden activity even more, thereby making the avoidance of the activity all the more difficult.

A young, ambitious assistant district attorney presented for treatment because of periodic episodes of problematic drinking. The young man, Jerry, feared that he might make a "serious mistake" during one of his drinking episodes that would place his legal career in jeopardy. Jerry confessed that his weakness was margaritas, which he tended to gulp down on an empty stomach, three and four at a time. In a discouraged voice, Jerry recounted the many attempts he had made to stop the problematic drinking episodes. He had tried to avoid thinking about alcohol and had stopped keeping liquor in his apartment. On a few occasions, he had been so desperate that he had even gone to another town to attend an A.A. meeting. However, all the talk about *not* drinking had made him want a drink so much that he had, in each instance, left the meeting and gone straight to a bar.

Together, Jerry and the therapist began to explore what Jerry wanted to accomplish while in treatment. Jerry immediately said that he wanted to stop the pattern of problematic drinking episodes. Recognizing that such a goal was not "well-formed," the therapist asked Jerry what he would be doing when he was no longer troubled by these episodes. Jerry complained that he no longer enjoyed the taste of the margarita because he consumed them so quickly and because he worried so much about his "problem." He then volunteered that instead of "gulping down" three or four drinks he would take the time to enjoy them. In addition, he would invite others to go out for a drink with him more often. At home, he said that he would fix something to eat instead of drinking on an empty stomach.

Over the course of therapy, with the goals for treatment stated positively, Jerry was able to implement the behaviors he described during the first session and overcome his problematic drinking episodes. At last report, Jerry continues his new eating and drinking patterns.

The process of helping a client state the treatment goal as the presence rather than the absence of something is demonstrated in another case involving a 16-year-old named David who was brought for treatment by his mother because of his problematic use of alcohol and his withdrawn behavior. At the outset of the session, David stated that he did not have a problem and that he did not want to participate in the session. David's statement was accepted by the therapist and the conversation shifted to his mother. In the following excerpt, the therapist works together with David's mother to negotiate a positive goal:

Therapist: So, Mrs. L, what do you suppose you will see David doing differently when we are finished with our work here so that you don't have to come anymore?

Mother: I don't want him drinking and so withdrawn. He hardly says anything to the family when he is home. He shuts himself up in his room and doesn't come out.

Th: So, when David gets the right kind of help from coming here, what would you see him doing instead?

M: Well, uh, I probably will see him like he was before. He used to be a lot of fun, always joking. I think he is really broken up about his girlfriend.

Th: So, when he is back to his old self, what would you notice him doing differently than he does now?

M: Well, oh, I suppose he will be more cheerful. I know he is a teenager and he will have mood swings, but he will at least talk to us and have dinner with us sometimes.

Th: Okay, what else?

M: He will come out of his room and at least say "hi" to us and we will have those conversations like we used to and he will tell me what his plans for the future are and where he is going with his life.

Th: Anything else?

M: Well, I suppose he will continue to go to work and school and all that.

With the goals stated in such a positive fashion the chances are higher that David's mother will notice and recognize when a small change occurs. In addition, when she sees that David is changing, she is more likely to respond in a positive manner toward her son, thereby reinforcing the small changes and facilitating a "ripple effect." If, on the other hand, the goal is negotiated in negative terms, any small changes that are made by David are likely to go unrecognized by his mother and be discontinued because of a lack of reinforcement.

5. A Beginning Rather Than an End

The ancient saying, "A journey of a thousand miles begins with one step" means that no matter how large or complex our goal, it can be accomplished if we concentrate on starting it, rather than on its eventual outcome. Similarly, goals must describe the first small steps the client needs to take rather than the end of the journey. When clients initially present for treatment they often describe their goals in completed form (i.e., sobriety, happiness); in other words, in terms of the end result they hope to achieve. While this can be considered a sign that the client is able to perceive the possibility of a different life, unless she is helped to define the movement toward those goals in a step-by-step fashion, her goal may remain just a possibility and nothing more. While the client's perception of the end result should be accepted, the therapist must work together with the client to specify exactly what steps will need to be taken *first* in order to accomplish that desired result.

In another excerpt from the case of David and his mother, Mother describes the hope she has for her son. Up to this point in the session, David has sat quietly, looking bored and sullen, without participating in the discussion.

Mother: David has so much . . . I want him to be all that he can be (looks at David).

David: (looks away from his mother)

Therapist: I can see that you see a lot of potential in David.

M: Of course I do. I keep telling him what a smart person he is. He is really very smart.

D: (looks down at floor)

Th: So, what would be the first sign to you that David is heading in the right direction?

M: Well . . . I suppose I will see him living up to his potential.

Th: I see . . . and what will be the very first, small sign that David is "living up to his potential"?

M: The first small sign?

Th: Yeah, what will be the first small thing that David will do that will say to you, "Hey, he is beginning to live up to his potential!"

D: (turns head slightly toward mother)

M: Well, he would . . . he would just smile more and, uh . . . he used
    to get along well with his brother, and they used to be very close.
    So I suppose, another small sign will be that he starts getting along
    with his brother again.

Th: Good.

M: And, like I said earlier, he would have dinner with us when he can.
    I can't expect him to do that every night because he works after
    school and on Saturdays.

Th: Right, so, when you see him smile more, and get along with his
    brother, and when he joins the family for dinner, that will be the
    first small sign?

M: Yes.

D: (looks surprised)

Over the course of this exchange, the mother's beginning goals become more clear. In addition, David appears to become somewhat more
engaged in the treatment process, albeit on a nonverbal level. In the
dialogue that followed, David finally began participating in the discussion. In fact, the therapist was able to work with David to negotiate
some small beginning goals of his own. We frequently find that clients
who are initially hesitant about treatment are often more willing to
participate once they recognize that they are not going to be asked or
forced to be "cured" at the end of the session or to set unreasonably high
goals.

6. Realistic and Achievable Within the Context of the Client's Life

When working with the problem drinker, it is important that the clinician cooperate in determining what is and is not realistic and achievable
within the context of the client's life circumstances. While some clients
may have difficulty identifying what is realistic and achievable, in most
cases we find that the client is the single best source of information
about what he can be expected to accomplish. We recognize that many
problem drinkers have a reputation for making grandiose promises that
they frequently fail to keep. Our view of this negative reputation, however, is that it is due in large measure to the unrealistic and unachievable
goals that treatment professionals have traditionally demanded (e.g.,
lifelong abstinence, etc.), rather than an inherently negative characteristic of the problem drinking population.

When a client does present an unrealistic or unachievable goal, the therapist must work *with* the client to negotiate a goal that is more manageable. We find that most clients either know beforehand or recognize very quickly when their initial goal for treatment is unachievable and are willing to negotiate a more realistic alternative. For example, when a problem drinker seeks treatment after his spouse has left, it is not uncommon for him to state initially that his only goal for treatment is to "get my wife back!" Very often, however, this goal is not realistic. After listening and empathizing with the client's plight, we find that most recognize this fact and are willing to negotiate a different, more realistic goal. The few remaining clients are generally willing to consider a more achievable interim goal (e.g., make changes in their problem drinking behavior) if they believe that this will increase the chances of restoring their relationship.

7. Perceived as Involving "Hard Work"

The final quality of a well-formed goal is that the goal must be perceived as involving "hard work." We frequently remind both ourselves and our clients that the changes the client will be attempting to make will require "hard work." This idea may seem contradictory given that we have previously advocated that the therapist negotiate goals that are small and achievable. However, in addition to these qualities, we find that acknowledging the "hard work" involved in making changes serves a number of important functions.

The first, and perhaps most important, of these functions is the protection and promotion of the client's sense of self-worth and dignity. Stating at the outset of treatment that the client's goal will involve "hard work" serves to protect the client's sense of dignity in the event that she is unable to reach her desired goal. In such circumstances, failure only means more hard work remains to be done, not that the client cannot accomplish her goal. In a similar fashion, a client's sense of dignity can be bolstered by attributing past failures to the difficult nature of the problem.

In our clinical experience, we find that the problem drinker always benefits from having some graceful and acceptable way to acknowledge that he has failed in the past. In the traditional model, the problem drinking client has always been able to salvage some of his self-respect by blaming his failures on the "disease of alcoholism." In general, however, we have found this approach less effective in promoting subsequent personal responsibility. In contrast, when the goal is described as a "difficult" one that involves "hard work," the client is forced to internalize responsibility for achieving his goal while simultaneously having a way to maintain his sense of self-respect in the event of failure.

Phrasing goals as "hard work" also parallels the client's past experience of dealing with her drinking problem. Before coming to treatment, most clients have already tried and failed numerous times to solve their problem. Stating that the client's problem is difficult and will require "hard work" is very often a point on which the client can readily agree. In addition, we find that this serves to instill hope in the client that her goal is attainable with the requisite amount of hard work. We further find that this hope helps to motivate the client to achieve her goal.

Most problem drinkers have been told repeatedly that what they have to do is very simple if they would only do it! For example, all they need to do is, "just say no," "live one day at a time," or "follow the program," and so forth. At best, such statements are disrespectful, as they underestimate how difficult it can be for the problem drinker to put such simple solutions into practice. At worst, such statements may exacerbate feelings of hopelessness and despair associated with previous failures. Indeed, these statements imply that if the client fails then it is because he is stupid, unwilling, or characterologically flawed. Returning to the "Big Book" once again, recall the explanation offered about those individuals who are unable to benefit from the "simple" approach offered by Alcoholics Anonymous. According to the book, these people are "constitutionally incapable of being honest with themselves, . . . [they are] born that way . . . [and are] naturally incapable of grasping and developing a manner of living which demands rigorous honesty" (p. 58). This view allows very little opportunity for the client to maintain a sense of dignity and self-worth, much less a feeling of hopefulness, in the event that he is unable to follow the A.A. model.

Emphasizing "hard work" when negotiating treatment goals puts the client and the therapist in a "win-win" situation. Whatever the outcome, the client and the therapist are able to view their efforts as successful. If the client does not reach the goal this is simply a sign that more hard work remains to be done. However, if by chance the client is able to solve her problem very quickly then she can be given extra credit and praise for having figured out how to solve a very "difficult" problem in a short period of time. And, finally, if the client makes slow, steady, even progress then this can be accepted as normal and the client can be complimented for her hard work.

4

Negotiating and Cooperating: Goals and the Client-Therapist Relationship

If you keep saying things are going to be bad, you have a good chance of being a prophet.

— Isaac Bashevis Singer

Too many therapists take you out to dinner and then tell you what to order. I take a patient out to a psychotherapeutic dinner and I say, "You give your order."

— Milton Erickson (1973)

WE WOULD LIKE TO STRESS THAT EVEN well-formed goals must be implemented in such a way so as to fit each client-therapist relationship in order to be effective. Such efforts to individualize treatment require considerable clinical skills in not only adapting to what the client wants, but also negotiating with her concerning her potential for success and her willingness to arrive at workable goals. In this chapter we will describe some common clinical situations that were presented as problematic during our teaching and supervisory sessions.

GOAL SETTING WITH AN INVOLUNTARY CLIENT

It is no fun working with involuntary clients. It is more rewarding and easier to work with clients who value our professional knowledge and expertise. Unfortunately, because excessive use of alcohol creates legal and ethical problems, many treatment programs must treat clients who are often described as "involuntary." It is possible that the negative reputation that problem drinkers have among treatment professionals is actually the result of the professionals' misassessment of the therapeutic relationship and unwillingness to accept the clients' goals as worthy of merit or useful as a starting point.

45

Working with an involuntary client who denies or minimizes the serious consequences of his drinking, for himself and those around him, requires the therapist to make a paradigmatic shift in order to increase treatment effectiveness. Without such a change, the therapist can easily become discouraged and overwhelmed and can end up feeling hopeless about the client.

A common therapist reaction to such a client is to become more upset about the client's drinking problem than the client, overreacting to the client's minimizing. The *therapist* can easily become a "customer" for her own services.

GOAL SETTING WITH A VISITOR-TYPE RELATIONSHIP

When working in a visitor-type relationship, therapists are particularly vulnerable to telling clients "what to do." The outcome of this type of intervention is quite predictably negative. In order to avoid such tendencies, it is important to be aware of the pitfalls and take steps to guard against them.

When viewing the dramatic and serious physical and psychological damage caused by the prolonged abuse of alcohol, it is easy for a therapist to impose goals on the client. The therapist may see that there is a great deal of potential for the client to become productive and whole again. A therapist can also see the suffering inflicted on those around the problem drinker (e.g., the husband, children, employers) and on the drinker herself, and indignation can cloud the best clinical judgment. Many professionals become surprised and angry when the client does not follow the goals already set by the therapist or by the treatment program — without the client's input.

It is our belief that the bad reputation of the problem drinker develops because clinicians often misjudge a client as being a "customer" when, in fact, the client may be a "visitor." When the therapist proceeds to discuss the client's need to take steps to join A.A., to take steps towards sobriety, to become more responsible, or to take treatment more seriously, the client is most often less likely to participate with desired responsiveness. Therefore, accurately assessing a visitor-type relationship and proceeding accordingly will enhance the client's motivation and will enhance his feeling of being respected.

Instead of becoming frustrated with such clients, the following are some techniques not only to set the relationship on the right track but also to help clients decide on goals that they believe will be helpful for moving in a more positive direction.

Find Out What the Client Wants

The most helpful stance a professional can take with the visiting client is to be sincere, genuine, and respectful of his self-determination in setting goals, and to trust that he has enough intelligence to figure out what is good for him. When the therapist has made it clear that she has genuine regard for the client, she should then find out what is important from his point of view. Our clinical experience indicates that all clients want something from coming to see a therapist, even if it is a reassuring phone call to his probation officer or employer.

For some clients, being a good father and family man means being a stable financial provider. Others may view relationships with friends who engage in outdoor activities as important. Another important goal may be keeping a marriage together or holding onto a job. For some, it may be staying "independent" and not "being told what to do."

At times, finding out what the client wants is not so easy because the client often does not know what she wants. For example, a 24-year-old civil service worker, Cindy, was very guarded initially and had difficulty describing what she wanted. It appeared that her drinking had escalated during the three months just prior to our first meeting to the point where she failed to show up for work. When her supervisor demanded that Cindy present medical excuses for her excessive absences, she was unable to produce one because in reality she "partied" all night and often didn't get any sleep. Various questions designed to generate her supervisor's goal for her coming to treatment produced only a vague notion about wanting to "feel better" about herself and become more assertive. Yet when asked about how important it was for her to "feel better" about herself later on during the interview, Cindy's ranking of it was rather low, while she indicated that her keeping her job was more important. At the same time, Cindy indicated that because she was a member of a civil service union, her job was protected and that she was not likely to lose it. Much of the information she provided was inconsistent. We decided that she was not clear about what was important to her, and therefore, not ready to commit to treatment. It took Cindy and the therapist two sessions to clarify what was important to her.

Agree with the Client's Goal and
Be Sympathetic to His Plight

In order to achieve the goal of getting someone "off my back," the client must follow certain rules, such as not drinking and driving, not coming home drunk, not coming to work drunk, or making sure that he shows up for appointments. Even though we may hope that the client will strive for more ambitious goals of confronting problems, the goal of "avoiding trouble" may be good enough for now, because in order to do this, the client must control his drinking. Find out what the client is *willing* to do and then work to achieve that goal, setting aside thoughts of what he *should* do.

Nobody likes to be told what to do, and your client is no exception. Clinicians must take a sympathetic attitude to the client's plight of having someone rule her life. Try to utilize the technique of empathy and imagine how difficult it must be to be sitting in your office. Be sympathetic, and be on the client's side. Do not defend the employers, the drunk driving law, the judge's mandate, or the "unreasonable" family demands.

Compliment the Client

The client who comes to treatment under duress should be complimented on taking the time and effort to come to the session. Such an effort can be viewed as a willingness to get along with someone (e.g., employer, judge) who is in a position to demand that the client take steps, or as a way to avoid unpleasant or unhelpful consequences. The client had the choice of not complying with the mandated demands and could have taken the consequences of such a choice. The motivation behind coming to the session is clearly a desire to minimize conflict in his life — this is clearly a positive step. Clinicians must be sincere in their belief that the client has something worthwhile to be complimented on; therefore, a therapist may have to look for things to compliment.

The client expects the clinician to react in the same way everyone else in her life has, to be critical and to "tell her what to do," which will remind her of her failures. It is not surprising that a client will be astonished when you say something complimentary to him, by pointing out some genuine efforts he has made. Clients are often caught off guard when this happens; some clients react in intensely emotional ways. A client may start to cry, to smile, or to confirm the therapist's comments by agreeing and repeating how tough it was for him to come to the session. A client may say, "You know, I know I drink too much. I know it's not good for me. Actually, I should do something about my drinking."

Take a position, until proven otherwise, that what the client wants to do is good for her. When a therapist takes such a position, it is easy to be respectful of the client and to see what positive things she is doing in her attempts to solve her problems.

The client can be complimented on showing up for an appointment. Even though he had the option of taking the legal consequences (such as losing a license or going to jail), he is doing the right thing by coming to class, coming to therapy, making an effort to keep his job, or trying to please his family. Even though a client may have failed before, he is now making an effort.

Anything the client is doing that is good for her, including attempts to manage her life and drinking habits, should be highlighted and given credit. Other things to compliment include a client's having stayed at a job for a long time or having achieved a certain level of proficiency in a job or academic, athletic, or social endeavor. For example, after meeting with Cindy, the civil service worker who was sent to treatment by her supervisor, the therapist complimented her on coming to the first session even though it was not her own idea. We agreed with her that her wanting to feel better about herself and her wanting to keep her job were certainly the first steps toward doing what was good for her. Because the client was vague, we decided to match her vagueness, while still suggesting to her that her feeling better about herself and wanting to keep her job was doing what was good for her.

Ask About the Client's View of the Referring Person's Demands

Since most clients in this category of initial "visitors" see themselves as being coerced into treatment, they are not likely to be cooperative, open, or honest about their drinking problems. However, they are often willing to correct someone else's mistaken notions about themselves. Asking the client about his perception of someone else's demands, mandates, or requirements, can prove to be productive. When the client feels he has been wrongly categorized, he is usually anxious to correct any misperceptions.

Case Example: Tough Mother

Derrick, age 17, was sent to a session by his mother, a single parent, for suspected drug and alcohol use. He seemed sullen and uncooperative as he stretched his tall, muscular frame out in a chair with a defiant look on his face. The therapist decided to start the conversation by being sympathetic:

Therapist: I guess you have better things to do on a day like this than to
   sit and talk to some strange counselor. So, what do you think your
   mother believes has to happen here so that she will say you don't
   have to come here anymore?

Derrick: Huh?

Th: What do you suppose your mother will have to see happen for her
   to believe that you don't have to come back to see me?

D: You can't tell her nothing. She thinks I'm a dope addict or something.

Th: It's good that you are not. What will convince your mom that you
   are a sensible person?

D: You can't talk to her, man. She is always going off, hollering, and
   screaming about nothing.

Th: Sounds like you have a tough situation at home. I'm sure it's no
   fun.

D: No, it ain't. She needs to chill out. She yells at little stuff, like when
   the dishes are not done right away, and stuff like that.

As can be seen from this exchange, the initial concern for Derrick was
not related to drug or alcohol abuse but to getting his mother to "chill
out" and not yell at him. Had the therapist delved into his drug and
alcohol use, Derrick probably would have refused to talk or refused to
return for a second session. When the therapist agreed with what was
important to him, Derrick was less resistant to the idea of returning.
Since his interest in returning enhances the possibility that Derrick may
become interested in looking at his drug and alcohol use, this is a good
beginning for goal negotiation. By recognizing Derrick's reluctance to
acknowledge his substance abuse problems, the counselor remained
sympathetic to Derrick's plight of being "misunderstood" by his mother
as "a dope addict."

The following questions are useful in negotiating goals with those
mandated to come for treatment.

1. Whose idea was it that you come here?
   Who suggested you come here? (Who made you come here?)
   What makes _____ think that you need to come here?
   What does _____ think is the reason that you have this
   problem?

2. What has to happen for _____ to leave you alone?
   What will convince _____ that you don't need to come
   here?

What do you suppose _____ will say you have to do for him to think that you don't have to come here?

What do you suppose _____ will say about how your coming here will be helpful to you?

3. What does _____ say you need to do differently?

4. What do you suppose _____ will say she needs to see you do that will tell her this is helping you?

5. When was the last time you did this?

What was different then?

How did you do this?

What was most helpful in getting you started?

What do you suppose _____ would say he noticed was different about you when you did this?

6. What is the first step you need to take to get started?

How confident are you that you can repeat what helped you again?

What do you suppose _____ would say it would take you to do this again?

What do suppose _____ would do differently then?

7. What will be different in your life then?

What will be going on in your life that is not going on now?

What difference would it make in your life then?

8. How will you know you have done enough?

Who will be the first to notice the changes you will make?

What do you suppose _____ will say is different about you then?

What difference would it make in your relationship with your family (your boss, your friends, your children) then?

What will you be doing different that you are not doing now?

The following dialogue illustrates how to put these questions together.

Therapist: So, how can I help you?

Client: I'm not sure. What is your name again?

Th: Sorry. I thought you knew. My name is . . . I am wondering what it is that I can do to be helpful to you?

Cl: I'm not sure. Everybody says I have a drinking problem, but uh . . . I'm not stumbling around or anything like that . . . you know . . . I don't have to drink every day. I can stop drinking anytime I decide to.

Th: Whose idea was it that you come here today?

Cl: If they think I'm an alcoholic, they are wrong.

Th: So, what do they think you have to do here so that you don't have to come here?

Cl: My supervisor has in it for me, you know, he never liked me from the first day. He thinks I'm an alcoholic.

Th: What do you suppose makes him think that you have a drinking problem?

Cl: Well, sometimes I don't make it to work on Mondays.

Th: How is that a problem for you?

Cl: I can't afford to lose this job. I guess I shouldn't drink on the weekend. I read it somewhere, uh, that it is genetic.

Th: So, what do you have to do to keep your job?

Cl: I have to convince my supervisor that I don't have a drinking problem.

Th: That's a good idea. So, what do you suppose your supervisor would say you have to do to convince him that you can handle your job?

Cl: Well, uh, I suppose he thinks I will have to show up for work on Monday morning all full of pep and energy, uh, be a "team player," that's his favorite words.

Th: So, what else do you have to do, in addition to showing up for work on Mondays, to show him that you are a "team player"?

The above dialogue clearly demonstrates a frustrating beginning with a client. The client could easily have been dismissed as someone who was "in denial"; however, then the therapist would lose an opportunity to help him become a customer for some other issue than his drinking. It would make a therapist's job easier if the client saw things as "they really are." But, as can be seen from the dialogue, even when a client refuses to acknowledge a problem with alcohol, the therapist's decision on which way to go with the clinical material can make a difference. The therapist showed genuine respect and curiosity about how the client saw things differently from his employer. When the therapist saw the client's problem from the client's perspective, the client eventually decided on a goal that could be followed through on.

Sometimes, even when the client comes to treatment "voluntarily," it is still necessary to assess his view of how much of a problem drinking is for him and how much he sees himself as a part of the solution to the drinking problem.

Case Example: An Ambivalent Client

The following is an excerpt from a session with John, who was referred for treatment "at his request." Notice that the client's ambivalence and the tenuous nature of his commitment to treatment had to be fully explored before he could come to a decision that would enable him to be successful in addressing his problems. Pay particular attention to how the therapist stays focused on what the client says, thus giving credence to the client's views, while at the same time gently challenging those views.

Therapist: How can I help?

John: I'm not sure. I want to get on some type of program.

Th: What type of program do you have in mind?

J: For drug and alcohol problems.

Th: What kind of drug do you use mostly?

J: Cocaine mostly, and alcohol.

Th: How do you get money for that?

J: Well, I know a lot of people who have connections. When I am around, they might let me do some things.

Realizing that John was becoming more hesitant and vague, the therapist recognized that perhaps she was too intrusive too soon in the session. Recognizing this, the therapist decides to drop the issue of where he gets the money for cocaine and instead to focus on goal negotiation.

Th: So, what kind of help were you looking for when you came here today?

J: Well, I don't know myself what I am looking for.

Th: You mean you don't know if you want to quit drugs and alcohol?

J: That's just it. I don't know what I want. I tell myself I want to quit, but I don't know. I know a lot of people who tried to quit but couldn't quit.

Th: So, talking to your social worker had something to do with wanting to quit drugs and alcohol use? Or was it about something else?

J: The social worker said you people try to help people like myself. I want to do something, but I don't know. I'm having a hard time right now.

Th: You mean you have a hard time deciding which way you want to go?

J: Yeah, I don't know what I want. I know that I shouldn't be doing drugs. I don't like how things are going right now.

Th: What does your brother think you should do?

J: Well, he doesn't say much about what I should do anymore. But sometimes he asks "When are you going to get a job?" I gather that he thinks it will be good for me to get a job.

Th: Obviously he wants you to do what is good for you. What do you think will be good for you to do?

J: I know what I would like to do, and that is to go back to school someday.

Th: So, what do you have to do so that you can go back to school? What would it take you to do that?

J: Well, I will have to be more stable, and have a place of my own. And stop drinking and stop drugs.

Th: So, what will help you make up your mind to go one way or the other?

J: That's just it, right there. I don't know. I really don't know.

Th: I appreciate your being honest about that. You know you could be giving me a lot of bull. I can understand that there is a good reason for doing drugs and drinking and a good reason for not using drugs. So, what would you say is a good reason for doing drugs?

J: Let me see. A good reason would be because I feel comfortable doing that.

Th: There must also be other side benefits.

J: You know, it makes me feel like I'm somebody. You know the type of people I hang out with. It helps me to relate to other people.

Th: Okay, that's a good reason. Any other good reasons?

J: Not really. It's something I've been doing all my life.

Th: You have been at it a long time.

J: Yeah, I started in junior high and it's like a habit now.

Th: Junior high kids don't know any better, so they start something. But you've been at it for a long time. So, you must have a good reason for continuing. You seem like the sort of person that wouldn't do things without good reasons.

J: I never really thought of it like that. I've been doing it so long that it is something I do.

Th: You mean you are doing it just out of habit, just because you've been doing it so long?

J: It's like this. Like today. When I'm tired of sitting around, I go over there and I do drugs.

Th: You mean when you are bored. Okay, that's a good reason. Can you think of any other good reason?

J: When you say "a good reason," I never thought of it like that. A good reason.

Th: You seem like a reasonably smart guy and you don't seem like the kind that will do things without good reason.

J: It really don't seem like a good reason. I'd be just doing it.

Th: Maybe it's a good reason. To make you feel more comfortable. Can you think of some other good reason?

J: Not really. Not right off.

Th: You don't seem like the kind of guy that will do things with no good reason.

J: Okay. I read a long time ago that people who abuse drugs are suicidal, that they are tying to kill themselves. I agree with that because sometimes I feel like killing myself. In fact, I tried to kill myself but couldn't do it. Since then, I decided I was too much of a coward to kill myself, so, I'm not going to do it.

Th: Okay, that's good. I'm glad to hear that. Now, let's think about good reasons for not doing it.

J: Not doing it? Let me see. I know I will have more money in my pocket. Probably will have more respect from people.

Th: Who?

J: My family. My sister, especially. And my father. I will probably have my health.

Th: Your health, which is the most important thing. Probably more important than anything. Okay. Anything else?

J: No, I don't think so.

Th: So, when you look at both sides, good reason for doing it and good reason for not doing it. How will you decide which is better for you?

J: How will I decide? You mean which way I will go?

Th: Yeah.

J: It really doesn't seem like a hard question, but it is hard. Because I do miss certain things, but it is hard for me to say which way I will go. It's hard to decide.

Th: Yeah, you've got a tough problem, deciding which way to go. Now, are you the kind of person that once you decide which way to go, you can stick with it? Or even after you decide, will you change your mind?

J: I change my mind.

Th: But you stuck with the program for seven months before.
J: It wasn't that hard. I stuck with it even though it was tough some-
   times.
Th: Let's get back to this. How will you decide which way to go?
J: It seems like the right and wrong thing. I seem to do the wrong thing.
   I know what is right for me. I want to stop using drugs and alcohol
   and start doing something positive.

By posing the decision to enter treatment as a difficult choice between equally attractive options, the therapist not only respectfully
points out that the client's choice of drug use was made at a very young,
inexperienced age, but suggests that now he is smart enough to make a
wiser choice. This allows the client a graceful way to remake his choice
not to use drugs. It also implies that this time he will make a better
decision, one based on what is good for him. The emphasis here is on
what will be ultimately good for the client, from *his* point of view.

Allowing the client to weigh the merits of both options while recognizing and trusting that he will make a wise choice, puts a tremendous
pressure on the client to make a wise decision. Our clinical experience is
that when clients are given such choices, contrary to our worst fears
about their making a poor choice, they make good choices. This certainly restores our faith in the human spirit.

The therapist recognizes that the client is ambivalent about which
direction to take and that pushing him to a certain direction would only
increase the resistance. The therapist compliments the client on being
respectful enough to be honest and acknowledges that the client has a
serious question to ask himself during the coming week.

The following week, John came back more cheerful and upbeat,
reporting that he cut down on his drug and alcohol use considerably (on
his own) by keeping busy looking for a job. He discovered that it was not
as difficult as he thought it might be.

GOAL NEGOTIATION WITH A COMPLAINANT

Frequently confusing to therapists, the "complainant" type of client-
therapist relationship can become frustrating if not clearly assessed. As
discussed fully in Chapter 2, clients in such a relationship seem to separate the cause of problems from their solutions. Therefore, a client's
view frequently is that she is a "victim" of someone else's drinking and
other related problems and, therefore, the solution to her problems
should lie with the drinker. In other instances, the client may agree that

her drinking is a problem but that because it is caused by genetic predisposition, she has no viable means to solve the problem. One client proclaimed, "I'm an alcoholic. They say it's genetic. So, what do you want me to do?" This is an extreme example of someone who does not yet see the connection between the problem and the solution. A complainant initially sees no discernible connection between the problems and his own role in solutions. At times, this type of client-therapist relationship is difficult to identify, because, while the client clearly states there is a problem, he either sees no solutions or feels helpless to do anything. He may have come to this conclusion because many attempted solutions did not work, and it may require a cognitive shift in order for him to see the connection between the two.

Because of their tendency to look at solutions as lying in someone else's hands, clients' initial solutions usually center around trying to help someone else change instead of focusing on changes in their own lives. Parents, for example, will complain about the bad influence of their child's friends and feel impotent to do anything about it. The spouses of alcohol abusers, feeling helpless to do anything about the drinker's problems, nonetheless expend a great deal of energy trying to change the drinker's behaviors. These family members believe that the problem is inflicted on them, but that the solution lies elsewhere. In the literature these types of clients are commonly misunderstood and described incorrectly as "codependent" or "enablers."

Such clients need to be empowered by a therapist who will help them recognize that there are changes they can make so their lives will be better. At this point, the suggestion to join an Al-Anon group may not make any sense to the client. Even though it is an excellent resource, a group may require too big a shift in thinking about the client's part in the solution patterns. Such clients require interim help in order to make the intellectual leap to seeing themselves as needing help.

Case Example: Sullen in Black

Sara, age 17 and a senior in high school, looked sullen and answered only "yes" or "no" to questions. Although it was the middle of an August heat wave, she was dressed in black with dyed black hair and harsh, mostly black makeup. Sara was uncooperative and uncommunicative, and her verbal and nonverbal clues indicated clearly that she did not want to be there. Mrs. T, Sara's mother, was very talkative; she described all the problems she had had with Sara over the years, particularly since Sara began to hang out with "bad friends." Mrs. T felt hurt and rejected by Sara, because all of her hard work in trying to instill Catholic values in her daughter was going nowhere.

When asked what would be helpful to Sara, Mrs. T went on in detail about the mistakes her previous therapist made with Sara, which had given Sara reasons not to return. Mrs. T also described Sara's father's insensitivity to her needs and his tendency to bury himself in his business. However, it appeared that the parental conflict centered on their mutual criticism of each other. Each parent accused the other of not showing affection. Now, faced with Sara's serious drinking problem, Mrs. T was frantic and agitated. The mother expressed feeling overwhelmed with a sense of failure and guilt, and acknowledged that she tended to scream and "become bossy" when stressed out.

Two days before the session, a police officer had found Sara throwing up in the neighborhood McDonald's bathroom; Sara appeared pale and sick, and the officer escorted her home. Mrs. T went on at length about Sara's long-standing problems of "attitude," her lack of feminine traits, and most of all, the bad influence of her friends. Nothing her mother did was enough to persuade Sara to drop her "bad" friends. Mrs. T even gave up her job and stayed home, "watching Sara like a hawk." In her mother's view, Sara's drinking was "a complete surprise." Sara finally told her mother, with anger and defiance, that she had been drinking for two years and that no amount of therapy was going to stop her — if she wanted to stop drinking she would do it without her mother's help. Deciding that the conjoint session with mother and daughter was likely to increase the level of anger and hostility instead of leading to a viable alternative, the therapist chose to see Sara and her mother separately.

The individual session with Sara indicated that since the McDonald's episode, Sara had attended N.A. (Narcotics Anonymous) meetings on her own, had made new friends there, had stopped drinking altogether, and was looking for a job. "Why N.A., instead of A.A.?" the therapist asked. "Just to be different," replied Sara. Besides, she "liked the kids there better than the A.A. kids." Sara was clearly finding it helpful to attend N.A. meetings where her newfound friends were. Sara's only goal was to leave home when she finished high school, which was about nine months away. Again, she made it clear that she was only coming to the session because her mother made her, and then reassured the therapist that she would never like coming to a session.

It was clear from the beginning that Sara was a "visitor" to the session. Since Sara found N.A. helpful and had already started to abstain from drinking, the therapist decided to support Sara's taking charge of her own problems through N.A.

In order to support and maintain Sara's tentative steps toward sobriety, it was crucial that her parents become less critical and more supportive of Sara's initial efforts and, furthermore, find ways to enhance her self-esteem. Clearly Sara needed a more positive and encouraging relationship with her parents, and not one of criticism and mutual blaming. Therefore, the therapist decided to support the parents because if they felt supported and understood it would be easier for them to be supportive of Sara and of each other.

In a summary statement with both mother and daughter together, the therapist was sympathetic to Mrs. T's dilemma and complimented her on having tried many different things for Sara under very difficult circumstances, thus showing that she still had faith in Sara's ability to change. It was pointed out that Mrs. T had provided some important and useful information about the seriousness of Sara's problems and about how best to help her daughter. Mrs. T was complimented on having been so watchful of Sara, which was clearly a difficult task under any circumstances. Sara was complimented on having come to the initial session even though she did not agree with her mother's idea of what would help. Sara was also complimented for taking control of her problem by stopping drinking, going to N.A., making new friends who were nondrinkers, and doing many other things that were good for her. She was encouraged to continue with N.A.

Future sessions focused on the parents' working together to become a parenting team to help Sara maintain her sobriety and reestablish her positive identity. There was a total of seven sessions. A one-year follow-up indicated that Sara was continuing to do well with her sobriety, had her first alumni meeting at N.A., had graduated from high school, and was working, but still living at home. The parents were having more fun and had resumed social activities with other couples.

Therapeutic Activities

When working with someone in a complainant-type relationship, the therapist's attention should be directed toward helping the client claim ownership of solutions by bypassing the discussion of problems as much as possible. However, when a therapist mistakenly assumes that all clients are the same, and insists that they take ownership of their problems, they may unwittingly create a "resistant" client. When blamed, all clients become defensive. In order to protect herself and to correct the therapist's misunderstanding, the client may become even more adamant about how her problem is someone else's problem. A good strategy to help the client take ownership of her problems is to gently steer her toward finding solutions.

It is important to see family members as an important alliance for treatment, not as a hindrance to what the therapist is working toward. Many family members have made numerous attempts at convincing the problem drinker to stop, all with varying degrees of success. Family members can give objective information on what worked and what did not work. It is particularly useful to involve family members when the initiative for treatment comes from the family member, and not the client. Because of the strong emotional bond among family members it is helpful to see the spouse or other family members as a potential resource for finding solutions until proven otherwise. This is particularly true when working with adolescents. As David Treadway (1987) often says, "Blood is thicker than therapy"; even though there may be serious parent-child conflicts that have been exacerbated by the alcohol or other drug problem, parental support is crucial in maintaining the gains a treatment program makes. Positive and supportive alliances with family members reinforces gains clients make in treatment. This is also true of spousal relationships. As long as the couple expresses the desire to stay together, it is crucial that the nonabusing spouse (who may appear to be the complainant initially) become a strong partner in treatment when that treatment is designed to elicit support for the recovery process and for new ways of staying together as a couple.

The nonabusing client's view is that he has suffered much and that his life is full of frustrations and inconveniences as a result of someone else's problem drinking. It is helpful to recognize as positive the investment of energy, time, and commitment to helping the abusing member of a family and see it as an indication of hope for the drinker. We generally tend to view the invested, nondrinking family members as expert in knowing what would be the most helpful treatment for the client. Since complainants tend to give detailed descriptions of how their lives have been troubled (through no fault of their own), it is helpful for them to know that the therapist does not see them as "nagging" or "controlling." It is easier to detach when the person, who is often described as codependent, feels understood rather than criticized. One must look for positive qualities in the client and see that those qualities can contribute to finding solutions.

Clients are often surprised and pleased to hear that someone finally recognizes what they have sacrificed. Clinicians need to start seeing what the client is doing as being positively motivated. However, this is not the same thing as "positive reframing" which will be discussed more in detail elsewhere. As a therapist you must really believe that the client's intentions are positive; only the outcome of his positive intentions is "unproductive," or as one colleague put it, "backfires on him."

Once the therapeutic relationship is established, it is fairly easy for a complainant to begin to see that her efforts at solutions are not working and that perhaps she needs to look for some other approach. Frequently, a client asks the therapist, "I know that nothing I try works. What have I been doing wrong?" or "Do you know what will work better? Nothing I do seems to work." At this point, the client has willingly become a "customer" looking for a more effective approach to solving problems. Until there is an indication that the client is beginning to see that he can become part of the solution-finding process, a therapist should refrain from suggesting quick and easy solutions.

GOAL SETTING WITH A CUSTOMER

A customer-type relationship is the ideal of every clinician. Most professionals strive to have one. "Customers" will take responsibility not only for the problem but also for taking steps to find solutions to the problem. Thus, they become active participants in their own treatment. Clients are, for example, willing to abstain for 30 days, to go to 90 A.A. meetings in 90 days, and to actively search for ways to change their life styles.

"Customers" clearly indicate readiness to take steps to find solutions to their problems. "Something has to be done," "I am running out of ideas of what to do," "I have to do something," "This has to stop," "I am killing myself and hurting everyone," and "I cannot go on like this," communicate that they realize they have "hit bottom" and cannot go on any further.

In addition, "customers" will mention that they have made a number of attempts to solve problems, acknowledging that these previous measures have not worked and conceding that they are now ready to hear some other ways to find solutions. At times, "customers" may blame their past, poor parenting, early deprivation, abuse, a spouse, genetic endowment, a work environment, or something else, but the important element is their willingness to take responsibility for changing the *future*.

Because the client is ready to take steps toward a solution, the changes can be very rapid and significant. Once the changes begin, the major task of the clinician is to support, reinforce, and then "get the hell out of the way," as a former client suggested.

What Is the Next Step?

Even when clients take ownership of the problem and are willing to take steps toward solutions, some will still try to negotiate and find ways to "cut down on drinking" and not give up alcohol use entirely. We contend that the client must reach the point of deciding on his own that abstinence is the only viable solution, then have a clear commitment to carry out what it takes, and not feel coerced into that decision in order to increase his chances of success (Hester & Miller, 1989; Miller, 1985).

Although a client is motivated to take responsibility, the therapist still needs to pay attention to maintaining the customer-type relationship throughout the treatment process. What follows are suggestions for such activities.

> a. Compliment the client on the attempts he has made to try to solve his problem. Point out any successes he has had, however small, either on his own or with help. Complimenting is particularly important when the client has had numerous treatment episodes before and is now trying one more time. A client needs to be encouraged to try again.
>
> b. Agree with the reason for treatment. Even if a client is interested in treatment only because she is close to losing her driver's license, job, or marriage, focus on things that are important to her.
>
> c. Focus on everything the client did to be successful, even for a short period of time. If the activities are those that he can repeat, the better the outlook. Building on past successes increases self-esteem and confidence and makes the task easier because he has done it once already. Repeating what the client knows how to do is much easier than starting something brand new.
>
> d. Use the seven qualities of well-formed goals, described in Chapter 3, in order to negotiate realistic, achievable, and measurable goals. The client needs to be successful, which will encourage him to go on. When there are some successes, it is easier to manage the inevitable disappointments and failures. ,
>
> e. Use a cautious approach in setting goals, and monitor progress.
>
> f. Find out the details of the client's life and work circumstances and the new patterns of success she is developing. When the client is aware of the patterns connected with success and failure, she is empowered to make wise choices.

g. Ask detailed questions about patterns, such as who did what, when, and how, and with what results. Small details count. Clients do not know enough to ask about these questions on their own. In the process of having to answer them, clients learn about their own patterns. Asking these questions increases and heightens clients' awareness of their own specific solutions.

Looking for the "Hidden Customer" in the "Difficult Client"

"Categories" of client-therapist relationships need to be thought of as guidelines for pacing movement during the course of treatment. The categorization is dynamic and may fluctuate back and forth between "visitor" and "customer." When used in this way, the therapist can make an assessment of the changing relationship between herself and the client and suggest tasks accordingly.

The following case illustrates the idea of the "hidden customer." The client was referred for treatment because there was a dispute between him and his supervisor about his showing up for work with "alcohol breath." The client, Sheldon, insisted that he had a stomach problem that caused the alcohol breath and that, in fact, he did not "touch the stuff." The therapist was convinced that Sheldon was lying. Of course, Sheldon kept insisting that something was wrong with his intestinal system which caused the bad breath. The therapist, frustrated by Sheldon's dishonesty, sought the "truth," and insisted that Sheldon undergo extensive medical examinations to prove that he was lying. This took considerable time, energy, and expense. During this prolonged process, Sheldon's alcohol breath mysteriously disappeared. In hindsight, had the therapist agreed with Sheldon and shown concern about his unusual medical condition, together they might have been able to negotiate goals that included stopping drinking.

So, what are the clues that indicate that a professional may have misjudged and failed to "cooperate" with the client? A good indication is when a therapist says to himself or to colleagues such things as, "I am doing all the work, and he just sits there," or "I am working harder than she does." Other signs are when the therapist secretly wishes that the client would cancel the appointment, or when she thinks of referring the case to someone else. Any therapist who runs into a client like Sheldon and reacts in a similar fashion is very likely to use these phrases to describe his frustrations with his client.

When a therapist finds herself saying or thinking these things about a client, she should stop and review what the client is willing to work for and not what she, the professional, thinks the client should be working for. She should then go back and renegotiate the goals using the guidelines described earlier in this chapter and look for anything the client is "willing to be a customer for." Cooperating with the client by accepting his goals, however absurd they may seem initially, will allow the therapist to join with the client's view of what is important to him.

GOAL NEGOTIATION WITH NONABUSERS

Most treatment models tend to focus only on the abuser. They ignore the nonabusing family members or employers, by relegating them to the sidelines, or viewing them as codependents or enablers, thus, losing valuable resources for a successful treatment outcome. In the following section we would like to discuss frequently observed clinical phenomenon and offer suggestions on ways to initiate changes.

There are clinical situations where the abuser is unwilling or not ready to enter treatment on his own. The most common response in such a situation is to encourage the nonabusing family members to attend Al-Anon meetings, which we believe is a good option. However, therapists can do more. Clinical reality is that as nonabusing spouses become educated about alcohol abuse, they enter treatment on their own. However, some nonabusing family members will not avail themselves of Al-Anon for a variety of reasons. Instead of waiting until these family members "hit bottom" and, out of desperation, agree to attend Al-Anon, we believe it is much more humane and economical to prevent the problem from becoming worse. The Al-Anon principles and the Twelve Steps can be adapted to clinical treatment situations easily as a one-on-one treatment model.

The nonabusing spouse seeks help for a variety of reasons. He is usually looking for ways to either contain the damage already done to the family or to make a decision about whether to stay or leave the relationship. In most situations, a nonabusing spouse reports that the abusing family member either refuses to participate, or outright denies or minimizes the damage his drinking problem inflicts on the family.

Most clinicians either give the nonabusing spouse a strong nudge to leave the relationship or label her as codependent and suggest treatment for her. She is thought to have personality defects that require long and extensive treatment. These are appropriate responses in many situations. We caution, however, against making a blanket recommendation without a careful assessment of what the goals for such a suggestion may be. It not only may be a disservice to the nonabusing family member but also may result in the loss of an important opportunity to make significant changes in treatment. Like all clients, the nonabusing spouse has specific goals in requesting service.

This may sound elementary, but the way the nonabusing family member views the abusing member determines how willing the non-abuser is to solve problems and what she is willing to do. Does the nonabusing client seeking help say, "I have a problem with my wife's drinking," "My husband has a drinking problem," or "My teenage son is influenced by the bad friends he hangs out with." Depending on which view the nonabusing family member takes, the steps that are necessary to solve the problem will be very different.

One client indicates that he needs to take steps to solve his problem related to his wife's drinking. The second client sees that it is her husband's drinking that needs to be changed. The third client feels helpless in the face of the strong influence her son's friends have on him and may need to be helped to focus on what she can do. Therapist techniques need to be different, depending on which position the client eventually takes. For example, with the first type of client, the definition of his goal may begin with:

a. How is your wife's drinking a problem for you?
b. What do you suppose your wife will say is a problem for her?
c. What do you have to see different in your life for you to say to yourself that the problem is starting to change?
d. What have you done about your problem with your wife's drinking?
e. What do you suppose your wife would say that you do that is most helpful? Least helpful?
f. What do you suppose your wife would say you need to do to be more helpful to her?
g. What have you tried that worked?
h. What do you suppose your wife would say that she needs to do differently for her to stop drinking?
i. What do you suppose your wife would say how your family life would change when she stops drinking?

These questions will help the client sort out what his problems are, what his wife's problems are, what he needs to do differently, what he can change, what he cannot change, and so on. It will also help him clarify what his wife's view of the problem and solutions are. When the client can put his responsibility and solutions alongside his wife's problems and solutions, it will help him sort things out more clearly. This will help establish goals that are within his capacity to accomplish.

The questions that will help the second client may go something like this:

a. How does your husband's drinking problem affect you?

b. What do you suppose he would say about how his drinking affects him? His family? His life?

c. What do you suppose he would say he is willing to do to solve his drinking problem?

d. Who do you suppose he would say is more invested in him stopping drinking, you or him?

e. What do you suppose he would say you can do that is most helpful to him right now?

f. What do you suppose he would say he is willing to do to stop drinking right now?

g. What do you suppose he would say that you are willing to do if he doesn't stop drinking?

h. How serious do you suppose he would say your threat of divorce is?

i. What do you suppose he would say would convince him that you really mean business about divorcing him?

j. When you finally convince him that you really mean business about your threat of leaving, what do you suppose he would say he will do?

k. What do you suppose it will take for you to convince him that you mean business?

l. What do you suppose he will say that you will be like when you finally learn to detach yourself from his drinking?

The decision to take steps to solve a problem may rest with the nonabusing family member doing something different from what she normally does. This could include taking steps to detach, taking care of herself, developing supportive social relationships, and becoming and feeling more competent about herself.

Useful questions for the third client might be:

a. What do you suppose your son would say it would take for him to stop drinking?

b. How badly do you suppose your son would say he wants to be a part of the family?

c. What do you suppose your son would say it will take him to become a better student (worker, family member, etc.)?

d. What will be the first sign to you that your coming here is useful to you?

e. What do you suppose your son would say you will do differently as a result of coming here?

f. What do you suppose your son would say the chances are that he will give up his friends?

g. What do you suppose he would say your main objections to his friends are?

h. What do you suppose he would say is the worst possible thing that could happen to him if he doesn't give up his friends?

i. What do you suppose he would say is more important to him, the friends or his drinking?

These questions direct the parents to see the drinking and the "friends" issues both from the son's perspective and, therefore, help them arrive at the most realistic solutions.

These questions direct not only the negotiation of the client's goal for his or her life, but also the course of action he or she wants to take in order to change. The questions that therapists ask about relationship issues provide rich material about the issues between clients and their abusing family members. For example, a client might report that his wife would say that "I have to stop nagging about her drinking." The following question might be, "So, what would it take for you to stop nagging?" or "Suppose you stopped nagging. What do you suppose your wife would say about how things will be different between the two of you?" These questions help target the treatment and provide direction for the necessary changes.

Asking these "relationship questions" indicates to the client that the problem and the solutions lie solely with him, either with his taking different steps than what he tried previously or, if he has not taken any steps before, what the beginning moves toward change might be. Therefore, it is possible to generate solutions even when the abusing member is not present in the session. When the client takes certain steps, such as detaching, not "nagging," not reminding the problem drinker to not drink in front of the children, to go to work on time, or to show up sober at a social gathering, the nature of the client's interaction with the abusive family member changes. Such change creates the possibility that the abuser will realize that she must take control and find solutions that can be maintained in her life.

5

Orienting Toward Solution: How to Interview for a Change

"I never learn anything talking. I only learn things when I ask questions."

— Lou Holtz, *The New York Times*

A young man wanted clear statements about Erickson's method. Erickson interrupted the discussion and took the man outside. He pointed up the street and asked what he saw. Puzzled, he replied that he saw a street. Erickson pointed to the trees that lined the street. "Do you notice anything about the trees?" The young man eventually noted that they were all leaning in an easterly direction. "That's right, all except one. That second one from the end is leaning in a westerly direction. There's always an exception."

— Jay Haley, *Advanced Techniques of Hypnosis and Therapy* (1967)

SOME YEARS AGO, WE DECIDED TO SENSITIZE a group of beginning therapists to the process of solution-focused interviewing by showing them a videotape of a family interview. The family on the tape were actually neighbors of ours who had volunteered to come to our Center to have a videotape made of a typical family meeting. The purpose of the meeting was to plan an upcoming family picnic. We asked the family members to be themselves as much as possible and then turned on the camera. The Kellys did their best to simulate their usual family interactions in planning the picnic.

We then showed the videotape of the Kelly family to the trainees with instructions to describe, *not explain*, what they observed. We purposefully withheld the information about the real purpose of the tape as well as any identifying information about the family.

Very quickly, trainees began to describe what they "saw." Some of the

68

students noticed that the mother was an "angry and controlling woman" who seemed frustrated in her marriage. Another group pointed out how the husband was distant and aloof because he seemed to them almost reluctant to be pulled into the family interactions. Almost every trainee saw a strong alliance between the mother and the children and saw this bond as being possibly causally related to signs of behavioral problems in the children. Signs of problem drinking were soon identified in the father, and the mother appeared, to the training group, to enable him in maintaining his distance from the family by taking over the management of the children. Some trainees even speculated about whether there was sexual abuse of the daughter. Evidence of this abuse was based on an interpretation of the way the daughter ignored the father's suggestions and instead sided with her mother. As the tape progressed, the group of students continued to find more and more evidence of pathology and problems in this family.

This experience was truly an eye-opening lesson for us about how easy it is to move from the simple description of an event to causal hypotheses and explanations. In reality, the Kellys are a well-functioning family that we know very well. The speculations made about the Kellys raised serious questions about how observers arrive at conclusions, verify the truth of their conclusions, and how such conclusions affect clinical work.

According to Einstein, believing is seeing. In other words, what we believe dictates both what we choose to see and what we choose to ignore. Just as in the videotape, though the family was normal, because the trainees believed there were problems and pathology they were able to find them. Such selective attention gives us the means to organize the information entering our senses in a logical and coherent fashion and is a normal process. Given this knowledge, however, we must be careful to bring balance to the pictures we construct about the people and families we work with. Certainly, our views will affect our judgments about those people and the nature of our interaction with them.

THE PURPOSEFUL INTERVIEW

Interviewing is a complex process. What is said, what is not said, how it is said, who said what about what, when, and how, all convey information between the client and the therapist. Communication flows in both directions (Weakland, 1991). What the therapist decides to ask, what she ignores, what she highlights, the inflection of the voice, facial expression, body postures, subtle and not-so-subtle nuances of tone, convey to the client what the therapist thinks is important and related to achieving the client's goals.

Views of the therapeutic interviewing process have undergone a tremendous shift in recent years. In the earlier days of Freudian training, the therapist was thought to be a "blank screen" onto which a client's psychopathology was projected. Therefore, it was important for the therapist to maintain his "objectivity" and remain "value free." However, beginning with such pioneers as Karen Horney and Harry Stack Sullivan (Horney, 1937; Sullivan, 1952, 1954), therapists began to see the interviewing process as an interactional relationship. This opened up a new view of how the therapist participates in the client's construction of problems and solutions to problems (Anderson & Goolishian, 1988; de Shazer & Berg, in press; Efran, Lukens, & Lukens, 1990; O'Hanlon & Wilk, 1987).

Currently, many thinkers view the interview as a "therapeutic conversation" in which the therapist actively participates in the process of defining what the problem is and how it is to be solved (Anderson & Goolishian, 1988; de Shazer & Berg, in press; Penn, 1985; Tomm, 1987a, 1987b; Weakland, 1991). In solution-focused therapy, the therapist and client join together to form a therapeutic unit based on mutual trust and cooperation. The conversation of the participants in this therapeutic system jointly constructs what is problematic to the client and how both the client and therapist will cooperate to find a solution to that problem. Since the interviewing process cannot help but influence the client's view of the problem or potential solution, a method of interviewing has been developed to influence the client's view of the problem in a manner that leads to solution. In this process, we have found five questions to be exceptionally useful in fostering conversations that lead to solutions.

FIVE USEFUL QUESTIONS

Each question the therapist asks conveys to the client what the therapist believes is important in accomplishing the treatment goals. We believe that the therapist must select questions that are useful in finding solutions to the client's problems. Notice that the questions a therapist asks a client are based on assumptions and beliefs about what will be helpful to the client. The types of questions used in the solution-focused interview are based on our assumption that the best way to help clients is to capitalize on their existing strengths and resources.

1. Questions That Highlight Pre-Session Change

As indicated in Chapter 1, one of the basic tenets of the solution-focused model is that changes occur constantly. And indeed, we frequently observe that clients have made changes in existing problem patterns prior to coming for their first session. So common are reports of pre-session change that we now routinely ask clients to watch for evidence of it when scheduling their first session.

Not infrequently, problem drinking clients have started their first session with comments like, "I was wondering if I should have come because since I made the phone call I am drinking much less" or "I don't know if I am doing the right thing. Maybe I am wasting your time." Rather than interpreting such positive, pre-session change as evidence that the client is "resistant," "in denial," or lacking the necessary commitment for treatment, we have found it useful to use such change as a building block for attaining future goals. This was certainly the case with a client seen recently at the Center:

Client: Since I called, I have cut down on my drinking because of a friend.
Therapist: Well, tell me more about that. What do you mean?
Cl: I drank all my life, all hard stuff. I got started in the army when there were cheap drinks from the PX. I drank all the time, man.
Th: So, how have you managed to cut down on your drinking since the phone call?
Cl: I haven't had anything hard to drink for two weeks now because of that friend.
Th: That is incredible. You didn't drink anything hard for two weeks? Sounds like this friend is really important to you.
Cl: She is. She wants me to stop completely.
Th: So how much are you drinking now?
Cl: As I said, I used to drink all hard stuff. A lot. Too much. I been drinking only beer now.
Th: You gave up hard liquor?
Cl: Yeah.
Th: Was it hard, I mean, not to drink?
Cl: Not really. When I am with Sally I don't drink at all. I only drink when I hang out with my brother and friends.
Th: So, what do you suppose Sally would say is different about you when you don't drink at all?
Cl: She would say I'm a different person. I don't have a bad attitude.

Studies do support our observation that clients make significant changes in their problem patterns prior to coming for treatment (Bloom, 1981; Kogan, 1957a, 1957b, 1957c; Noonan, 1973; Talmon, 1990; Weiner-Davis et al., 1987). Such changes, however, are rarely reported spontaneously by clients. For this reason, it is crucial that the therapist inquire about the existence of such changes! In his studies, Talmon (1990) found that when a therapist makes a point of asking clients about pre-session change nearly two-thirds of the clients report some sort of change. Moreover, such change is usually in the direction desired by the client.

We think a client who makes changes on her own needs to be encouraged, because when the client has made these changes, it is easy for her to take ownership of the solution to her problem drinking. When the therapist helps the client claim her own solutions, the client is more likely to maintain those goals. Frequently, it is a profoundly emotional experience for the problem drinker to take credit for the solutions, since it is rare that she is given recognition for success when it involves her drinking. In addition, since the solutions found are already natural to her way of doing things, the client is more likely to succeed in maintaining these solutions.

The first method of discovering if pre-session changes were made is to ask:

> "It is our experience that many people notice that things are better between the time they set up an appointment and the time they come in for the first session. Have you noticed such changes in your situation?"

This sets up an expectation and an assumption that it is quite normal and expected that their serious problems may have eased a bit since they made the appointment.

Client reactions are quite varied, as one can easily imagine. Some clients are clear that "things are a little bit better" but are not sure how much to trust such good fortune, and they wait for the professional opinion. Other clients are more cautious, because a change has happened before and then the problem usually became worse. Therefore, the client with such experience is still somewhat skeptical of how long lasting the improvement will be. She seems to be more hesitant, especially when the positive changes involve other members of the family. When the pre-session change involves her having taken active and deliberate steps she is more willing to trust such changes as indicative of a move in a positive direction. When the client is in a "complainant-type" relationship, meaning the problem involves others (such as the spouse or children), she tends to be more skeptical of such changes having a lasting effect.

We both prefer the second method of investigating the pre-session changes. That is, instead of immediately asking a direct question about any pre-session changes, we find it less intrusive to wait for the right moment to ask about the pre-session changes. Not only is this approach more fluid and natural, but it also becomes a journey of discovery for both the client and the therapist. The following example illustrates this technique.

Case Example: After the Party

Therapist: So what would you like to have changed as a result of coming here today?

Client: Well, I'm not sure. I was just coming out of a bad state when I called you people. Maybe I just scared myself. I knew I was drinking too much. So I just cut out drinking altogether. It's been four days now and so far I seem to be doing it.

Th: So, how did you do that?

Cl: You know, I was just drinking too much and I had to do something.

Th: So, how did you manage not to drink for four full days?

Cl: One thing I did was I called here. Then I decided that if I'm going to be serious about it, I better start right then and there. So, I just stopped drinking.

Th: Is that different for you?

Cl: Yeah, it sure is. I am one of those people who believes in solving your own problems. But this is the first time I realized that I needed some help. It is really hard for me to accept help from anybody. That's why I can't go to A.A. I don't want to hear about other people's problems and I don't want to spill my guts to strangers.

Th: So, how did you manage not to drink for four days now?

Cl: It wasn't easy, I will tell you that. But it is getting easier.

Th: How did you get the idea of getting a head start on this? Some people drink more when they are getting ready for treatment. Are you the type who takes the bull by the horn and runs with it?

Cl: Well, I never thought of myself like that. But I always knew that I had to do something about my drinking, so I just decided it might as well be right now.

Th: So, suppose your wife was here—if I were to ask her what she
    noticed different about you, what do you suppose she would say
    that's been different about you these four days?
Cl: She probably would say that I'm more relaxed. I know I've been
    pretty jumpy lately.

The therapist empowers the client by asking more about the steps he
took to arrive at this decision. Asking about other family member's
perceptions not only verifies the information the client is giving the
therapist, but it also directs the client to be aware of how his behavior
affects others. The next step is to help the client find ways to maintain
this sobriety he has started on his own.

Th: So, what do you have to do so that you can stay on this track?
Cl: I've been wondering about that myself. (Pause) I guess I will just
    have to keep doing what I've done for the past four days.
Th: So, what have you been doing for four days? That's a long time not
    to be drinking for you.
Cl: I just kept busy. Actually I've been feeling pretty good. Just know-
    ing I'm doing something good for myself and my family helps a
    lot. It also helps to see that it makes my wife happy with me.

The therapist spent more time asking in detail about what the client
needed to do to maintain this nondrinking life-style. At the end of the
session, the client was given compliments and then had homework suggested to him in the following manner:

> "We are very struck by your determination to do what is good for you and
> your family even though it is tough to do. It is clear to us that you are the
> kind of person that will solve problems your way and not follow the
> crowd. It is also clear that you are a man of action and when you make up
> your mind to do something, you take the bull by the horns and go with it.
> "Because you realize that you need to take one day at a time and be on
> guard [these are the client's words], and because you realize that you need
> to go slowly, we would like to have you keep track of all the things you are
> continuing to do in order to stay sober. You may even discover some new
> things you haven't tried yet."

When the client has found ways to take charge of his drinking, it is
helpful for the therapist to give full credit to the client. This empowering process enhances the client's self-perceptions. When the client

owns up to the solution, it is easy for him to own up to the problems, too.

As you can see from this case, when there is a clear pre-session change in the direction the client sought help with, and when the client is confident of staying on course, the next step for the therapist is to help the client remain on the course that was started before the first session.

Each subsequent session is spent in reviewing and discovering any new changes the client makes, and how the family members react to these changes, and what needs to be modified in order to stay on course.

2. Exception-Finding Questions: Enhancing Existing and Past Successes

Just as we value the pre-session change as a context marker (O'Hanlon & Wilk, 1987), the exception to the problem needs to be pointed out and labeled as such by the therapist. This approach capitalizes and utilizes (Dolan, 1991) the client resources, thus enhancing the client's self-esteem.

An exception to a problem occurs when the client engages in non-drinking behavior, either spontaneously or by taking some concrete and measured steps. Therefore, when asked about an exception, some clients can describe in detail how they managed either to reduce their drinking or to abstain altogether by taking specific steps. For example, a client described her exception to problem drinking during the weekdays in the following manner:

Case Example: Deliberate Exceptions

Therapist: So, I am curious about your nondrinking days. How do you do it?

Client: I never thought about it like that before and so I'm not sure if I can tell you exactly.

Th: You mentioned that you don't drink on weekdays.

Cl: I haven't done that for years. How do I do it? I have to do it. I just make up my mind that I'm not going to touch any alcohol. Then I don't think about it. So, I tell myself it's not an option.

Th: Wow! That's amazing. How do you do that?

Cl: Don't give me all that much credit. I had to work very hard at it.

Th: That is even more amazing to me; that you worked so hard to be where you are at.

Cl: Sometimes, I get tempted when I'm out for parties or meetings and there is drinking. Then, I make sure that I only drink Coke, stay away from those who drink and concentrate on getting interested in people. I try to find at least one person to talk to and then just concentrate on their stories.

Th: That's amazing. How did you figure out that doing that helps?

Cl: It didn't come easy. I tried many things. I decided that I am going to concentrate on my career during the weekdays. In order to get ahead in my job, I have to put everything into it.

Th: I'm sure it's true. So, what do you do when you are home during the weekdays so that you don't drink?

Cl: I just concentrate on what I have to do: cooking, any homework, writing a letter or report, calling my friends, taking a bath, shopping, and all that needs my attention. I just remembered. I joined the health club. That really helps. I feel good about myself when I work out. When I feel good about myself I don't have to drink.

Th: What do you suppose your co-workers or friends would say they notice different about you when you are doing all those things?

Cl: I doubt that they even notice anything different about me. I told you that when I drink, I drink only on weekends and when I'm alone.

Th: I remember you did. So, what would it take for you to not drink on weekends also?

Cl: That's just it. (Pause) Well, I suppose I could pretend it's the same as weekdays. I will just have to have the same mindset I have on weekdays and maybe I should save some of my chores for the weekend. You know that is when I get bored and lonely. That's when I get in trouble. I should go work out on weekends, too. Actually, it will be good for me to be interested in life and not wallow in my sorrows on the weekend, too.

The client, an ambitious and attractive career woman, recognizes through this conversation that she manages her weekdays quite well. In the process of responding to the therapist's questions about what she does to not drink, the client becomes aware of all the activities that are part of her life. As she explains these activities to the therapist, she is beginning to construct her successful strategies for what to do on the weekends to avoid drinking. A client may need some help in this recounting (in a positive and helpful way) so that he will discover what he can repeat. For this client, the vulnerable points she identified were her feelings of boredom and loneliness. Her solution was going to the health club on the weekend and getting "interested in life." Sometimes the solution is simple and within very easy reach of the client.

Sometimes it is clear to the client that there are times when he is able to curtail or refrain from drinking. However, when asked, the client is unable to describe or retrace the steps taken to abstain. The most common response is "I don't know, it just happened. I just woke up feeling good." Some clients attribute the exception to events that cannot be repeated regularly. For example, Darryl makes sure that he does not drink during Lent because of his religious beliefs and values. George never touches alcohol when he goes out to dinner with his boss, no matter what the circumstances. He explains that he is expected to not drink, and everyone at dinner drinks only mineral water, tea, or coffee. It has been that way ever since the company president first stopped drinking after his heart attack. George is not able to describe what he does during those times, except that he does not crave alcohol.

Because these clients are not able to describe the steps they take when there are exceptions to their drinking, or because the exception is perceived by them as being other-dependent, it is difficult to replicate. Therefore, these are not very useful exceptions. As will be described in Chapter 6 on solution-focused interventions, when the therapist is faced with such a situation, he may find a prediction task useful. In Chapter 6, we will describe more fully how this prediction task can be applied with clients who have spontaneous exceptions.

The solution-focused interviewing technique magnifies and enhances a client's successes through repeated emphasis on those few, but important, exceptions. When repeated often and examined in detail, the client's successes become more real to her. When the client can "see" her success and recognize that she has actually taken steps to implement it, she is forced to face the reality that she does know how to stop drinking. When the client recognizes this reality it can easily become a self-fulfilling prophecy.

3. "Miracles Do Happen": Miracle Questions

As mentioned throughout this book, the miracle question may be the most important question of the model. It orients the client to a future state when the problem is solved and he can start to savor the successful completion of therapy. The question may be phrased in the following manner.

"I want to ask you a slightly different question now. You will have to use your imagination for this one. Suppose you go home and go to bed tonight after today's session. While you are sleeping a miracle happens and the problem that brought you here is solved, just like that (snapping a finger). Since you were sleeping, you didn't know that this miracle happened. What do you suppose will be the first small thing that will indicate to you tomorrow morning that there has been a miracle overnight and the problem that brought you here is solved?"

Time and time again, the most incredible thing happens. A client starts to dream about an alternate reality and begins to have hope for himself. Then he begins to detail how his tomorrow will be different. As he continues, he begins to smile, his eyes begin to sparkle, he sits up straight, and actually seems to glow as he describes the changes he imagines.

Often, this is a powerful new experience for the client. When a client can project to the future and imagine a transformation of her painful, hurt, and damaged life into a more coherent, harmonious, and successful life, it is an empowering experience. We believe this is the most important gift a therapist can give to a client: hope and a vision of possibility. Clients respond by being hopeful about their lives and about themselves.

"First of all, I will have had a restful night and so I will wake up in a good mood and say 'good morning' to my wife. Maybe even give her a kiss and we may even hug each other. We may discuss what is coming up for the day. I will get up without a hangover and look forward to the day. I may even help my wife by making coffee, help the kids with their breakfast, send them off to school. Maybe even give my wife a chance to sleep late for half an hour. She will like that. And I will go off to work in a good mood."

"A miracle? A real miracle? You probably won't notice it until I come home because I leave for work before everybody gets up. Yeah, that's when it will show. I will be nicer to my family. I will treat my family like they should be treated. They will know because they won't be afraid of me. How can they tell? Well, I will be relaxed. That's it. I will be calm, talk in a calmer voice to them. I won't swear at them. But most of all, I won't be drinking."

"I'm not sure. I never thought about that. Boy, that's hard. My girlfriend will say I am cheerful, more ambitious about myself and not talk down about myself. Yeah, more upbeat generally. That's it. I will feel good about myself. I will go places, I mean, with my job. I'm at a dead-end job now but I would feel like I'm going someplace with my life."

"My boyfriend will stop drinking. No, before that, he will admit that he has a drinking problem and not brush it off as if it is nothing. I suppose when he does that, I won't nag him. Then, we won't fight all the time. Yeah, more peace and quiet. Like we used to be when we first met."

"A true miracle? I believe in miracles. But miracles come slow. So, I suppose the first thing is I will feel like caring about myself. Personal grooming, I would say. No, that's what my husband would say. I will feel like taking care of myself, get dressed in bright clothes, get my hair done. Get some exercise, get interested in gardening. Taking care of my children. That will be a big miracle."

"A miracle? I will win the lottery and quit working. Seriously, my husband will have a stable job and contribute to the family. He will laugh again. I will see his eyes twinkle and see smiles on his face. That will be a miracle in our house."

Even though it is labeled as a "miracle," by and large clients are amazingly realistic and down-to-earth about their picture of the "miracle day." When someone starts to enjoy a pipe-dream or a pie-in-the-sky dream, the therapist can gently bring him back to reality either with humor, or by normalizing his wish to win the lottery, to have a yacht, and to live in a castle. But most clients know that it is just a fantasy and quickly settle into painting a more realistic miracle.

What is amazing, from our clinical experience, is that "miracle pictures" are quite realistic, detailed, and achievable within the context of the client's life. Since the image is generated by the client, it fits naturally into his life-style and, consequently, is achievable. As with the exceptions to the problem, it is within the client's ability to perform the miracle. The miracle picture is most useful when it is described in detailed and measurable terms. Inner feelings generated by a miracle image should be described as an outward sign of the changes that will take place. Therefore, when the client answers: "I will feel better, more peaceful, more relaxed," he needs to convert those ideas into outward manifestations of internal changes. Another good question to ask is:

"Suppose you find this inner peace (or feel content with yourself, or you feel like your old self again) tomorrow after the miracle, what do you suppose you will notice different about you that will tell you that you have this peace?"

We believe that the client with a drinking problem needs some external signs of how her internal self is changing. Because a client has ignored and masked these internal emotional reactions to her environment for so long (with alcohol use), she needs to learn to connect her internal emotions with her behavioral manifestations, or her drinking patterns with the consequences.

The next step for the therapist is to take advantage of this miracle and start to implement this information. Implementation could be facilitated by utilizing a form of the following dialogue:

Therapist: So, when would you say was the last time when part of this miracle happened, even a little bit?

Client: I will have to say, it was two weeks ago.

Th: Tell me about that. What did you do to have a little bit of a miracle day?

Cl: I am not sure. I would say it was on the weekend. I decided that I've been pretty selfish and made up my mind to spend the day doing what my family wanted me to do for a long time. We cooked together, went for a walk, and went grocery shopping. It sounds silly but we really had a lot of fun. It was a good day. We even agreed that we should do more of those things.

Th: So, what would it take for you to continue to do what you started that day?

Cl: You know, now that I think about it, not much. Just schedule and do it.

Th: What do you suppose your family would say it would take for you to repeat this?

Cl: Umm, that' hard. My wife will probably say the same thing. We did it, so, we will just have to do it.

Th: What is the first step you will have to take?

Cl: I have taken the first step already by coming here. So, I guess I will have to take the second step. Just plan it and have the babysitter lined up and take my wife out for dinner and a movie.

If there is a pre-session change or past success to rely on, the miracle day can easily be implemented. Because it is within his repertoire of available behavioral resources, it is fairly easy to repeat the "exceptional day" in a step by step fashion. In order to show clients that this is possible, the therapist needs to ask for detailed information about a small segment of behavior they initiated.

When the client reports no past successful period or there is no exception to the problem, the next step for the therapist is to help the client to project success into the future. Again, detailed descriptions are useful.

Therapist: So, what do you suppose is the first small step you have to take to make a little bit of the miracle happen?

Client: That's tough. I suppose I will have to stop drinking.

Th: That sounds like a big step to me. What do you suppose has to come before that, something small you can do right away?

Cl: Feel good about myself first. I have to feel good about my work. I know I should do better on my job. I can't goof off any more.

Th: So, after the miracle, what would you do different about your job?

Cl: Well, I will come to work with a good attitude.

Th: What do you have to do so that you will come to work with a good attitude?

Cl: Stop blaming my parents. I guess I have to grow up and face the fact that I have to support myself.

The therapist reinforces the idea that the client is ultimately responsible for shaping her own future. Just sitting around and talking about what could be different is useless unless the client actually takes steps to make things happen.

Now that the client has the image of the "miracle" picture, it is time to turn him into a "miracle worker." The next step is to transform the small portion of the miracle into reality and to help the client imagine what will change in his life when he actually takes steps to make the miracle happen.

Cl: You know what my miracle is? Do you really want to know?

Th: Why not? It's a true miracle and the problem that brought you here is solved. What would be the first small sign to you that your problem is beginning to be solved?

Cl: Jerry will serve breakfast in bed. It is something I dreamed about as a child. To me it is so romantic. Yeah, I want more romance in my life. When we first got married, he used to do it. I was so happy in those days.

Th: So, pretend that a miracle happened and Jerry served you breakfast in bed one day. What do you suppose you would do that you are not doing right now?

Cl: I won't be so angry with him.

Th: What would you do instead of being angry?

Cl: I would encourage him to spend more time with his family, to go along when he visits them.

Th: What else?

Cl: I would be loving toward him. I will put the past behind us and go on with our life.

Th: What will you do different then?

Cl: I will show more interest in his work, and be more responsive when he approaches me sexually. I may even suggest we go to the movies together without the kids.

Th: So, when you take the first step, what do you suppose Jerry would say he notices different about you?

Cl: He will say I'm happier, smile more, am nicer to the kids, and more loving toward everybody.

Notice the questions the therapist asks are phrased in such a way that it is possible not only for a miracle to happen, but also for the client to behave differently. "When" the miracle happens, not "if" it happens is the way the question is stated. "What *would* you do differently?" is a question that will gradually change to "What *will* you do differently?" Repeated questions are also designed to elicit repeated answers. When clients repeat the answers to these questions in an affirmative way, it becomes their own idea to make these behavioral changes. Questions are phrased in such a way so as to elicit information as well as make a strong suggestion that the client start new and positive behavior, behavior that is likely to make the miracle a reality.

Professionals who have observed our clinical work comment frequently about how patient we are when we ask these questions. We truly believe that even though it may seem to slow things down at first, it ultimately has the effect of speeding things up.

Instead of asking for detailed information about a client's problem areas or past history, we believe that repetitive questions about potential solutions is more productive. These questions work as a cognitive rehearsal and help map out the details of a solution. The more a client repeats the successful outcome verbally, the more real it becomes to her.

4. Scaling Questions

There is magic in numbers. When the client is asked to put his problems, priorities, successes, emotional investments in relationships, and level of self-esteem on a numerical scale, it gives the therapist a much better assessment of the things he has to know. The following are some of the applications we have used that we find helpful in assessing the relationship. Again, as in all other questions the therapist asks, the scaling questions are designed to inform the therapist and also are used to motivate, encourage, and enhance the change process.

Scaling questions can be used to assess the seriousness of the problem.

Therapist: Let's say, 10 means how you want your life to be when you solved the problem that brought you here, and 1 means how bad things were when you picked up the phone to set up an appointment, where would you say the problem is at today between 1 and 10?

Client: I would say it's at 3.

Th: What did you do to move up from 1 to 3 in such a short time?

Cl: I had to do it. My life was in shambles. My husband and I had a long talk.

Th: Is that unusual for you to have such a long talk?

Cl: The first time in years.

Th: What else have you done to go up from 1 to 3?

Cl: I also went to an Al-Anon meeting. I stopped going years ago. But I felt better.

Th: So, what would it take to go from 3 to 4?

Cl: I will have to detach myself more from Jason.

The following example illustrates how a client rates her investment in a relationship.

Therapist: Suppose 10 means you will do anything to keep this relationship with Lee, and 1 means you are just going to sit and wait for something to happen, where would you say you are at right now?

Client: I would say I'm at 9.

Th: Where do you suppose Lee would say he is at on the same scale?

Cl: That's hard. I would guess he would say at 2.

Th: You mean you are far more invested in this relationship than Lee is?

Cl: I guess so, now that I think about it.

Th: Where do you suppose he would say he is at, if I were to ask him?

Cl: I think he would say he is at 2, maybe 3.

Th: Where do you suppose he would say you are at, from his point of view?

Cl: He would say I'm at 10. He knows I love him more than he loves me. He tells me not to do that all the time.

Th: So, how do you explain that you love him so much more than he loves you?

Cl: I am beginning to wonder about that. Maybe because I'm afraid of the unknown? Because of the kids? I will have to think about that very hard.

These questions startled this client into thinking about the hopelessness and the one-sidedness of her "carrying the torch" of love for someone who is not reciprocating her love.

The evaluation for progress in treatment is an ongoing process and is monitored continuously throughout treatment. We find the scaling question useful in individualizing the treatment process because it helps the client take ownership of her treatment, by allowing her to take the responsibility of evaluating the process. Because the rate of progress in treatment is determined by the changes the client is making, it is appropriate that the client take the major burden of assessing her own progress. Also, because the client is the consumer of the professional service, we believe that she needs to be in charge of the rate of change she is making. When the client can assess her own progress, the therapist can better help her determine what might be the next step in the treatment process.

Therapist: Let's assume that when you first started therapy the problem that brought you here was at 1 and where you want to be after you finish here is 10, where would you say you are today, between 1 and 10?

Client: I would put myself at 4. I have a way to go yet.

Th: Okay. What would you say you have to do to move up from 4 to 5?

Cl: More time. Definitely more time. I have been at this point many times before. I have to go slow this time, to make sure that it sticks.

Th: I absolutely agree with you. So, how much time do you have to stay at 4 before you are ready to move up to 5?

Cl: I would say two months.

Th: Sounds reasonable. So, let's imagine that you have moved up to 5, two months from now. What do you suppose your family will notice different about you that will tell them you are at 5?

Cl: They will say I will be more responsible, will pay my bills, won't leave the kids alone, won't get kicked out of my apartment. Of course, it means I won't drink any more.

Th: Wow, that sounds like higher than 5 to me, more like 7 or 8 to me.

Cl: Yeah, I'm anxious to get going with my life. I'm so tired of all this mess. I want a normal life like everyone else.

Th: So, when you do all of these things, what would be different with you?

Cl: I will have more confidence in myself. I will look forward to getting up in the morning, will be a good mother to my kids, will see my family more often. I will have a normal life.

The therapist helps the client chart her future in the direction she wants. The more the client repeats what she wants during the conversation, the more convinced the client is that these goals are exactly what *she* wants for herself. This increases her motivation and her confidence that the change is something she can carry out and maintain.

Our view is that the client investment in treatment is not static, nor is it solely dependent on the client personality (Miller, 1985), rather, it is in a constant state of fluctuation and change. Client investment in recovery seems to fluctuate and change according to many variables that are beyond the control of treatment or the therapist. Continuous and periodic assessment that measures the changes in the client's progress provides the therapist with a useful sense of normal fluctuation. Periodic assessment also provides ways to accommodate and adapt therapeutic practices to the changes in the client; such monitoring allows the therapist to encourage the client to "hang in there" when she becomes discouraged. The following are examples of how to use scaling questions for assessment purposes.

Therapist: Suppose 10 means you will do anything to stop drinking, change your life around, and do what is good for you and 1 means all you are willing to do is to sit and pray, where would you say you are at today?

Client: I have tried to sit and pray before and it doesn't work. I will say I'm at 5 because I have been at this for three months and that's the longest period of sobriety I have had so far.

Th: So, you've come a long way. What do you have to do next for you to move up from 5 to 6?

Cl: Just stay at this space longer, maybe like another month.

Th: So, if I were to ask your children and if they could verbalize things to you, what do you suppose your children would say they notice different about you that will tell them that you have moved up one more point?

Cl: They will say that I am more cheerful, more loving toward them. More dependable. I will be there when I say I will be there. They will really like that.

Th: What about your mother, what would she say she will notice different about you when you go up from 5 to 6?

Cl: She will say that she will get her old daughter back. I was a very responsible and nurturing person before I started drinking so much.

Th: Who else would notice the difference in you when you are at 6?

Cl: My ex-husband, probably. He will say I won't blame him for everything and will take ownership of my own problems.

Th: So, when you do that, what do you suppose these people will do different with you?

Alcohol problems affect all facets of the client's life. Therefore, most clinicians meet clients who seem to have so many problems (marital, financial, health) that it seems impossible to sort out what must be done first.

If a therapist can become overwhelmed by the long list of problems, it is not difficult to imagine how the client can be immobilized by them. It is crucial that the therapist provide the client with ways to organize his priorities. We find the following method useful.

Th: I realize that it may be difficult to put numbers on all of your problems. Suppose I ask you to put numbers on each of the problems we discussed. Say, 10 is the most urgent and 1 the least. Where do you suppose you will put the drinking problem? Problem with the marriage? The kids? Money? Health? In-laws? What number would you give to each of these problems?

Cl: I would say the problem with my daughter's running away, that's 10. I know it has to do with me and my wife fighting. But we have to straighten out Heather's school problem before we do anything. She has to finish high school and she doesn't have much time to mess with.

Th: So, what do you suppose Heather would say how important it is for her to finish high school? On the same scale, where do you suppose she would say she is on the school problem?

Cl: She probably would say she is on 5. Heather would say, though, our fighting is at 10.

Th: What do you suppose Heather would say will be different when you two stop fighting?

Cl: She would probably say that if we stop fighting she can do her school work better. She just hates it when we fight. That's when she runs away.

Th: So, what would it take for you and your wife not to fight?

Cl: I will have to cut down on my drinking. If I know it's going to help my daughter I'm willing to do it. I love my kids. She shouldn't throw her life away like I did.

Th: So, what would Heather say you can do to be more helpful to her so that she can finish high school?

Cl: She probably would say I have to stop fighting with my wife and stop drinking.

From this conversation it becomes clear that his daughter's success in life is more important than anything else at this time. It is more useful to go along with his goals for the stated purpose as an initial starting point. When the client recognizes that his drinking interferes with what he values the most — in this example, his daughter's completing high school — it will be easier for him to stop drinking *because of his daughter* and not because he is an "alcoholic." Therefore, *not drinking* becomes a means to being a good parent. His willingness to consider what is good for his daughter certainly is the beginning motivation and it may change as he realizes what other positive changes will follow.

The application of the scaling question to the assessment of self-esteem was first described to us by a talented therapist, Ron Kral (Kral, 1988), in his work with children in school settings. Since then, we have adapted this to working with adults as well as children.

Therapist: Let's say, Tracy, that number 100 stands for the ideal person you always wanted to be, you know, the kind of person you always dreamed about becoming. How close are you to being at 100 right now?

Tracy: Well, I would say I'm at 25 today. I feel very low about myself today.

Th: So, what would you say was the highest number you have ever reached close to 100?

T: I would say about 50. That was the best or the highest I have ever accomplished so far in my life.

Th: That's pretty good, considering all the tough breaks you have had in your life. But how did you do that?

T: That was when I was going to A.A., I didn't drink for a long time, had a steady job, I felt like I was going somewhere in life. That was three years ago.

Th: What else was going on in your life, then?

T: I was involved in a relationship. I had reason to live. I was making progress in life.

Th: So, what would it take for you to be at 50 again? Since you did it once only three years ago, it means you can do it again.

T: I never thought of it like that. I suppose the first thing is to start to going to A.A. meetings again.

Th: Okay. What comes after that?

The fact that the client was at the halfway point one time in her life becomes an exception to her view that she has messed up her entire life. Remembering and describing what she did to be at the halfway mark give clues on what she needs to do (i.e., start attending A.A. meetings). This question not only gives the therapist some sense of how the client evaluates her own goal, but it also points out the exceptions and possible solutions as realistic and achievable.

5. Coping Questions

In consulting and supervision sessions with therapists, we find that many professionals feel that the most difficult clients are those with hopeless views of themselves and their futures. This kind of client cannot be comforted and/or reassured that there is hope for him. This client is often described by clinicians as a "very depressed and very depressing" type of person to treat. The therapist often dreads the sessions, secretly hopes the client will fail to show up, blames the client or attaches serious-sounding diagnostic labels, or keeps trying to reassure him again and again without success. As a result, the therapist may end up feeling as hopeless as the client does.

On the client's part, she may claim that there is no hope of her ever stopping drinking, or that her life will not improve no matter what she tries. This client's rationale is that because life is not likely to improve, why not just "drink life away and suffer in quiet desperation."

Of course, any client with this much of a pessimistic outlook is difficult for a therapist to face because it is exactly the opposite of what most therapists believe about their work and their clients. The therapist's most frequent reaction is that such a client "has to hit bottom" before he will accept that he has a drinking problem. It is a difficult notion to contemplate—that not every client can be helped regardless of what treatment model is used. Before giving up on this type of case, we suggest that a therapist try one other type of question.

When faced with such a discouraging clinical situation, we find that coping questions are often successful in gently challenging the client's belief system and her feelings of hopelessness while, at the same time, orienting her toward a sense of a small measure of success.

Therapist: Having heard about your terrible experience and your family's drinking history, it is understandable why you believe that nothing will help. So, tell me, *how* do you keep going everyday?

Client: I barely survive. You know about my history. Nothing will change. I will never be different. I will be like this for the rest of my life. It is sickening to think that I'm doomed to live like this for the rest of my life.

Th: So, how do you manage to keep going? (with a look of curiosity and amazement)

Cl: I keep telling you that I just live from day to day with no hope of my life improving.

Th: I can see why you believe that. So, what do you do to barely cope from day to day?

Cl: I drink. That's how I do it. What's the use? There is no hope for me. Coming from the kind of family I come from, nothing will change. It was hammered into my head that I will not amount to anything.

Th: I'm not sure if I agree with that, but, that's beside the point. So, what do you do so that you get through each day? How did you manage to get up in the morning?

Cl: I have to, don't I? I force myself to get up and barely get myself to work. It's an effort. I shouldn't have to do this. Life should be a joy. I should be glad to get up in the morning and look forward to the day.

Th: I agree. Absolutely. So, how do you force yourself to get out of bed and get to work every morning? I am amazed, considering what you have been through, the abuse, the alcoholic parents, no nurturing, and all the hell you've been through, I sometimes wonder how you manage to keep going everyday.

Cl: It's really no big deal. I just force myself to get out of bed and think of all those people who depend on me. I haven't missed a day's work this year yet. I rarely use my sick days.

Th: That's what I mean. How do you do that? I know a lot of people who have difficulty getting to work on time even without your background.

Cl: Well, you make it sound like it's a big thing. I just do it.

Th: You mean, you are the type of person who makes up her mind and
    then just does it?
Cl: Not because I enjoy it, but because I have to; I just do it.
Th: That's great.

The client is asked to describe *how* she "barely copes" with such a serious
lifelong problem, she begins to describe a small step that enables her to get
through each day. Clearly this small "barely coping," step she takes each
day becomes the foundation for what she needs to continue to do.

However small it may seem, the small things the client does to "barely
cope" are the very things that the client must do more of "one day at a
time" in order to create a basis on which to build more successful measures. Such a client needs to be reminded and encouraged to barely
cope. It is true that she deserves to enjoy her life more, but that comes
later. The first step is for the client to recognize that she has coping
skills.

Clients frequently are surprised when we ask this question. Their
common nonverbal expressions convey a message of "You've gotta be
kidding" and then they slowly begin to recognize their inner strength
and resources. Here is an example of this recognition:

Therapist: I'm confused, Lisa, from what you have said so far, most
    people would find their lives a lot worse than what you have, given
    the same set of circumstances. How comes things aren't worse?
    What are you doing to keep them from getting worse?
Client: You think so?
Th: Yeah, I sure do. Tell me again, what are you doing so that things
    are not worse?
Cl: I keep reciting the Serenity Prayer and keep the spiritual side to my
    life. I try to remember things to be grateful for every day.
Th: That's a lot. How did you figure out that doing this would help?
Cl: These are the things that I learned in A.A. I forget to use them,
    though.
Th: So, what do you need to do so that you can continue to remember
    to use these things?
Cl: I will post the Twelve Steps on my refrigerator door. I have all those
    pictures my kids drew. I will make room for it.

As the above example shows, the variation on the coping question of
asking, "How come your life is not worse?" is used to "blame" the client
for her success which she does not see. Such positive "blame," as de-

scribed by Kral in his work with children and teachers in a school setting (Kral, 1988) assigns the responsibility of the positive or helpful behaviors to the client. It is used not only to affirm what the client is doing as being successful, but also indicates to the client that the therapist has confidence that she knows what she needs to do to solve her own problems.

We find the coping question very useful when treating a client in acute crisis. Before hastily reassuring the client that he has survived the trauma (which can range from a physical assault to a natural disaster), the use of a coping question uncovers and then utilizes what the *client* did to survive the crisis or trauma. The emphasis in such a situation is on conveying to the client that she somehow survived the crisis and managed not to make things worse. We have used this coping question strategy in crisis debriefing with success.

Case Example: Homicide Before Breakfast

Early one morning a man called the office asking to be seen as soon as possible. He indicated on the phone that he had nearly killed his wife and himself and that he needed to see someone right away. He sounded tearful and was in a great deal of emotional distress. We agreed to see him as soon as he could get to our office.

Sean, a factory worker, had had "on again, off again" marital problems because of his wife's drinking. The combination of his unstable job history and his wife's drinking caused considerable tension in the marriage and long-standing financial difficulties. Sean had also accused his wife, Connie, of having an affair, which she repeatedly denied.

The night before we saw him, Sean had returned home unexpectedly early from his "graveyard shift" only to find Connie and his best friend in his bed. He reported that his immediate impulse had been to grab his shotgun and shoot both them and himself but somehow he managed to control himself and ran out of the house — he had been afraid to return home since. His fear was what he might do out of rage more than what he might find at home. Instead, he reported that he had been "walking the streets" all night and called our office when he thought it would open.

It would have been easy for the therapist to focus on his rage, how he may have contributed to Connie's drinking problem, the marital tension, lack of money, and a host of problems that were apparent. The therapist realized that in the state Sean was in, what he needed was crisis management.

Therapist: Let's see. It is now a little after eight o'clock and you are saying this happened around one o'clock. So, what have you been doing since one o'clock to cope with this?

Sean: I have been walking the streets. That's the only way I managed not to kill anyone, including myself.

Th: You mean, you've been walking for seven hours?

S: Yeah, I couldn't go back there. I knew I saw red and I would do something I shouldn't do.

Th: So, how did you know that you had to leave the house? What gave you the idea to leave and not get into an argument with Connie or with Jim (his best friend)?

S: I know my temper. I just knew I had to get out of there. I couldn't sit down. I had to walk. I've walked everywhere, all over town.

Th: I'm still amazed you had enough sense to know that you had to get out of there. How did you do that?

S: I just knew it. Something inside me told me that if I stayed there, I would do something terrible.

Th: So, even in such a situation you had enough sense to listen to yourself. Did you know that about yourself?

S: To tell you the truth, no, I didn't know that. I always had a temper since I was young and that got me into a lot of fights.

Th: So, how did you know that you had to run out of the house when you did?

S: I thought about my kids. That's what I did. I didn't want my kids to grow up without their mother or father. It would break my heart . . . to see my kids get hurt from anything I do that is stupid.

Th: If I were to ask your wife, what do you suppose she would say you did that was most helpful?

S: She probably would say that I left. She is scared of my temper. She has always told me that the kids shouldn't see me lose my temper. So, I guess she would say that helped. But I don't know what I am going to do about this mess. I have to go home sooner or later and face the problem. I can't wander the streets any more. I have to find a solution to this problem.

Th: So, suppose a miracle happened while you were walking around all night and the problem that brought you here is solved. What do you suppose you will notice yourself doing differently?

S: First of all, I will handle myself calmer and use my head. I will sit down with Connie and talk to her, ask her, and not tell her what she wants to do about her drinking problem.

Th: What do you suppose she will notice different about you that will tell her that a miracle happened?

The client certainly did the right thing by running out of the house. His concern for his children became the important point to compliment the client on and became the focus for what his next steps would be. Because he took the right beginning steps, the next therapeutic task is to assess and plan subsequent steps in achieving his goal. The miracle question would indicate his ideas of how his life would be different when the problem is solved. The use of scaling questions would indicate how willing he or his wife are to solve this serious marital problem. Since the client is beginning to identify his temper and Connie's drinking as the important factors in their marital problem, the assessment of which problems must be solved first and who is willing to take what steps first can be negotiated through various questions.

The Therapist's Stance in Using These Five Useful Questions

The most striking comments and reactions therapists have when they observe our clinical interview is how the client responds to our repeated use of variations on these five useful questions during the single interview. At first, we were somewhat puzzled by these reactions. As we continued our dialogue and paid close attention to what the observers pointed out, it became more and more clear to us that our attitudes towards a client seemed to make the crucial difference. We are told that our respectful approach to the client and our genuine curiosity about what a client describes as her unique way of solving problems seem to make it impossible for the client to object to repeated questions. Frankly, we believe that the more the client is asked to repeat her success stories, the more convinced she will become that the solutions she implemented were exactly right for her. What better way for the therapist to empower a client to take control of her life and to solve her drinking problem?

At this point in the interview, it should become fairly easy for the therapist to assess the client-therapist relationship we described in Chapter 2. Depending on how willing the therapist is to negotiate goals with the client, the nature of the relationship changes dramatically. By reviewing what is most salient to the client, and how willing the client is to take the first small but significant step toward solving his problem, it becomes relatively easy to assess what that first step should be.

6

The Components, Types, and Delivery of Treatment Interventions

> You cannot solve a problem with the same kind of thinking that created it.
>
> — Albert Einstein

> I have been waiting for twenty years for someone to say to me: "You have to fight fire with fire" so that I could reply, "that's funny — I always use water."
>
> — Howard Gosage, *Zen to Go* (Winnokur, 1989)

LIKE OTHER ASPECTS OF THE SOLUTION-FOCUSED therapy model, our view of therapeutic intervention has evolved over the past 20 years. In the earlier years, we tended to view the intervention* and the homework assignments we suggested at the conclusion of the session as the means to solving the client's drinking problem. Therefore, we put a great deal of thought and energy into devising the right homework tasks. We focused on inventing the most clever, witty, and creative ways to present our tasks to the clients. Because so much energy was invested in creating these homework tasks, we tended to give much weight to whether the client carried out the suggested task or not, and if not, why not.

Our thinking about therapeutic interventions has changed a great deal. Our current belief is that all solution-focused interventions, both the interviewing and the homework task components, are designed to elicit, trigger, and repeat exceptions the client generates. In this process, the therapist performs the function of tipping the first domino. This is

---

*We wish to emphasize a clear distinction between what is known as "intervention" in the field of alcohol treatment and our ideas of therapeutic intervention. We refer to intervention as a part of the treatment strategy in which the therapist assists the client in discovering his own solutions to his problem.

based on a more fundamental shift in our thinking—instead of putting emphasis on *stopping* the problematic drinking, the more effective, economical, and efficient treatment approach is to *elicit and enlarge upon* the existing successful solutions that the client has generated. That is, the traditional emphasis on *stopping* drinking requires both the therapist and the client to focus on negative goals. As discussed in Chapter III, such a prohibitive approach will, by necessity, only emphasize failures and problems.

Consequently, we have come to view the interviewing process as a crucial means to uncovering, creating, and, at times, challenging the client's beliefs, and as a means to negotiating the treatment process based on the client's unique solutions and her world view. Thus, it only makes sense that when following the philosophy and assumptions we subscribe to, the logical conclusion would be to consider the interview process as very important. Frequently, the sheer act of identifying what the goals are can be tremendously therapeutic.

In this chapter we will discuss the types of interventions that are individualized to each client, based on the therapist's assessment of the kind of client-therapist relationship that exists. This is the fourth step in the solution-focused model. The following is a list of therapist behaviors that are designed to enhance cooperation in treatment while allowing room for the therapist to individualize the homework task to fit the type of relationship the therapist and client have.

INTRASESSION CONSULTATION AND TEAM APPROACH

As described elsewhere (Berg, 1988a, 1988b, 1989, 1991; de Shazer, 1985, 1988, 1991), one of the important and innovative techniques borrowed from the family therapy field is the notion of intrasession consultation with a team behind a one-way mirror.

The team approach utilizes a one-way mirror and a telephone hookup between the therapist and a team of therapists acting as consultants behind the window. The idea behind this innovation is that it offers multiple views of the problem—and, thus, multiple views of the solution—what de Shazer calls, a poly-ocular view (de Shazer, 1982). Such use of the team offers a more objective and varied view of the client's problems. The therapist, therefore, is less likely to become "stuck" with attempting the "same damned thing" that does not work. Many creative and innovative ideas have emerged from such use of the team, for example, the "reflecting team" (Andersen, 1990), the Milan team's idea of neutrality (Boscolo, Cecchin, Hoffman, & Penn, 1987), the Greek chorus model (Papp, 1980), and other teaching and treatment models developed from this format (c.f. Madanes, 1984a, 1984b; Watzlawick, Weakland, & Fisch, 1974; Weeks, 1991). There are also other ways the team approach can be useful in treatment strategies, such as the split-team intervention, which will be described later in this chapter.

About 45 minutes after the beginning of the usual 60-minute session, a brief period of time is scheduled for a "consultation break" when the therapist leaves the room for 5 to 10 minutes. During this period, the therapist meets with the team to review the session and to compose feedback and homework tasks to suggest to the client. The client can sit and wait in the therapy room or have a cigarette or coffee break on her own. This short thinking break allows the therapist to process the session free from the immediate task of attending to the client's needs and the influence of the immediate interaction with the client.

A therapist working alone without a team can also use the intrasession consultation with herself by taking time out to think, to review whether there are well-formed goals, the type of client-therapist relationship that exists, to develop compliments the client will accept, and to decide on the kind of intervention that would fit the client.

This short pause heightens the client's anticipation of what the therapist will say upon her return. Clients are usually eager to hear the feedback and concentrate on every suggestion the therapist makes. As they are preparing to receive the feedback, a common response from the client is, "So, tell me what a rotten person I am" or "Tell me, Doc, how bad my problem is" or "I guess I really messed up my life." When the client expects the most awful and dreadful pronouncement from the "expert," and the therapist gives the unexpected feedback described below, usually starting with the positive things the client has done, the response is dramatic and emotional. The following describes the components of this message and method of delivery that enhance the power of solution-focused intervention:

1. The therapist should point out any positive, successful, or useful efforts the client has made in his desire to move toward his goals. Anything the client is doing that is good for him, should be highlighted and given credit.

2. Whenever possible, using the words the client uses enhances client cooperation. Any therapy jargon is better translated into everyday conversational language so that the client feels understood. The therapeutic task at this point is to convey to the client, as clearly and simply as possible, that the therapist is cooperating

with the client. When clients have idiosyncratic ways of using words, it is helpful for the therapist to imitate and incorporate what the client says, wherever possible. This joining maneuver engenders in the client a feeling of being understood and reassured by the professional, thus reducing the client's need to defend her position.

3. The therapist should agree with the client's goal and should phrase it in a positive way. For example, stating the goal as, "We agree that your burning desire to stay sober is difficult but worthy of strong effort. What you would gain from such hard work would seem worthwhile, given the fact that you love your family very much and you want to do what is good for you and your family." "Staying sober" is a better way to phrase the goal than "stop drinking." He has already tried to "stop drinking," but "stay sober" requires a different frame of mind and a different focus.

4. The therapist emphasizes that the goal will be difficult to accomplish, that it will take hard work, and that the problem is a difficult one to solve. In reference to our discussion on guidelines for well-formed goals, this emphasis on hard work enhances client motivation and helps him to "save face" in regards to past failure.

When appropriate, complimenting the client for having tried many things to solve her problems or "hanging in there" when it would have been easier to just give up is helpful. Such statements reflect the client's perception of herself as being motivated to solve her problem and makes it seem natural for the client to cooperate.

5. Always give a rationale or explanation for suggesting homework. Even if the only reasonable goal that emerges at the end of the session is to have the client return for a second session, it is helpful to offer a rationale for returning. A simple statement such as, "Since there is a serious disagreement between you and your probation officer about what kind of treatment you really need, I would like to have you return next week so that we can get a better idea of how to accomplish both," is needed to explain the therapist's thinking on a reason for the client to return. Such a rationale must make sense from the client's perspective and thus must fit with her view as reasonable and worthy of doing.

A helpful bridging statement may begin with the following statement, repeating what the client stated during the session: "I agree with you that you worked very hard to . . . " or "Because many things you have tried did not work . . . " or "Since your boss misunderstands about your drinking problem. . . . "

6. Since it is difficult to separate the message from the messenger, the therapist's style and manner of delivery adds to the significance of the message and the suggestions offered to the client. Our recommendation is that the therapist speak in a deliberate manner, slowly and with authority.

INDIVIDUALIZING THE TASK

The therapist must always take into consideration the type of relationship she has with each client and adapt homework tasks accordingly. The following guide is designed to provide the therapist with a thumbnail sketch of what to do.

Visitor-Type Relationship

When the therapist determines that a visitor-type relationship exists, then it is likely that she and the client have not created a workable goal, and that the client is not likely to carry out any suggestions or tasks that the therapist may offer. One can describe the therapeutic task of the client-therapist relationship at this stage as that of establishing a workable goal, that is, establishing with some clarity what the client is seeking by coming to therapy. For instance, if a client, whose therapy is mandated by someone else (probation officer, employer, parents), disagrees with the goals the mandating agent has set for her, the therapist would be prudent not to repeat what others have done without success, that is, to mandate and demand that the client follow a suggestion. We are frequently dumbfounded during consultation sessions by how often therapists unwittingly repeat the same old efforts that did not work in the past, only to be frustrated even more.

Giving frequent positive feedback on what the client is doing that is helpful to her encourages the client to become more interested in treatment because she sees herself as cooperative, hard working, and interested in doing what is good for herself. Sometimes the therapist will have to search for small things: the client chose to come to therapy even though it was not her own idea, or the client is making an effort to eat healthy, exercise, or maintain social relationships with nondrinkers. If the client has held down a job for six months and this is the longest period he has had a job, and he acknowledges this as a positive move on his part that took much effort, then the therapist needs to make much ado about this as a small but significant step toward success. Successes, whether big or small, need to be highlighted and the suggestion should be made that they be continued. The following is an example of how we ended the session with a client who came to fulfil his probation obligation. This message was given to the client following our "thinking break."

"Curtis, we are very impressed that you are here today even though this is not your idea. You certainly had the option of taking the easy way out by not coming. Your willingness to put up with many demands that seem unreasonable, including being here today, shows that you are the kind of person that wants to do the right thing. It has not been easy for you to be here today; having to give up your personal time, talking about things you really don't want to talk about, having to take the bus, and so on. But we are impressed with your willingness to cooperate with us today.

"I realize that you are an independent minded person who does not want to be told what to do and I agree with you that you should be left alone. But you also realize that doing what you are told will help you get these people out of your life and you will be left alone sooner. Therefore, I would like to meet with you again to figure out further what will be good for you to do. So, let's meet next week at the same time."

In addition to complimenting the client for the positive things he is doing, it is prudent for the therapist to refrain from making any suggestions that require behavioral changes the client is not likely to make.

Although professionals fear that they are condoning and reinforcing the client's continued drinking with compliments, this type of message delivered at the end of a session with a visitor-type client has two benefits. First, when this approach is used, the problem drinker is much more likely to return for second and subsequent sessions. Contrary to what the client is accustomed to hearing (reprimands, pleas for abstinence, threats of an ultimatum, and reminders of their past broken promises), these messages strike the client as being really new and different. If nothing else, it catches the client's attention, which is the first necessary step in making changes. Second, this type of message seems to facilitate client cooperation and willingness to participate in the treatment process.

Even if the client drops out of therapy prematurely, our clinical experience indicates that this approach increases and enhances the possibility that the client will return to see the therapist in the future when she decides that she is serious about solving her drinking problem. It seems the client remembers the first and only encounter with our center because it was so positive. Clients also tend to return much sooner should there be other problems, perhaps not related to problem drinking.

Complainant-Type Relationship

This type of relationship is created when, by the end of the session, the therapist has helped the client to identify what the solution would look like (using the miracle question) and to develop some expectations that the problem that brought him to therapy can change. However, since the client still believes that the solution lies in someone else taking steps, the awareness that *he* needs to take steps to solve his own problem is not fully developed yet. Thus, the client may look to the therapist to convince his spouse to stop drinking, force her to go A.A. meetings, and so on. The therapeutic task at this point is to shift the client perception of problem and solution. As a result, clients often begin to understand that only they can take steps to find solutions to their problems.

Complimenting the client for having suffered a great deal because of a family member's drinking problem, and for having offered many helpful observations and analyses of the drinker's history, is the beginning step with this type of relationship. It is also useful to give credit for having kept faith and hope in the problem drinker despite many difficulties, and having attempted many different things to solve the problem. Any suggestions a therapist makes to the client in a complainant-type relationship are directed toward changing the client's perception of herself from that of a helpless victim to that of someone with a solution to carry out on her own. Because the client in this type of situation is typically an *observer* of the problem drinker, any suggestions for a task should be limited to *thinking and observing*.

> "It is clear to us that you have given a lot of thought to your husband's drinking problem and noticed many things that are helpful to understand his problem. It is clear that you have tried many different things to convince your husband of the seriousness of the problem because you love him and are very concerned about the welfare of the family. It is also clear that in spite of everything you have been through, you still have hope that he may realize some day how serious the problem is.
>
> "At the same time, we are impressed that you have come to finally accept that only he can stop drinking and that he needs to learn to take the natural consequences of his drinking. We agree that this is what growing up is about. We think that your being here today is the first step toward healthier future for both of you, and that right now is the best

time to start detaching yourself from his drinking and concentrate on learning to take care of yourself. But as you know, it will not be easy. Therefore, we would like you to give some further *thoughts* to what else you will notice different about him that gives you hope as you continue to detach yourself."

Customer-Type Relationship

Because the distinguishing trait of this type of client-therapist relationship is that the client is willing to *take steps* to solve problems and sees himself as taking an active role in finding solutions, the therapist needs to adapt the messages accordingly. In addition to the now familiar suggestion of complimenting the client for his willingness to solve his drinking problem, the important therapeutic task for the therapist at this point is to identify, with the client, what might be the first active, behavioral step he needs to implement. Frequently for this type of client there already exist numerous examples of pre-session change and some deliberate exceptions, which the therapist needs to reinforce and support.

> "I am very impressed that you have finally recognized that you have to, stop drinking, be more responsible, and take care of your family. It takes a great deal of maturity and strength to accept the reality that you must start taking care of your business [these are the client's terms]. We agree that it will take hard work and the tough part still lies ahead, but your determination to be a better parent to your children than your father has been to you is very impressive. But, as you know, it will take lots of hard work and trial and error since you will be teaching yourself how to be a responsible father. The same will be true with staying sober. As a way of getting you started in the right direction toward becoming more responsible, I would like to have you continue to stay with your newly discovered healthy habits and also pay attention to what new ways you discover that increase your chances of success."

COMPLIMENTS: POWER OF AFFIRMATION

The team at the Brief Family Therapy Center has been using and studying compliments for close to 20 years, and we continue to be amazed at their therapeutic power and usefulness as an intervention tool. The compliment is used with all cases as described above, regardless of the type of client-therapist relationship, and throughout the treatment process. Except on rare occasions when the client is squeamish about receiving compliments, and in extremely rare situations where the therapist is unable to find anything positive at all, we find that using compliments enhances the cooperation with the client. Even when the relationship is already positive, it increases the already good working relationship.

Complimenting the client is not the same as condoning her destructive behavior. It simply acknowledges and gives credence to her view of her world, affirming her view of herself, accepting her "story," and soothing her frustration at having to admit to failures.

The use of compliments is one of many tools a therapist has at his disposal that takes advantage of socially accepted norms of discourse. We discovered through our cross-cultural and international presentations that all cultures use compliments as a means to cementing social relationships at all levels. However, the cultural norm dictates the manner in which compliments are presented. For example, a commonly accepted form of insuring a positive relationship in North America highlights personal achievements and individual traits: "You look good today, what's different about you?" "The color red looks good on you," "Your new tie really stands out, it looks good!" "That was a great presentation at the staff meeting, you did a good job!" "I like the way you spoke up for yourself to the boss, it's about time he recognized your good points," and so on. In other cultures, the compliment may be directed at what a person does on behalf of the family, the group, the clan, or the employer (such as sacrificing one's wishes for the benefit of the family honor) (Berg & Gilkey, in press). While North Americans value an open, clear, and direct manner of complimenting one other, other cultures are much more subtle about giving compliments. The compliment may be expressed with a look, a raised eyebrow, or a subtle smile. Such unique cultural and ethnic differences need to be taken into consideration when a therapist selects what to highlight and compliment the client on. A competent therapist with solid training in listening skills and with a respectful attitude toward the client will learn what the client will consider an acceptable and positive compliment. We cannot emphasize strongly enough that whatever compliments the therapist makes must be genuine, sincere, and honest in order to engender client confidence in the therapist.

AGREE WITH CLIENT GOALS

Empowerment of the client starts with honoring and following his lead in deciding what is important to him. This differs from the medical model of treatment in which the expert decides what is good for the patient and then prescribes a course of treatment for the patient to follow.

The treatment model we advocate is a collaborative one where the client and therapist work together to bring about the goals the *client* decides on. As is indicated elsewhere, the model not only respects the client's right to self-determination but also implies that she is the expert in her problem and she may already have solutions. Since the client will have to take an active part in finding solutions and implementing these solutions, the most prudent way to enhance self-determination and increase self-efficacy is to respectfully follow client's goals. This will help ensure a cooperative working relationship, reduce therapist frustration and burnout, and shorten treatment. In addition, our clinical pragmatism indicates that in most situations the client is likely to do what she wants to do anyway, no matter how much we want her to do or want something else.

Whatever the client's immediate goal, such as getting along with his family, keeping her job or saving money, it must be accepted as a good goal. As mentioned previously, any suggestions or tasks the therapist offers to the client need to be described as a means to achieve the *client's* immediate goals.

Case Example: Good Father

Jeff, a 37-year-old police rookie, was referred by the Employee Assistance Program because of a "domestic conflict." The referral information indicated that he was engaged in many high-risk activities, such as riding a motorcycle at high speeds without a helmet, flashing his service revolver while fighting with his wife about her affair, and drinking excessively while cleaning his guns. It was learned later that during the latest drinking episode he got into a fight with his wife and shot at the ceiling, barely missing her.

In negotiating goals for treatment, Jeff kept stressing his goal of being a good father to his young son. While skeptical of his goal of wanting to be a "good father" and wondering if he was "minimizing" and "denying" the seriousness of his problem drinking and his suicidal and dangerous behavior of drinking and driving, the therapist nevertheless negotiated with Jeff about his ideas of what difference it would make in his life when he became a "good father."

This turned out to be a very productive move. Even though the therapist was initially skeptical of Jeff's stated goal, the client was persistent in sticking with his goal of becoming a good father. This included learning how to be attentive to his son's needs, participating in child care, helping out around the house, not drinking, and teaching his son to negotiate disagreements without violence. These same qualities

also applied to being a "top-notch cop," another goal the client articulated.

Do More of What Works

The second rule of our central philosophy, "doing more of what works,"
is a simple idea but has had a profound impact on our approach to
working *with* clients. The premise of this idea is that there is no "right"
way to solve problems, whatever works is what should be repeated. This
is an important outcome of our deep respect for the client's ability to
solve problems and our willingness to learn from our clients.

Such a simple idea can be very complex. What is meant by "what
works," and how does one define what works from what does not work?
It depends a great deal on one's definition of what is normal and what is
"pathological." Another benefit of working with the solution-focused
model is that it allows a frame for working with a variety of cultural and
ethnic meanings around "what works."

This premise of doing more of what works is one of the simple,
commonsense ideas on which we base our work. Since many of the
details of how to implement these intervention techniques are described
in Chapter 5, we will list them here as a flow chart of intervention
strategies.

Triggering Pre-Session Change

It is estimated that as many as 67% of outpatient clients report some
"positive" changes between the time they call for an appointment and
their first session (Talmon, 1990; Weiner-Davis et al., 1987). What is
more surprising is that these "positive" changes were in the direction
clients sought help with in coming to therapy. We began to see these
positive pre-session changes as a foundation for life-style changes. Because the client has already made a movement in the direction of his
therapy goals, these small changes should not be dismissed, but further
changes can be built upon them.

In *Single Session Therapy*, Talmon (1990) not only capitalizes on and
utilizes these positive pre-session changes, but also adopts the approach
that a therapist can trigger this natural process by using a first-session
formula task described by de Shazer (de Shazer, 1985). During the
initial phone call the client makes to set up an appointment, the following task is given by the therapist: "Between now and the time you come
for your first appointment, I would like you to keep track of all the

things that go well in your life and that you would like to have continue." This initial phone conversation can be seen as the first session. Therefore, the first in-person session starts with asking what the client discovered about her life that she would like to have continued.

Even without being asked pointed questions designed to uncover any pre-session changes, clients frequently open their sessions with such spontaneous comments as, "On the way over here I was thinking if I should come today because since I made the phone call, somehow things are much better." Such comments can be easily dismissed as "flight into health" instead of being seen as a positive first step. Again, our preference is to wait for an opportune moment in the natural flow of therapeutic conversation and ask the client to elaborate on his mention of pre-session changes. When the therapist picks up on such a change, she might digress a little to highlight the change by asking such questions as, "You cut down on your drinking on your own? How did you do that? Wasn't it hard?" Enhancing and enlarging such pre-session change also makes the therapeutic task of offering compliments easier, because it is natural to compliment a client on having had initiative to start on his treatment process. Such a therapeutic stance enhances the poor self-esteem of most problem drinkers as it forces them to change their self-perceptions from "no good bum" to "self-starter."

When the client has taken positive steps toward achieving her goal, the therapeutic task becomes one of monitoring and encouraging the client to stay on track, doing more of what works. We are amazed at the infinitely creative ways clients solve their problems on their own. This is one more way we have come to respect the creativity and resourcefulness of even the most chronic problem drinkers to know what is good for them. The solutions generated by the client are easier to incorporate into his life-style than if they were suggested by an expert who is unfamiliar with details of the client's life. In addition, because it is his own solution, he is much more invested in succeeding.

Case Example: Doing Without Knowing

Calvin, a 29-year-old unemployed worker living with his divorced mother, came to therapy complaining of depression and "crying jags," which embarrassed and concerned him. Although Calvin had a long history of drug and alcohol use, he was initially more concerned about his depression than his substance use.

When asked what changes he noticed about his depression since he had called a week ago, Calvin stated he got a job working in a yacht club because he decided he was tired of being poor and that he had not used any drugs or alcohol for about a week. Amazed and curious about this show of initiative, the therapist decided to build on this pre-session change:

Therapist: Let's say, on a scale of 1 to 10, 10 stands for how you want your life to be at the end of therapy here and 1 means the lowest you have ever felt about your life, where would you say you are at today?

Client: I would say, I am at about 4 today.

Th: Wow, that's a lot of change in such a short time! What do you suppose you did to move up all the way to 4?

Cl: I took a good look at myself and decided that I did not want this kind of life.

Th: What do you suppose was different with you this time that made you say that to yourself?

Cl: Well, I am 29 going on 30 and I don't have anything to show for what I've done with my life.

Th: Sounds like something about turning 30 helped you look at things differently. Now, what do you need to do to keep this going, to stay on track?

Cl: That's just it. I know it's going to be tough.

Th: What do you suppose your mother would say that you have to do to keep on track?

Cl: She will say the main thing is the drinking. That's my downfall.

Th: So, how have you managed not to drink for a whole week?

When there is a clearly identified pre-session change, the therapeutic task becomes that of helping the client stay on his newfound path of staying sober. Subsequent sessions with Calvin was focused on reviews of how he managed to stay sober, and what new methods he was creating to stay on this new path. Each new problem and concern Calvin brought to the session — his depression, his need to socialize more, and his desire to save money — were all treated in a similar manner until Calvin was confident of maintaining progress on his own.

Look for Exceptions

The team at the Brief Family Therapy Center has been investigating the exceptions to problems for a number of years (de Shazer, 1985, 1988, 1991) and has decided that these exceptions fall into two types: deliberate and random.

Deliberate exceptions are those solutions that clients implement and are able to describe in detail. Paying attention to the details of exceptions is important because when the client can identify the steps she has taken, it means that she can repeat them, thus creating a solution pattern.

The following is a typical example of a conversation in which a deliberate exception is highlighted (the client is Calvin from the previous example):

Therapist: So, how did you manage to not drink for a whole week?
Client: It's only a week. I've done that many times. Sometimes, I go for a month, even a couple of months without drinking.
Th: That's amazing. How do you do that? Isn't it hard?
Cl: You know, once you make up your mind, you just don't think about it.
Th: You mean you don't have to fight it every minute of the day?
Cl: Yeah, I could if I wanted to. But you know, what works is just distract yourself from thinking about it and just keep busy.
Th: So, tell me, how have you been managing for a whole week this time?
Cl: I just keep positive thinking. Whenever I pray, it helps. Going to A.A. meetings helps. I've been really busy. When I feel productive, I don't need to drink.

Through this kind of investigation the client comes to realize that indeed he has managed to stay sober for a whole week. In addition, more important than the relatively short period of sobriety is his discovery of how he stayed sober. If the therapist had not asked for details, this client probably would not have thought about what he actually did to stay sober, nor attach any significance to it. As the client becomes more conscious of his own strategies, such as keeping busy, going to A.A. meetings, not thinking about drinking as an option, etc., he discovers that he is developing some useful ways to stay sober.

Case Example: How Do You Do It?

Mark, a hardworking and ambitious young man in his late twenties, was concerned about his drinking. He reported that he and his girlfriend, whom he loves very much and wants to marry someday, get into frequent fights over his drinking. Even though she used to drink with him when they first met, she is now "domesticated" and has "calmed down," according to Mark, and becomes very upset with his drinking. From the description of his drinking pattern, the therapist agreed with her view that Mark needs to take appropriate steps.

A detailed account of Mark's drinking revealed that he drank to excess only on weekends, and even then only when he and his girlfriend were out "partying" with others. Their severe fights, during which each threatened to leave the other, followed these drinking episodes. Having just started a new real estate business, Mark attended such parties frequently. When he and his girlfriend were home together or went out for dinner on their own, his drinking was moderate, usually no more than a couple of drinks. Already his description indicated exceptions. The therapist decided to pursue Mark's nondrinking pattern in more detail.

Knowing that being in the real estate business means having to work on weekends, the therapist asked Mark what he was like when he had to work on weekends. Mark reported that when he was "on call" on weekends, he never got drunk, even at "wild parties" with free drinks. Surprised to hear this, the therapist asked how he managed to not drink then. Mark explained in a serious tone that it was very important that he succeed in this new business venture and that he did not want to risk incurring enormous debt and loss of credibility in the real estate business. Therefore, when he was "on duty" or when he had an important presentation to a potential customer on a Monday, he did not drink at all on weekends. The therapist kept asking exactly what he did in order to abstain from drinking when the temptation was great. Mark detailed what he did to stay sober at these times. They included only drinking soda, staying close to his girlfriend, or making sure he went to the parties in a relaxed frame of mind.

The therapeutic intervention with Mark centered first on his enhancing his awareness of his ability to control his behaviors related to staying sober and then, on what he needed to do in order to repeat these nondrinking behaviors at other parties.

Case Example: Deliberate Exceptions on the Road

Jim, a long-distance truck driver in his early thirties, requested emergency service immediately following a violent outburst of temper during which he struck his wife and sent her to the hospital. He was remorseful about his lifelong problems controlling his temper. It repeatedly got him into fights—during one fight, he had come close to killing someone. His loss of temper became worse when he drank, even though it also occurred when he was sober.

The therapist was curious about how Jim's hot temper affected his on-the-road behavior as he was on his own between 5 and 30 days at a stretch, and had to deal with a variety of traffic conditions in all types of weather. Jim reported that he managed to control his temper as well as his drinking while he was "on the job" with no difficulty; losing his temper was not an option for him at these times. In fact, in his 12 years of truck driving he had never had an accident and had received many safety awards. Another exception we discovered was his behavior with his sons, ages five and seven. It was clear that he loved them very much and there had been no incidents of his losing his temper with them, which was another indication of a remarkable degree of responsible behavior.

Recognizing that long periods of driving must be extremely stressful and boring the therapist expressed amazement at and curiosity about how Jim might explain the differences in himself between the times he was "on the road" and "off the road." Without hesitation, he answered that the main difference was that being "on the job" and being responsible for the costly truck and its cargo allowed him to be detached about the stupidity of other drivers on the road and that the choice of drinking did not even enter his mind. Still unconvinced about this remarkable degree of self-monitoring, the therapist probed further into Jim's understanding of these differences. Jim related that he needed his job in order to support his family, particularly his two boys whom he loved very much, and it was his job to bring home the money. Therefore, he kept his temper in check with other drivers who irritated him on the road, and he was not tempted to drink because it would jeopardize his job. His boys did not provoke him because he usually saw what they did as being more funny than irritating.

These two cases are clear examples of deliberate exceptions. Because both clients already had developed successful strategies on their own that worked remarkably well, the therapist needed to support and encourage them to "do more" of what worked and to expand on the exceptions they identified.

At the end of the session, Mark was complimented on having taken the time to come for the appointment in order to do what was good for him. It was pointed out that he clearly valued his relationship with his girlfriend and his commitment to success in his new business was important to him. He was also complimented on having figured out what his priorities were: his strong desire to succeed both in the business and in his personal relationship. Because we decided that our relationship was a customer-type, we suggested that during the coming week he continue to do what he found worked for him and also to "keep track of what other ways you manage to keep your drinking under control." We then agreed he would return one week later. When he returned with information on new and different ways he had discovered to control his behavior at parties, termination came rather rapidly.

Jim, the second client, was complimented on his decision to seek help, which was an outward sign of his recognition of a serious problem with his temper and his drinking. The therapist was again amazed at his ability to stay focused on being a good "family man" and at how he managed to earn an "excellent driver" award. It showed that doing a good job as father and family man was important to him. The next therapeutic move was to expand his definition of "on the job" into his family life. Deciding that he was clearly in a customer-type relationship, Jim was asked to continue doing what worked for him and to pay attention to what else he was doing while he was "on the job" at home. When he returned with an impressive list of strategies, the therapist and Jim studied each item on it and discussed what he needed to do to transfer them to his "job" at home. The case terminated in four sessions.

Random exceptions are those instances when the client reports obvious exceptions to her drinking but is unable to describe the steps she took to bring them about. From her point of view it appears that these events occur spontaneously; she just finds herself mysteriously not drinking. Frequently clients attribute this abstinence to chance: They did not have money to drink, or they found themselves in a situation that lent itself to not drinking. Just as they see themselves as having no control over drinking, they also see themselves as having no idea how they stop or curtail their drinking.

Because such a client sees himself as not responsible for exceptions to his drinking, by implication he also denies his responsibility for drinking. Such a client needs to be helped to recognize that he manages to not drink on his own accord and, therefore, can turn such chance occurrences into more deliberate ones. The client needs a therapist's assistance to discover that she has a substantial degree of control over her drinking, perhaps more than she thinks she has, which is the first step toward owning up to her responsibility for her problem drinking. This approach holds clients accountable for their drinking and nondrinking behaviors.

Case Example: Only on Weekdays

Gail, in her mid-thirties, came to therapy complaining of depression. She was not sure exactly what was causing it and was able to describe it only in a global manner, saying that her life was not going well generally and that it was not turning out as she wished. She went on to describe her complaints. She was not happy with her professional position, which seemed to be at a dead end. She had worked hard to get through college, believing that it guaranteed fulfillment and happiness, but it was not turning out that way. Her relationships with men were "so-so." Life was not what she thought it would be, and she was generally disappointed and apathetic about her future.

When the therapist asked Gail how she coped, she answered, "Not very well." In fact, she said she had become somewhat concerned about drinking too much. Having come from a family with a long history of problem drinking, Gail was concerned about her tendency to drink when she got depressed and wondered if she had a drinking problem.

Further discussion about her depression and drinking revealed that Gail's complaints were generally vague and unclear. The connection between her depression and her drinking was also unclear to her. Because she was not quite ready to say that her drinking was the problem, the therapist asked if there were times when Gail managed not to drink, even when her life was "just so-so." Gail replied that there were many occasions when she did not drink even though her life was not going well. For example, she had attended a social gathering the previous week where drinking was going on and she "somehow" managed not to drink at all. On the other hand, at an office party some months ago, she had made a fool of herself and had been embarrassed to face her colleagues the next day. Generally, she was vague on what made her drinking and nondrinking days different.

It was necessary for the therapist to help Gail articulate her goals more clearly, to clarify the source of her vague dissatisfaction, and to highlight the patterns of exceptions. The therapist made the following comments at the end of the first session.

"Clearly coming here today was not easy for you but I am glad that you decided to take some steps to do what is good for you, that is, to do something about your depression and drinking. One positive indication is that there are days when you just lose interest in drinking but it is not clear what the relationship between the depression and your drinking is. It is still something of a mystery that you manage to have good days and bad days without clear connection to other parts of your life. It seems to me that we both might benefit a lot from knowing more about your nondrinking days. Therefore, during the coming week it would be helpful to keep track of all the things you do when you run into a drinking situation but manage not to drink. Keep a detailed log of what you do instead of drinking. We will review it next time we meet."

Gail returned with an impressive list of detailed information about her behavior on the days when she did not drink. Therefore, what appeared at first to be a chance occurrence of not drinking became a deliberate exception, which the client could replicate now that she knew more clearly what steps she needed to take. When she kept a log of her days, she also discovered that her depression was related to her drinking days. Thus, she realized she had to implement more deliberate exceptions to her drinking in order to achieve her goal of managing her depression.

Because a detailed discussion of our current view, that interviewing is the path to finding solutions, is laid out in Chapter 5, we will limit our discussion to reminding the reader of the infinite opportunities the interview offers for influencing the client's decisions about her future, her self-perception, and her own influence on those around her. The following are several useful interviewing strategies for the therapist who views the interaction with the client as an intervention.

Most alcohol-abusing clients are very sensitive to others' opinions of them, even though they may initially minimize this. The client's perception of others in his life becomes real for him and the nature of his interactions with those around him are based on these perceptions. What we see influences what we believe, and what we believe influences what we do with those around us. This, in turn, influences how others behave toward us, which in turn affects what we see (Mead, 1934). This loop of interactions is important data, which clients use to construct and modify what is real for them (Watzlawick, 1984). Therefore, it is prudent for the therapist to help the client not only recognize his perception of others' perceptions of himself, but also see this as a potential source of improving his interaction with his significant others.

The following are examples of exception-finding questions that the clinician might ask the client:

Therapist: You mean you did not drink for two years? How did you do that, with all those hassles going on in your life?
Client: It was no big deal. I just decided I was tired of it.
Th: How do you suppose you did that I mean, not drinking?
Cl: It wasn't that hard. I had to test myself whether I could do it or not. And I found out that I can do it.
Th: If I were to ask your wife, what do you suppose she would say it took for you to stop drinking in those days?
Cl: I suppose she would say it wasn't easy. I was a mess. She helped a lot. I just kept busy, stayed away from my drinking buddies,

worked out a lot. Actually, I got pretty healthy. I liked working out and really getting into the healthy life. I ate better and even quit smoking for a while.

Th: What do you suppose your wife would say was different about you in those days?

Cl: She probably would say I was calmer. Maybe even more sure of myself. I spent more time with the kids.

Th: What do you suppose she would say was different about your relationship with her during that time?

Cl: She would say that she was not as angry in those days. Actually, we got along much better.

Th: What do you suppose she would say it will take for you to get back into doing that again?

Cl: Actually nothing. I just have to want to do it. I did it for two years.

Th: What do you suppose your wife would say it will take you to get back into doing it again?

Cl: I will just have to get up early tomorrow morning and go jogging. If I tell my kids that I will be home by a certain hour, I will do it. I hated it when my father disappointed me, and I promised myself when the kids were born I would always keep my promises to them.

Th: Being a good father means a great deal to you, doesn't it?

Cl: Yeah, they need me. They are so small and helpless. I'm their hero right now. I know it won't last, but by golly, I'm going to enjoy it while I can.

Th: So, I know that your children will not be able to put it into words, but if they could, what do you suppose they would say was different about you during those two years when you stopped drinking?

Cl: They probably would say that I came home early, was happy with myself and with them, more confident about myself, and they were not afraid of me.

Th: What do you suppose your children would say about how they were different when you did not drink?

Cl: I suppose they would say that everyone was calmer. They were calmer, too. Come to think of it, they actually did better in school, too. You know, I really should stop drinking altogether. I did it for two years. I can do it again.

Th: So, what do you suppose is the first step you have to take to stop drinking?

Cl: I will just have to stop, pure and simple. I know what I have to do.

Th: So, what would be the first sign to your wife that you stopped drinking again?

Asking questions related to the client's perception of others' perceptions of him generates many useful ideas about solving problems. This client realized, through having to answer these questions, how his wife and children saw him during the period while he was sober and what effect it had on them. It frequently has a startling impact on the client, who has been preoccupied with himself, to discover that there are other people in his life who are affected by his drinking problems. We find that this is a more powerfully effective method than confrontation or lecturing.

Looking to the Future: After the Miracle

In this adaptation of the "crystal ball" technique, based on the work of Milton Erickson (Rossi, 1980) and adapted and amplified by de Shazer (1985), the solutions derived from the "miracle question" are implemented. The results are often striking, as the following exchange shows.

Case Example: Miracle for the Family

Therapist: What will you notice that is different, that will tell you this miracle has occurred?

Client: Gosh, I am not sure. I suppose the first thing I will notice is that my wife is cheerful. Uh, I might say "good morning" to her, we may hug and kiss, and discuss what's coming up for the day. I will get up and get the kids breakfast and give my wife a break so that she can take her time getting up. I will go off to work. The real miracle will happen in the evening, though. I will come home on time, and the kids and I will play while we wait for dinner.

Th: What do you suppose your wife would say she would notice different about you on this miracle day?

Cl: I'm not sure, but she would probably say that I will be coming home sober, in a good mood and on time.

Th: Suppose you came home straight in a good mood. What do you suppose she would do different that she doesn't do now?

Cl: She will probably be shocked at first, but I guess she will be really happy to see me in a good mood. I don't do that very often, you know.

Th: What do you suppose the children would notice different about you on this miracle day?

Cl: First thing the kids would notice, I would guess, is that we are not fighting. We will be calm and my wife and I will get along and we won't be mad at each other.

Th: What do you suppose is the first thing you have to do in order to have a miracle day?

This last question assumes that the client will take steps to implement his "miracle day." In the process of answering this question, the client is engaged in looking at his own future behavior, therefore assuming the posture for taking responsibility for triggering this successful interaction.

By asking, "When was the last time you had a day like that?" the therapist directs the client to review his past successes and exceptions to his drinking, thus slightly altering his self-perception as someone who has never had a successful day. This question presumes that the client *did* have a successful period but somehow has forgotten about his own success. When pursued successfully, this question implies "What do you have to do to bring back that successful period?"

When the therapist asks, "What do you suppose your wife would say it will take for your family to have a miracle day?" the focus is on the family as a whole, and because the client's miracle picture included the family, it is a viable alternative to pursue. Therefore, it is useful to ask when ongoing assessment indicates that the client values his marriage and when his wife is an important source of support.

Whichever of the three possible questions the therapist decides to ask will lead to a different path. Decisions regarding which path the therapist decides to take and which to ignore will depend greatly on her clinical intuition, timing, and other clues on how to adapt to each client.

When the client has a clear, concrete, and detailed image of how he will behave differently after the problem is solved, and the nature of the client-therapist relationship is the customer-type, the therapist may direct the client to "pretend a miracle happened while you were sleeping and that the problem that brought you here is solved." This follows the compliment andthe bridging statement that provides the client with a rationale for the directives. An important addition to this suggestion is to direct the client to "observe what difference it makes in your life and come back and tell us." Notice that this question indicates that future sessions will focus not on the client "pretending" that a miracle happened but *the difference this makes* in his life.

Many observers of our work are surprised at the striking changes this task brings. Clients report more deliberate exceptions to their problematic behavior, which they can trace back and report in detail because of this exercise.

During subsequent sessions, clients are further helped to look at those changes they initiated and the positive results of those changes they observed. The most frequently heard comments from clients are that when they kept the picture of the miracle in their heads they were able to focus more on what they had to do. Clearly this fosters positive self-esteem and increases a sense of confidence in their ability to control their problem drinking.

DO SOMETHING DIFFERENT WHEN NOTHING ELSE WORKS

There are, of course, exceptions to exceptions. All clinicians are familiar with situations where the client is unable or unwilling to create the miracle picture, where there is no useful exception to build on, or there is no pre-session change to repeat. In such situations, both the client and the therapist need to *do something different*. The following are some examples of solution-focused interventions that utilize different strategies that are likely to increase the chances of success. These gentle and humane approaches enhance the possibility of badly needed successes for the client. The result is that the treatment becomes shorter, and, what is more important, the client takes full responsibility for his own treatment.

Keep Track of What You Do When You Overcome the Urge to Drink

With this approach the therapist's emphasis is crucial: By use of inflection, she implies that the client will *do* something positive *when* she overcomes the impulse to drink. The therapist is not postulating "if" but "*when*," as if it is a most natural and expected occurrence that simply requires monitoring. This suggestion reflects the model's underlying assumption that the client can and will know what is good for her.

This intervention is strongly influenced by the field of hypnotherapy. The intention of this suggestion is to focus the client's attention on successful activities he already may be engaged in without being aware of, thus highlighting successful strategies for his life instead of problematic behaviors. This task, when delivered in the deliberate manner, conveys to the client that the therapist is confident that client will be successful in achieving his goal.

Keep Track of What Goes Well in Your Life

First used as a "formula first session task" (de Shazer, 1985), this suggestion was one of many interventions that spearheaded the evolution of the solution-focused model. The following is an example of how we adapted this task into a message.

> "Clearly you have a very complex and difficult problem to solve. We are just beginning to grasp the complexities of all the issues involved in your drinking problem, and we would like to make a suggestion for you. It would help us understand your problems a little bit better. We have gained a fairly good idea of what the problem might be and we need to understand the missing piece here to get a more complete picture. So, we want you to *keep track of what goes well in your life that you would like to see happen again and again between now and next time we see you.* Make a list of what you notice, and keep it to yourself. Do not discuss it with your family."

This task is designed to create a concise "success list." Because most clients tend to become preoccupied with and overwhelmed by their "laundry list" of problems, we prefer that they make an inventory of successes while being focused on the future. Notice the wording of this task. The suggestion is designed to direct the client's focus to successful aspects of her life that will go on between now and the next meeting. By the absence of references to the past (de Shazer, 1985), the therapist implies that the emphasis is on the future.

This task is particularly applicable to situations where the client has multiple problems and is unable to focus on a reasonable, realistic goal. Another clinical situation that lends itself well to this task is when the client feels under siege from multiple sources that demand that she change "or else" face dire consequences. The directive given at the end of this message — not to discuss the task with others — seems to encourage a new and different interaction pattern with those significant others, thus further increasing the chances of success. This is designed to extinguish the nonproductive interaction patterns.

This task can be easily modified to fit the client's pressing presenting problems. For example, if the client presents loss of temper as the urgent complaint and the immediate goal is to solve this problem, the therapist can suggest that the client "Keep track of what goes well in your life when you keep your temper under control." What is implied is that temper control is bound to happen, and the client's task in solving the temper problem is to notice all the things he does when his life is going well. Noticing and keeping track of all those things related to not losing his temper will highlight the client's successes and provide directions for what he needs to "do more of."

Therapist-Team Split

Imagine a clinical situation where a couple is caught in a deadlock about who has to change first, either the husband has to stop drinking or the wife must stop nagging; or a case where parents demand that their teenager prove trustworthy before they will allow him the use of the family car, while the teenager insists that the parents' lack of trust makes him feel like "What's the use? I can't convince them. Why give a damn?" Picture a nondrinking spouse caught in the dilemma posed by the equally attractive and repulsive options of leaving the marriage and risk facing the future alone or remaining married to the problem drinker and facing an equally unpredictable life with him. Clients who are faced with two equally compelling reasons for making an "either/or" choice and as a result are unable to make any choice commonly present in the treatment of problem drinking.

These situations offer clinicians numerous invitations and opportunities to act as referee, mediator, or even judge. They are tempted to become the expert and pronounce final judgment on various dilemmas clients present. And, of course, experience shows that giving in to such demands or temptations is the most countertherapeutic move a therapist can make, let alone the most frustrating because responding in such a manner does not work. Yet, when faced with the struggles and pain the client suffers from, especially when the solution seems so simple and obvious to the therapist, it is not difficult to understand how a therapist might resort to giving advice. We must confess that we are no exception to this clinical pitfall and have made our share of mistakes. We also have studied many such mistakes that therapists have made during the consultation and supervision of "difficult cases." When faced with such clinical situations we find the following method of presenting and reflecting the client's dilemma very helpful. It also affirms for the client that her struggles and frustration are reasonable, given the impossible circumstance she is faced with. By mirroring and heightening the dilemma and ambivalence the client is contending with, the therapist affirms and agrees with the client that the solution is a difficult one to find and to carry out.

The therapist and the team take opposite positions regarding the dilemma. It is important, however, that this polarization between the team and the therapist be presented honestly to the client, as the following example shows.

Case Example: Two-Way Split Between the Therapist and the Team

A young couple came to therapy, each claiming the desire to stop drinking. Yet both enjoyed the taste of alcohol immensely and were having difficulty limiting their drinking, which frequently escalated into violence. Feelings of deprivation and the long-standing competitive strain in their relationship gave them the further edge in their demand that the other person stop drinking first. The couple reported that whenever one spouse stopped drinking first, the other tended to drink more, thus sabotaging the first spouse's effort. Before long, they found themselves resuming their usual pattern of drinking. Their sense of failure and feelings of betrayal compounded their difficulty. Both agreed, however, that an alcohol-free environment would greatly improve their health and marriage and surely would contribute to their decision to start a family. The couple could not decide who should stop first, and yet each was equally concerned about the other's drinking and interpreted the other's ability to start a healthy life-style as an expression of commitment to the relationship. Exploration of exceptions and a miracle picture produced no workable clue for the therapist. After meeting with the team, the therapist reported to the clients in the following manner.

"The team and I are very impressed by your strong desire to continue your efforts in spite of your long struggle to maintain a healthy life-style. Both of you realize that exchanging your "bad habit" for a healthy life-style will be not only good for your individual health but also good for the relationship. Clearly your disagreement about who should stop first is out of your concern and care for each other.

"The team and I, however, disagreed on who will start sobriety first. The team thought that Tom, you will take the leadership position and start your healthy life, not only for your sake but also for Darlene's sake as your way of showing how much you care about her and your future together. On the other hand, I think that Darlene, you will start the sobriety first as a way of showing commitment to Tom. We couldn't agree on which side was right. So we would like you to reflect on this and come back next week and tell us who decided to show the stronger commitment by sticking to the healthy life-style first."

Treating couples whose primary energy seems to be directed toward competing about who is "more right" or "more committed" is a nightmare for most clinicians. When the therapist tries to mediate who is right and who is wrong, the situation becomes hopeless for both therapist and clients. The immediate temptation is to see the partners separately under the false assumption that what needs to be resolved is their individual personality problems rather than the interaction within the relationship. When the therapist treats such couples separately, she invariably is forced to take sides in the couple's competitive fights, thus escalating an already difficult situation. If such a mistake is made, one partner's "winning" the competitive struggle is only a hollow victory. It is more profitable to treat the couple conjointly and highlight their dilemma by using the two-way or three-way split team intervention. It directs their competitive energy in the positive direction of who will do more to build the relationship, in such a way that they both can "win." This therapist-team split is successfully used when the therapist-client relationship falls into the complainant category because the message offers the possibility of changing the client's view of the problem.

In some instances the two-way split team is not enough. Because the purpose of most therapeutic suggestions is to increase the options or paths to solution and enhance the client's competency and freedom of choice, the three-way split frequently offers more opportunities and possibilities. What follows is a good example of how this intervention can be a useful tool.

Case Example: The Three-Way Split

Carey brought her husband, Kevin, to therapy seeking the therapist's assistance to convince him that he should attend A.A. She was convinced that his attending A.A. meetings was the only way he would cut down his drinking because that was exactly how she had succeeded with her goal. Carey reported that A.A. saved her life, and in addition, she learned about herself. Therefore, as far as she was concerned, until Kevin attended A.A. meetings, she would not rest from trying to convince him of this. Kevin, on the other hand, was equally adamant against going to A.A. meetings. His argument was that they each had a right to choose the method of attaining sobriety, and Carey should respect his choice of not going to A.A. Indeed, he agreed with Carey that going to A.A. had been good for her and the marriage; however, no matter what anyone said, he was not going to A.A. He further related that he had been "roped into" going to a couple of A.A. meetings, which convinced him that it was not for him. He was willing to come to therapy and obtain help for his drinking problem, with the goal of learning to moderate his drinking. Kevin echoed a familiar refrain of the more "she nagged" or insisted on his abstinence, the more rebellious and obstinate he became and the more he drank. He prided himself on being independent-minded and on being "a man who won't be pushed around by no woman." Other clinical indications were that his drinking was problematic only where it concerned his wife and when they fought. The wife agreed that indeed his drinking was not problematic in other aspects of his life. Each spent a considerable amount of energy not only disputing the other's point but also defending their respective positions.

This couple's standoff called for a three-way split. As is true in most clinical cases that present rigidly defined options, the most helpful suggestions the therapist can offer initially is to nullify (or to deconstruct) both options as not being viable and to suggest alternatives to them. The team and the therapist were sympathetic to Carey and Kevin's dilemma and saw the disagreement as each partner's intensely strong desire to remain independent within the marriage, knowing that this contributes to the integrity of a marriage. However, when it came to the question of what to do, half the team thought the husband was right, while the other half thought that the wife was right. The therapist was confused and had no idea of what to suggest. However, both the team and the therapist agreed there must be a third alternative. That is, if they could get along better before trying to resolve the A.A. or no-A.A. issue, perhaps it was possible that they might come up with solutions that they both could accept. In subsequent sessions the couple reported that they started to go out together, had more fun at home, and that the husband was able to limit his drinking to two drinks once a week, which the wife reported was a vast improvement.

What to Do When There Is No Team

In spite of the fun, excitement, and creativity generated when working with colleagues using the team approach, we are restrained by economic reality, as are most clinicians, and find that the team approach is not realistically viable on an ongoing basis. Therefore, there are many occasions when the staff at the Brief Family Therapy Center conduct therapy without the benefit of a team. Frequent questions are raised about how to utilize the split-team technique in a clinical setting without using a team. Adaptation of this technique is rather simple. When the therapist determines that a two-way split is called for, the following approach can be used:

> "Part of me is inclined to agree with your friends and family that you certainly deserve someone better than Pat and, therefore, you should leave. On the other hand, the other part of me can also see that it is not so simple or easy to do because you still love him deeply and can see the good qualities in him whenever he allows you to see that side of him. I am not surprised that you have been having a hard time deciding which way to go, whether to follow what your head tells you or to listen to your heart. Some decisions are made by the head and some by the heart, even though it makes no sense and may even look foolish to others. So, let's continue to think about this and get together again."

The clients usually respond with a sigh of relief. This intervention has the effect of reducing the client's internal pressure to make a decision — when this pressure is reduced, it is easier to make that decision.

The three-way split for the therapist who works without a team may go as follows:

> "I am afraid that I may not be very helpful to you today but let me tell you what my thoughts are. My many years of experience of working with your kind of problem drinking indicates that I should recommend that you abstain from drinking altogether. That would be the logical treatment. As you know, most people in the field would say that abstinence is the only solution for your situation. On the other hand, the more I get to know you and learn about the incredible odds against which you have come this far, the more I am not sure if total abstinence is the only solution, especially since you have had many good ideas on cutting down on your drinking and have had some remarkable successes from them, I can see why you think you can do it. So, I am real confused about what might be the best solution for you at this time. There should be a solution to this difficult choice for you but your unique situation is making it less clear about which way to go. There may even be a third option that we have not considered yet! So, I want you to think about it some more and I certainly will give it more thought and let's get together next time to discuss further what is best for you."

Surprisingly, clients usually return to report a decrease in their drinking and describe what they have done to accomplish this. Once these exceptions are described, the next therapeutic task is to think in terms of "do more of what works." The client who received the previous message came to the following session with many exceptions to his usual drinking pattern. Even though he objected initially when his physician insisted that he must abstain completely, the client eventually decided on his own that abstinence was much easier to accomplish than he imagined.

Coin Toss

Another suggestion to help clients to become "unstuck," which is applicable when there is a customer-type relationship, is the "coin toss." Following the structure of the intervention messages we have outlined throughout this chapter, the therapist might first compliment the client for anything he is doing that is good for him; second, provide a rationale for a homework task; and third, offer a suggestion in a positive tone. At times, such a task can be described as an experiment to find out more information or as a step toward achieving his goal.

The message might go as follows:

> "In order to help us get a better sense of what might be the next step, I would like to suggest the following for you to do between now and the next time we meet. The first thing you do every morning when you get up, toss a coin. If you get a head, that's the day you pretend that a miracle happened and do everything you would do on a miracle day as you described. If you get a tail, do everything you would do on your normal day. We would like you to pay close attention to what difference it makes with your drinking."

Most clients who are willing to take steps are intrigued by this suggestion. They are curious about what will turn up at the toss of the coin, and they look forward to finding out what their "luck" will be. Some clients even enjoy what appears to be a childlike game and get into the spirit of the suggestion, because they realize that their previous serious attempts at solutions did not work. Frequently, they report on their deliberate exceptions with great enthusiasm.

The versatility of this task allows the therapist to adapt it to the client's unique circumstances and issues. For example, a depressed young woman came to therapy and bitterly complained about her husband, who refused to attend the session because their problem was caused by her "stupidity" and "craziness." In fact, she reported that informing her husband of her decision to seek therapy would confirm his theory that she was "crazy"; she chose to keep it a secret from the husband in order to avoid further trouble with him. During the session she agreed that it was unlikely that he would ever change and that she might have to be the person to initiate change, however unfair that was.

She also agreed that perhaps she was more invested in making the marriage work than he was.

Following the compliment and acknowledgment that the problem would probably take hard work to solve, the therapist suggested that the client toss a coin every evening before going to bed. If the coin revealed heads, she was to pretend that a miracle had happened for both of them. If it came up tails, she was to pretend it was a normal day, while continuing to keep this task a secret from her husband. The client returned two weeks later, happy but scratching her head in bewilderment. She related how attentive her husband had been to her: He brought her flowers for the first time in a couple of years. They had enjoyed the best two weeks they had had in a long time; she had found herself calmer and feeling more positive toward her husband, and was "biting my tongue more about his drinking." To her surprise, she noticed that he drank much less. In addition to being happy about this positive change, the client was curious about how her husband changed as he still did not know that she had come to therapy. She speculated that perhaps he was responding to the changes in herself, more than he really changed on his own. Because she was confident that this change would endure in the future (this was determined through the use of scaling questions), the case terminated successfully in three sessions.

When clients are trying to decide whether they are ready to stop drinking and do what it takes to follow through, they can often be helped to make a decisive step through the use of this task. For example, on the day the client gets a "head" in the coin toss, he is to pretend that he decided to abstain from drinking that day, regardless of the circumstances. On the day he gets a "tail," he is to go about his usual routine, that is, to drink in his usual manner. The client is to return with the observation of what difference this made in his drinking. When asked what they learned about themselves between the sessions, most clients are usually amazed at how they decided not to drink on a day that they normally would have. Since the purpose of all tasks is to trigger deliberate exceptions to their drinking patterns, the insight gained from this task can be used to map out what the client needs to do to repeat this new nondrinking pattern.

Case Example: To Leave or Not to Leave

Lisa, who might easily be described as "codependent," vacillated for a couple of years between leaving her boyfriend, Tim, when he got drunk and wanting to marry him and start a family when he was sober. Her intense frustration with not knowing what to do was difficult to cope with. Lisa found herself on some days calling Tim at his favorite tavern and begging him to come home, and on other days becoming "bitchy" when he failed to show up at family gatherings as promised. She was always fearful of what shape he would be in when he came home. On the other hand, when he did not drink, sometimes for a week or two at a time, which he would do in order to prove to her that he was not "an alcoholic," they talked of saving money to buy a house, getting married, and having children. Tim was described as "when he is good, he is really good; when he is bad, he is really bad."

Lisa's goal in coming to therapy was to make a decision about the relationship. She was "not getting any younger" and she felt her "biological clock was ticking." An earlier therapist's suggestion of Al-Anon for Lisa was turned down since she saw her difficulty as a decision and it did not make any sense to her that she should try to learn to "detach" from Tim's drinking. From her point of view, the only way to "make it work" was for Tim to acknowledge his problem, receive treatment, and stop drinking altogether. However, Lisa reported that Tim refused to enter treatment, claiming that he could control his drinking any time he wanted to. He reportedly accused Lisa of trying to control his life and that she needed a "shrink" to solve her problems. The consistent advice from family and friends was that Lisa would be better off leaving Tim, which she did not want either, since she had invested two years of her life with Tim.

With the goal of helping Lisa come to a decision, the therapist suggested a coin toss. On the days she tossed a "head" Lisa was to pretend that she had made up her mind to stay in the relationship no matter what Tim did all day long and behave accordingly. On the days she got a "tail," she was to pretend that she had made up her mind to leave, independent of what Tim did.

This suggestion was intended to help Lisa find ways to detach herself from Tim's drinking by actually experiencing what she had only imagined. It was clear to us that her behavior was quite dependent on Tim; that is, whenever Tim returned home drunk, Lisa was predictably "bitchy" and angry. By contrast, Lisa felt out of control, that her life was unpredictable. In order to establish some measure of predictability, Lisa "nagged" and attempted to "control" Tim's drinking. Obviously, Tim controlled whether he and Lisa would have a pleasant or unpleasant evening.

Lisa returned to the next session two weeks later reporting her shocking discovery that the issue was more her problem than Tim's. She became acutely aware of her own reactions and insecurities, and how much she needed to know what Tim was up to and how intensely afraid she was of being alone. It became clear to her that perhaps she needed Tim more than he needed her and that it was a poor foundation for a solid relationship.

Prediction Task

The therapist utilizes the prediction task by suggesting to the client: "Between now and the next time we meet I suggest the following: Each night before going to bed, you make a prediction about what kind of drinking you will do the next day and keep a record of it. Next day you go about your day as usual but at the end of the day compare your activities with your previous day's prediction to see whether or not your prediction came true. Also, jot down on a piece of paper what difference you noticed about your life. Then make another prediction for the following day. We would like you to repeat this for a week and come back with the results. You may want to write it all down so that I will have accurate information."

Again, the therapist can suggest a variation of this task, tailoring it to the client's life circumstances. We find this suggestion very useful when the client's perception is that she has no control over her drinking and that she believes it occurs at random. Such clients believe that their drinking depends on others' behavior or chance happening that is outside of their control. We feel strongly that accepting such notions in therapy encourages clients to be irresponsible, and allows them to excuse their behavior with a "devil made me do it" attitude. We believe this is not only irresponsible but also unethical. Holding the client accountable for successes is a much more respectful way to approach this difficult issue.

WHAT TO DO WHEN NOTHING SEEMS TO WORK

Like all clinicians, we have had our share of cases that keep us humble and remind us of our limitations. We have also encountered and heard about numerous cases which baffled and frustrated many competent and skilled therapists around the world when we teach and consult. We have been curious about this phenomenon and think of these cases as offering us learning opportunities. When we study these cases, whether they are our own or other clinicians', there seem to be common points that remind us to rethink such cases.

Well-Formed Goals

One of the most frequent reminders that we encounter is related to the clarity of goals for therapy. Both the therapist and the client together need to review the goals for therapy frequently. We prefer to do this every session. With cases that are presented as being "stuck," the review of each step invariably leads us to examine the goals for therapy.

Whenever we are asked to consult or supervise on cases with our colleagues, we start the session with the scaling questions. For example, when we ask the client, "Suppose 10 stands for where you want your life to be at when you are finished with therapy, and 1 stands for where your life was when you first started with therapy, where would you say you are at today?" Most clients who are described by their therapists as "stuck" or "frustrating" cases answer, "I suppose I will say I'm at 7 or 8." Some clients even indicate they are at 9 or 10. When we ask "How long would you say you have been at 7 or 8?" the usual answer is, "Oh, I would say six or seven months." It appears that the client may be quite content with what she has achieved in therapy, while the therapist believes that there is more hard work to be done.

Another point is that the therapist needs to really *listen* to what the client says and not assume anything. Such a simple and basic premise of clinically sound therapy is often difficult to practice because clinicians are often several steps *ahead* of the client and decide what is in the best interest of the client. We are often reminded of how ambitious therapists tend to be for their clients, perhaps far more so than we have a right to be. Following closely what the client wants and not imposing therapist wishes, will insure successful completion of treatment.

$$7$$

Strategies for Maintaining and Enhancing Progress

"Nothing succeeds like success."

— Alexander Dumas the Elder, *Ange Piton* (1854)

"To promise *not* to do a thing is the surest way in the world to make a body want to go and do that very thing."

— Mark Twain, *The Adventures of Tom Sawyer* (1876)

AN IMPORTANT CONCERN FOR ALL PROFESSIONALS working with problem drinkers is the maintenance of treatment gains both during and after treatment. Setbacks during treatments are well-known to experienced alcohol treatment professionals and numerous studies have shown that an alarmingly high percentage (90%) of problem drinking clients experience some degree of failure to maintain gains following treatment (Gottheil et al., 1982; Helzer, Robins, Taylor et al., 1985; Polich, Armor, & Braiker, 1981). Given these results, a colleague of ours is fond of saying that "anyone can *temporarily* stop a problem drinker from drinking problematically . . . the real trick is helping them stop the problem drinking *permanently*."

One approach to this problem has been to establish follow-up and after-care programs. Such programs have traditionally been associated with inpatient and residential treatment facilities where formal treatment and after-care are separated because of the nature of the treatment setting. In the traditional approach, such follow-up programs usually consist of some combination of outpatient treatment contact and attendance at self-help peer support group meetings. No one can doubt the significant and positive impact that self-help peer support groups have had on the problem drinking population. For years, such programs were all that was available to problem drinkers, because they were largely ignored by the mental health profession. The main problem with this approach is that those problem drinkers most in need of the meetings are the least likely to follow through after the completion of the formal treatment process. For this reason, it can be argued that helping clients maintain their treatment goals should be an integral part of treatment.

Marlatt and Gordon (1980) first described another approach known as "relapse prevention" that has been widely copied and implemented in various treatment settings. Recognizing the high percentage of clients failing to maintain changes following treatment, these researchers and clinicians developed an approach specifically designed to reduce the probability and severity of such failure.

Whereas the traditional model held that the chronic, relapsing nature of alcohol problems was simply a reflection of the cunning, baffling, and powerful nature of alcoholism and evidence of the need for total commitment to the treatment model, Marlatt and Gordon (1985) postulated that relapse was a natural phenomenon due largely to defective, deficient, or absent client coping strategies for "high-risk" drinking situations. Based on this view, Marlatt and Gordon (1980, 1985) and others (Annis, 1982, 1986; Annis & Davis, 1989; Annis, Graham, & Davis, 1987; Marlatt & George, 1984) developed a system for classifying high-risk drinking situations and a treatment method aimed at helping clients develop coping strategies for dealing with them. The method is highly individualized and consists of such techniques as helping clients identify existing coping strategies that can be employed in high-risk situations, graduated exposure to high-risk drinking situations, and planning and rehearsing responses to high-risk situations.

As the name implies, relapse prevention focuses the bulk of therapeutic energy on *opportunities* for failure. Clients learn when, where, with whom, and under what situations they are most likely to be tempted to resume drinking. Clinical and personal time is then spent strategizing, rehearsing, and practicing what the problem drinker will do to *avoid* these potentials for failure. However, as we indicated in Chapter 3, attempting to prevent something from happening (e.g., a relapse) does not constitute a "well-formed" therapeutic goal. Such goals create a paradox in which the client is forced to keep thinking about a forbidden activity. Furthermore, attempting to stop someone from doing something is a much more difficult task than building on and enhancing activities that they are already doing (e.g, past and present successes). And finally, when the stated goal for treatment is avoiding or stopping something, it becomes difficult for both the therapist and client to determine when treatment is finished, as a "relapse" — by definition — may always occur again.

Regardless of how individualized the assessment, it is impossible to consider every contingency that might possibly trigger a problem drinking episode. For this reason, rather than focusing treatment efforts solely on "high-risk" situations, the solution-focused approach focuses on "high-success" situations. The majority of clinical time is spent enhancing and promoting those situations wherein the client is likely to be the most successful. When setbacks do occur they are viewed as normal and even as a sign of success (Sanchez-Craig et al., 1984). After all, one cannot experience a setback if there has been no success! Rather than spending a great deal of time analyzing why the setback occurred, treatment is immediately directed at orienting the client toward his previous level of functioning.

Our primary interest in helping clients maintain treatment gains rather than preventing them from relapsing led us to call the fifth step of the model "goal maintenance."

GOAL MAINTENANCE:
SECOND SESSION AND BEYOND

Frequently clients begin the second session by reporting one of three possible summaries of their lives since the first session: (1) "things are a little better," (2) "nothing is different," or (3) "it is worse than before." Our experience is that by and large the majority of our clients report that "it is a little bit better" when they return for a second session. Notice that when the presenting complaints are phrased in vague terms, such as "it" or "my life as a whole," it is easier to find something positive to build on. Regardless of the position the client takes, the therapeutic task is to help the client continue to take an active posture toward her own problem drinking and her life. As we pointed out earlier in Chapter 5, the client-therapist interaction loop allows the therapist considerable latitude on the content of what is to be talked about. The therapist's choice of what to pay attention to, as well as what to ignore, plays a significant role in deciding the focus of the session, as well as its outcome. Therefore, it is not unusual for a therapist at our Center to start the second session with the question, "What is better?" Clients are often disoriented momentarily because they still expect the therapist to focus on problems. The following is a typical client response:

Therapist: So, what's better?
Client: Huh?
Th: So, what have you noticed that's been better in your life since our
    last session?

Cl: Oh, um . . . let me see . . . I guess I will have to say I am not drinking as much, no, in fact, I haven't had anything to drink since I saw you.

Th: Wow, that's great. How are you doing that?

Cl: I am just concentrating on the work, thinking about things you wanted me to think about. . . . You know, it hasn't been bad at all.

Th: If your mother were here and if I were to ask her, what do you suppose she would say she noticed different about you during the past week?

One of our many visiting colleagues once observed our work and decided to call our therapy model "Wow Therapy." He explained that the therapist was in awe of the client's successes and kept repeating "wow" and "fantastic" every time the client mentioned a successful negotiation of a difficult situation with her problem drinking husband. We tend to agree with our colleague. Frankly, we are often amazed at the spirit and courage clients have shown in rising to the challenges of life, and we are often surprised by how well they are doing, given their incredibly difficult and painful histories.

When clients have had an opportunity to discuss their successes during the beginning of the session, subsequent discussions of other, more serious problems seem to be less overwhelming and discouraging.

Orienting the client toward discussing successful activities means staying close to the goal that the therapist and the client developed during the initial meeting. Each subsequent session should reflect on and monitor the progress the client is making, and should also involve "cheerleading" (Kral & Kowalski, 1989). The therapist should admire the client's resourcefulness, wisdom, and commonsense in having made small but significant progress toward his goals. The following dialogue is an example of how this might be achieved:

Therapist: So, what do you need to keep doing so that you can stay on track?

Client: I will just have to stay relaxed, keep working hard, and be good to myself. And to remember how I want to keep my family together and stay out of jail.

Th: So, how confident are you that you can continue to do what you have been doing last week?

Cl: Oh, yeah, your numbers. I've been thinking about that. I would say I'm at 5. I feel like I'm at about midpoint to where I want my life to go.

Th: Wow, that's big progress in one week, from 3 to 5. How did you do that?

Cl: I know. I've never been this confident about myself before. I think it is making a big difference that I am in therapy this time because I want to be, not because I am forced to be.

Th: If I were to ask your boyfriend where he thinks you are at, on the same scale, where do you suppose he will say he thinks you are?

Eliciting and amplifying the small but significant changes the client has made can be achieved by asking detailed questions regarding the events the client describes. This detailed questioning can easily last up to 20 minutes during the follow-up interview. Asking about the chain of events, sequences, and who else noticed the changes also amplifies the positive changes: When did this happen? What did you do? Who else noticed? What did they do when they saw you doing that? What tells you that they noticed the changes in you? What was going on at that place that helped you do things that way? What else did you do?

How Did You Do This?

We believe this simple question is the most empowering question a therapist can ask a client. Depending on the therapist's use of inflection, facial expression, and word choice, it can convey to the client a number of subtle shades of empowerment. Variations of this question are numerous and are all designed to suggest to the client that the positive changes she is making are initiated by her and not by the events, other people, or the situation. How did you know it would work? What gave you the idea to do it that way? You must have had some hunch that it would work, what told you that it would work? How did you think of doing it that way? Is that new for you? How did that help you? How did that help your family? What did your husband do when he noticed you doing it that way? How did that help him?

What Else?

This simple question is a valuable tool to help the client discover his own resources and strengths he may not have recognized. Our clinical experience is that unless this question is asked, clients tend to dismiss their successes as insignificant, trivial, or ordinary things that anybody can perform. Of course, life is made up of small, routine, ordinary things and doing these things well constitutes success. Professionals, as well as clients, need to be reminded that doing these ordinary, small steps contributes to a sense of competency and success. Questions like "You did what?" or "Say that again?" stated in combination with an incredulous or admiring look is a powerful way to reinforce the client's sense of competency.

Many professionals who are learning to adapt the solution-focused treatment into their practice are reminded to ask this question frequently. This question implies that the client has accomplished hidden successes and that the therapist is interested in every detail. When the client dismisses his success as unimportant or insignificant, the therapist can reshape the client's view by pointing out that not everybody can do what he did. These two frequently asked questions amplify not only the changes the client is making but also helps him take ownership of his successes.

Case Example: Warm Beer on the Fourth of July

32-year-old Andre is a hardworking young man who started drinking during his time in the military service. He reports the combination of loneliness, the drinking atmosphere of his barracks, and the availability of inexpensive alcohol from the PX got him started on his drinking habit. There had been several attempts at inpatient treatment and self-help groups, but after each he quickly resumed his usual heavy drinking.

He stopped drinking hard liquor on his own for five days prior to the first meeting with us to "get a head start" on treatment. There were many rich and detailed descriptions of successful strategies that he was able to identify, and because of his high motivation, the treatment had moved along successfully in the first three sessions. His goal for treatment was to overcome his "craving for the hard stuff." He made a clear distinction between craving for alcohol and thinking about drinking. He explained that he could manage thinking about drinking quite well but he failed at "craving." He had made good use of many successful strategies to distract himself from "thinking" about drinking and his confidence on the scale was rather high. However, he was not confident about handling the "craving." We saw the subsequent sessions as goal maintenance for handling his craving. The following conversation occurred during the fourth session.

Client: I have to tell you about what happened on the Fourth of July.
Therapist: Okay. Tell me what happened.
Cl: I was at a picnic at Dorothy's mother's. You know, it happens every year. I told you all her family are real heavy drinkers. I would

have usually joined them in their drinking as soon as I walked in there. But I got there late because I was fixing the bathroom. Anyway, when I got there in the afternoon they had run out of cold beer already because everybody had been drinking a lot. So, I grabbed a warm beer and sat on the lawn. You know, I didn't even finish that beer. I haven't done any drinking since then, even beer.

Th: Wow, that's amazing. Is that different for you to do? I mean not finishing that first beer at picnics and family get-togethers?

Cl: Yeah, man, I out-drank everybody and Dorothy would be all mad at me and then we would fight.

Th: So, how did you do that? What was different on the Fourth of July?

Cl: I don't know. (Smiling) It's the first time, man.

Th: I'm amazed. What do you suppose you did different this time?

Cl: I was relaxed. I finished the bathroom that Dorothy's been bugging me about for months. That felt real good. Maybe that was it. I felt good inside. You know, Dorothy even saw me grabbing a beer and she didn't say nothing. That helped, too.

Since the client attributes Dorothy's not nagging about his drinking as helpful, in addition to his feeling good inside about himself, the therapist decided to pick up on the changes in his relationship with Dorothy. The therapist was curious about how his newly discovered successful behaviors affected his relationship with Dorothy.

Th: What do you suppose Dorothy would say she noticed different about you on the Fourth of July?

Cl: She has been really good lately. She hasn't said a word about my drinking. I think she knows I'm serious about therapy this time. She knows I'm doing this for myself this time.

Th: So, what do you suppose Dorothy would say you do to let her know that you are doing this for yourself?

Cl: She would say I talk to her more. We talk a lot more lately and she likes that. I can tell she trusts me more and she don't check up on me like she used to.

Th: What do you suppose Dorothy would say you do that helps her to trust you more?

Cl: She don't have to drag things out of me anymore. I tell her more. I think that's the main thing.

Th: So, how confident are you that you can continue to do what you have been doing? Let's say, 10 means you are ready to put your money down that you can continue and 1 means you are very shaky about your ability to maintain what you have been doing, where would you put yourself on this scale?

Cl: I would say I'm at 6 or 7. I don't want to be too confident.

Th: I think you are being realistic. So, what do you have to do so that you can say you are at 7 or 8?

The therapist decided to focus on Andre's successes: what led him to decide to finally finish the bathroom, how he did not join the crowd, how he managed to stay relaxed, how he started to talk to Dorothy more, and so on. When approached in this way, we find that clients are more willing to discuss near mishaps and setbacks than they would otherwise be.

Since we discussed in detail in Chapter 3 how the therapist can help the client formulate treatment goals in such a way that she can make her own assessment of progress as she moves through the treatment process, the reader is reminded to review the guidelines for setting goals. We contend that helping clients to evaluate their own successes or failures in treatment rather than rely on the therapist's pronouncement of success or failure is a much more respectful way to cooperate with the client. Furthermore, it encourages responsibility for treatment and instills the concept of self-care. In each subsequent session both the therapist and the client evaluate the progress the client is making until both are confident that they can terminate. Our experience shows that, as the client increases the areas in which he is confident, the frequency of the sessions decreases. Therefore, it is common for the client and therapist to meet every other week, once every three weeks for a number of times, and then gradually decrease to a once a month check-up session.

"What Do You Have to Do to Stay On Track?"

Variations on this question are asked frequently throughout the remainder of the therapeutic contact, and particularly, immediately following reports of success. Once the goal of achieving sobriety is accomplished, even for a short period of time, the next focus for the therapist is to remind the client of her goal. Meanwhile, the task for the client is to "stay on track" or "do more of what works" until she is confident of having incorporated her new life-style into her everyday routines.

Detailed discussions during this period may center around the early clues that will alert the client or his family that the client is keeping a steady focus on the treatment goals. This step encourages the client to be responsible for various options of follow-up and self-care strategies that will help him to be focused on maintaining his initial goal.

Case Example: Long Track Record

Roger, a 54-year-old self-described "alcoholic" entered treatment in a 28-day inpatient treatment program following a two-month long "relapse." Roger had a lifelong history of problems with alcohol and multiple attempts at treatment had "failed." Hospitalization was considered "absolutely necessary because of the chronic nature of his alcohol problem and the failure of previous treatments."

As part of an insurance review, we met with the patient on the second day of his hospital stay. During this meeting with the patient, an inquiry was made regarding previous *successful* attempts to manage his problems with alcohol. At first, Roger appeared somewhat puzzled by the question. Apparently, no one had ever asked him this question before. In a surprised voice, Roger reported lengthy periods of time (e.g., months, years) during which he had successfully managed his problems with alcohol. In fact, just prior to the most recent episode, Roger had not had a problem with alcohol for 12 years. When queried in detail, he was able to specify what he had done differently during those times that contributed to his success. Roger indicated, for example, that he attended at least a few A.A. meetings per week, and prior to social gatherings he informed new friends about his own abstinence from alcohol. Finally, he noted that he had established a practice of "indulging" himself daily by preparing at least one "good" meal each day.

After finding out about what was different during his successful periods, Roger was simply asked what it would take to continue to do more of what had previously worked. Roger expressed relatively high confidence that he could at least begin doing some of those things. After receiving medical clearance, Roger was released from the hospital on the morning of the third day. Following his release, two further sessions were held with Roger. Over the course of these sessions, the successful periods were utilized as the basis for a successful treatment outcome. Some time following the last meeting, Roger sent a duplicate copy of his one-year sobriety token to the Center (Miller, in press).

What to Do When It Is Not Better

In the majority of cases, when the client reports that the situation is "not better," it means that the changes are not dramatic and fast enough to meet her expectations or that she is looking for big changes. Having lived with the problem drinking for many years, both the client and family members are impatient to bring about drastic changes quickly. Therefore, such feelings of frustration must be acknowledged, while at the same time the client's attention must be drawn to "small" changes she is making *and* these small changes must be highlighted as significant. Keep in mind that if the client has had an upsetting day just prior to the session, it may color his perception of the rest of the week, which may have gone reasonably well.

The helpful response in this case is to accept his perception as valid and review his week in detail. In this process clients often discover there were some instances, although small, where they behaved differently, thus creating some change. One of the basic premises we discussed in Chapter 1 is our belief that change is inevitable and constant and, therefore, what is therapeutic is to look for these changes as context markers (O'Hanlon & Wilk, 1987). When clients are helped to identify changes, they are more likely to behave in accordance with their perceptions. The following is a good example of how the second session proceeds even when the client reports that things are worse. Steve de Shazer is the therapist working with a woman who sought help with her confusion about whether or not to leave a physically abusive husband who was also a problem drinker.

Case Example: Developing Her Own Mind

Therapist: So, what's better since last time you were here?
Client: Nothing. You mean what's worse.
Th: Are you sure about that? (Smiling)
Cl: I'm positive about that. (Smiling)
Th: How can that be?
Cl: It just is. Nothing is positive at all (shaking her head).
Th: Let's see, you were here last Monday. How did Monday go?
Cl: It was okay. Just okay.
Th: How did you get that to happen?
Cl: Well, I talked more than I usually do. I talked to my friend, I guess more than I usually do.
Th: Okay. What about Tuesday?
Cl: (Looking up) Actually things did go well, Tuesday, Wednesday, and Thursday, up until Saturday. Everything was okay. I didn't have to listen to nobody, I did what I wanted to do. Then Friday was, ugh, not good.

Th: How about Saturday? Did it go back up again on Saturday?

Cl: No, sort of so-so. Sunday was sort of okay, too. Then I've been crying all day today, on and off.

Th: So, Monday, Tuesday, Wednesday, and Thursday went okay. So, how did you do that? You were saying, you were talking more, what else?

The temptation to discuss the details of what made the client "cry all day" is strong at this point, and succumbing to such temptation to focus on the problem talk would invariably end up with the therapist agreeing with the client that "it is worse." Returning to such "problem talk" should be delayed as long as possible, because when juxtaposed with the successes, the problem seems less overwhelming and more manageable to the client.

Cl: It was better because nobody bugged me about, I mean, all the stuff about what I should do or what I'm not doing well, and all that stuff. I was pretty much in control of my own self.

Th: How did you do that?

Cl: How did I do that? I have to get angry to do that. I'm like, forget it, I'm going to do what I want to do. I have to be pushed to that limit, though.

Th: But that was okay for you, though.

Cl: Uh, hum. I'm learning to know my own mind.

Th: So, you knew your own mind and stuck to it all day.

Cl: Right.

Th: And were you feeling less confused, too?

Cl: Actually, I wasn't confused at all, really, not since I've been here.

Th: How come? (Surprised and pleased)

Cl: It was good to talk to someone last week. It really helped.

The client still gives the credit for feeling more in control of herself to "talking to someone," that is, to something external. If not challenged, the client will continue to believe that the change (in this case, her "knowing her own mind" and being more clear about what she wants to do with her life), the client will continue to look to someone or something other than herself as a solution to her difficulty.

Th: Yeah, but you also had a whole week to get confused again, how come you weren't confused?

Cl: I don't know. You don't understand me? (Laugh)

Th: Not yet, but don't worry. So, Monday, Tuesday, Wednesday, Thursday, you weren't confused at all, you knew your own mind and you stuck to it. I am still wondering how you did that?

Cl: Weird, I guess. (Laughing)

Th: If you knew how you did that, you can do that all the time.

Cl: (Laugh) I know. People just upset me. I don't know how I did that. I just did.

Th: Um. Can you do that again? Would you know how to do it again, like last Monday, Tuesday, Wednesday, and Thursday?

Cl: I just did it. I am not sure how I did it.

Th: Um. Okay, let's call those days 10 and the worst days you had recently, say before you first came to see me are 1, where would you put Friday?

Cl: Friday was at 1.

Th: Where would put Saturday?

Cl: I would say about 5.

Th: And what about today?

Cl: I don't know where today is. I would say about 5.

Th: So, how did you get to go up from 1 to 5 on Saturday?

New Problems

Frequently clients will bring up new problems that they have kept on hold while dealing with the problem drinking. Now that the urgent issue of problem drinking is under control, the "real problem" or a long-standing major issue can be brought up. Agreeing to discuss each new issue that surfaces prolongs treatment and obscures the focus of the session. It is important that the client be helped to keep the miracle picture in clear focus throughout the treatment and avoid becoming distracted by many issues.

Case Example: Old vs. New-Fashioned Marriage

During the fourth session with Carole and Bob the "real issue" of their marriage surfaced, now that Bob had stopped drinking for two months. Carole had been angry at Bob for not "standing up and protecting me" against his former drinking buddies who "razz and harrass" Carole for being bitchy, bossy, and so on. Carole demanded that Bob stand up for her and tell his friends off, in order to let them know that he will not allow his wife to be mistreated by anyone. Bob's retort was that Carole was overly sensitive and reactive about what those "drunks" were saying and she should just ignore them. Carole reported that she always wanted to have an old-fashioned marriage in which she could feel protected by her man, while Bob felt that it was a silly notion in this day and age and that Carole should learn to stand up for herself. This led to a heated argument between the couple, each insisting that the other person change.

After considerable negotiation with the couple, we agreed that it was indeed an important issue for them to figure out what kind of marriage they wanted now that Bob was no longer drinking. Their sticking to these different ideas was their way of making sure that they each contributed to building the best marriage possible. However, we felt that they both needed more time to reflect on this important issue and longer time to negotiate how they would balance between the new and old ways to be married. We further offered our idea that because they were in a period of rapid changes in many areas, such as their new alcohol-free life-styles, perhaps they needed to go slower. In the meantime, they needed to concentrate on what *was* going well.

What to Do When a Client Reports a Setback

The Big Book, the foundation for A.A. and the Twelve Steps does not advocate a lifetime of abstinence as a goal. Instead, it advises that the true meaning of "one day at a time" is keeping an eye on each day's goal of maintaining and enhancing successful strategies of sobriety. Therefore, once the goal is attained, the therapist and the client need to review and recount the successful strategies and ways to repeat them.

Experienced clinicians know that a periodic setback from sobriety is a fact of life and is to be expected, not to be dreaded and feared. When a client is faced with a setback from her goal of maintaining sobriety, she loses perspective and immediately becomes overwhelmed with feelings of shame, disappointment, failure, guilt, and self-reproach. The sense of failure to live up to the promise to herself and to those around her often results in her feeling discouraged and hopeless about herself, and can lead to continued drinking. The therapist's role is crucial at this point in helping the client to see the successes she has had prior to the setback and in pointing out that the important task is to return to the original goals as soon as possible. The following questions are designed to achieve these purposes.

- How did you manage to stop drinking when you did? How did you know enough to stop at five beers?
- How did you manage to stop at five drinks and not go on to six? What did you do that was different?

- What clues did you have that told you to stop when you did? What told you it was time to stop? What are you doing to become more sensitive to these clues?
- What do you suppose your spouse would say you did different in order to stop at five drinks?
- What did your spouse do that was helpful to you during this period?

The assumptions behind these questions are that it is more useful for the client to focus on what she did to stop drinking rather than on what caused her to start drinking again. Our view is that each time the client has to justify her behavior she is forced to invent more and more plausible answers to questions. The more the client repeats these answers, the more convinced she becomes that these excuses are real. Again, it is important to gather information on the client's perception of others' views of her because of her long-standing tendency to please and adapt to others' demands on her. In the process of answering these questions the client will begin to change her sense of control over her life, thus regaining confidence that she can continue in her path of recovery.

- How is this setback different than the last one?
- What did you do differently this time (stopped drinking earlier, changed location, any sequence of events, and so on, in detail)?
- How did you figure out to do it that way so that you stopped drinking sooner?
- Who did what, how, when, and where to make things different this time?
- What do you suppose your spouse (parent) would say is different about you this time?
- What do you need to do to maintain this change?
- What difference would it make when you do this?

As described in Chapter 1, one of the basic assumptions we hold is adapted from the Buddhist premise that change is constant and that stability is an illusion. Since life is in a constant state of change, the client's drinking habit is also in constant flux. Therefore, the basic assumption we make is that each setback a client experiences is never the same. Something has changed and *will* change in his drinking pattern.

Discovering these differences allows the client to recognize that she is moving forward, that each time she has a setback she stops drinking sooner. Each setback is different because the client's subjective experience is different, even though external factors in her life may not have changed.

- What have you learned about yourself from this episode?
- Tell me about what this setback taught you about your drinking problem (stress coping strategies, self-esteem issues, personal care, etc.)?
- What will you do differently as a result?
- What do you suppose your mother would say you will do differently as a result of this new learning about yourself?
- What do you suppose she will do differently, then?
- What do you suppose your co-workers (spouse) will notice that is different about you when you implement this new way?
- What difference would it make in your relationship with your co-worker?
- How confident would your husband say he is that you will change the way you cope with your mother's drinking binges?
- What do you suppose your parents will do differently as a result of this?

A detailed discussion on what the client has learned about herself and her problem drinking from each setback is a gentle reminder to the client that change is constant and that she is learning and improving as she learns about how to live a new life.

Notice the manner in which the questions are asked. Asking, "Will you change your life-style as a result of this setback?" conveys vastly different expectations than "What will you do differently . . . ?" It conveys a gentle, yet persistent reminder to the client that she needs to adapt, grow, and change in small steps.

- What do you need to do more of?
- How will you make sure that you will do that?
- How do you suppose that will affect your life?
- What do you suppose your spouse would say you need to do more of?
- What difference would it make in your relationship with your spouse when you do more of that?
- What do you suppose he will do differently in response?
- What difference would it make in your relationship with him? With your children? With your employer?

Again the emphasis is placed on the client doing more of what is working for him, not on what the client needs to stop doing. Enhancing what works certainly is an easier way to succeed than trying to *stop* some undesirable behavior. Once a client knows what to do, then it is easier to figure out what path to take to move in the direction he wants to go.

- Could this be your unconscious way of reminding yourself that you still have a drinking problem?
- What other ways do you have to remind yourself that you still have a drinking problem?
- What do you suppose your best friend (spouse, parent, etc.) would suggest you do to remind yourself?

It is not infrequent for the client with a long history of problem drinking to test his level of confidence in maintaining his sobriety by attempting to drink again. The result is that a client discovers one more time that he has no control over his drinking. Some clients become quite discouraged and depressed at this rediscovery about the reality of their problem drinking. Instead of adding insult to the injury, the therapist can think of ways to turn it around and attribute positive motivation to this behavior.

The following case example illustrated the uses of these questions in detail.

Case Example: Just in the Nick of Time

Dotty, a 47-year-old Native American had been living with a man for a year. Her 14-year-old son had been placed in a foster home because of Dotty's neglect and abuse due to her problem drinking. Her desire was to have her son live with her again. Dotty was brought to the session by the nurse who visits her regularly as a part of the follow-up in her medical care. Apparently, during a recent visit with the nurse Dotty broke down and started crying about her uncontrollable urge to drink again, even though she had been abstinent for a year since her last bout with cirrhosis from which she "nearly died." The nurse became very concerned about Dotty and requested an emergency appointment. We learned that many of her women friends, often after maintaining sobriety for a year, had died from cirrhosis after they resumed drinking. Because she had been sober for about a year, she feared repeating her friends' fate when her cravings for alcohol returned.

Therapist: What would you like to see changed as a result of your coming here today?

Client: I don't even know why I am here myself. It's my drinking. Sometimes I wish I could drink but I can't.

Th: You don't drink?

Cl: I can't drink. Doctor's orders. I wish I could.

Th: So, how long have you not been drinking?

Cl: For over a year now. But I wish I could drink.

Th: Wow, for over a year?! How do you do it?

Cl: I can't. I will end up in the hospital and die. That's why I don't drink. I don't want to die. Do you?

Th: Of course not. So, how do you do it?

Cl: I guess I get so disgusted at myself.

Th: What about yourself?

Cl: I crave greasy food. I can't eat greasy food. I will land in the hospital again. I used to be on six or seven medications. Now I'm only on one for my blood pressure and I take vitamins.

Th: So, you are healthier than you used to be?

Cl: Yeah, I am doing much better now than I used to.

Th: Wow, how are you doing that?

Cl: What?

Th: Staying healthy. How are you staying healthy?

Cl: I have to. I just do it.

Th: But how are you doing that?

Cl: Well, I'm a grown woman. I'm 44 years old.

Th: So, you are saying you used to have a drinking problem, you used to have a lot of medical problems, used to be in poor health. And now you are doing better, all around doing better. How do you do it?

Cl: I just take better care of myself, that's all. I feel better about myself now, up here, too (pointing to her head).

Th: So, what did you do to be at this point today? You've come a long way.

Cl: Yeah, I think I have.

Th: How did you do that?

Cl: My boyfriend helps. He don't drink either. He used to be a big drinker but he don't drink now.

Th: So, is it good for him not to drink?

Cl: Yeah, of course, but he is helping me.

Th: Well, sounds like you are helping him, too.

Cl: I guess so. He used to drink a lot but he says he is not drinking because I'm not drinking. That's what he says.

Th: Well, he could be drinking a lot but he must care about you a lot.

Cl: Well, I don't know. I guess so. (Smiles broadly) He could drink if he wants to.

Th: So, he is deciding not to drink.

Cl: Yeah.

Th: And you are deciding not to drink.

Cl: Yeah, I am deciding not to drink.

There is a gradual shift in Dotty's perception of herself as the conversation continues. Initially, she "can't" do many things and the only reason for success is because of the prohibition imposed on her. However, the therapist refuses to accept her premise, since she has been sober for a year, and through repeated questions challenges her assumptions about her sense of lack of control. As the conversation continues Dotty begins to change her posture. The therapist joins Dotty's view and then challenges her to recognize that she is choosing *not* to drink, her boyfriend is also choosing *not* to drink, even though he has the option to do so. Each time Dotty repeats her decision not to drink, it becomes easier for her to believe that she is making an active choice and is not a passive recipient of her doctor's orders.

The therapist decided to reinforce her wisdom in choosing a man who loves her enough to not drink out of consideration for her and further complimented her on how she has been helpful to him, because it is good for him not to drink. This sense of reciprocity in her relationship with her boyfriend gently reminds Dotty that she is not just receiving help but is also contributing to his well-being. The therapist further elaborates on what Dotty chooses to do when she gets the urge to drink again. In the process, Dotty discovers that she has many good strategies, such as getting in the car and going for a ride, going to the shopping mall and walking around, going to a movie, visiting nondrinking friends, going for a walk, etc.

Client: Sometimes I get so bored, get so disgusted with myself that I just want to drink. Like today.

Therapist: So when you get so disgusted, what stops you from going like this (with drinking gesture)? How do you stop yourself from drinking?

Cl: I can't start the first. If I take one, I will drink more and more.

Th: So, what stops you from taking the first?

Cl: You know what stops me? I will tell you. It's my son. I want him to come back to live with me.

Th: You must love him very much.

Cl: Naturally. I'm the mother. Wouldn't you?

Th: Yeah, I would, too. So, you are doing many things that help you not to drink. Anything else you do that helps you not to drink?

Cl: I love to read. Mostly Westerns and love stories.

Again, a good portion of the session was spent in repeatedly listing what Dotty does to distract herself from the craving for alcohol.

Th: I am amazed that you have accepted the fact that you cannot drink. How do you accept the fact that you can't drink? How do you do that?

Cl: It's my doctor.

Th: He helps you do that?

Cl: Yeah, he does.

Th: What does he do right?

Cl: He just tells me alcohol is no good for you.

Th: And you listen to him?

Cl: Sure, I listen to him (with a smile).

Th: There are lots of people who don't listen to their doctors, as you know.

Cl: I know. But I listen to mine. Some of my friends didn't and now they are dead.

Th: You are smart.

Cl: Oh, yeah, I know.

Th: I mean you have common sense to listen to the doctor.

Cl: Oh, sure, I do listen to the doctor and do what he tells me.

Each time Dotty reverts back to giving the credit for her success to someone other than herself, the therapist repeatedly reminds her that it is she that makes choices to do many good things for herself. Later in the session the therapist shifts to what Dotty needs to do to continue her self-care and maintain her sobriety.

Th: So, what do you need to do to stay sober?

Cl: It helps to keep thinking about my friends who died.

Th: What about thinking about those friends helps you?

Cl: They drank a lot, all the time and now they are dead. I don't want to die.

Th: So, that helps. Remembering them. What else?

Cl: I go for walks, I go for a ride, we don't go to taverns anymore, I read a lot. I think about my son a lot. I want him home. He wants to come home, too.

Th: That's great. How confident are you that you can continue to do these things? Let's say on a scale of 1 to 10, 10 means you are very confident, 1 means you are not. Where are you on that scale today?

Cl: I would say I'm at 7 or 8.

Th: That's very high. In looking back, where do you suppose you would put yourself during this past year of sobriety?

Cl: I would say I was at 6 or 7. Sometimes low. Like the last couple of days, I was at 3 or 4.

From this conversation it is clear that the client's confidence has increased significantly during the session. By pointing out all the things the client did to stay sober during the past year it becomes clear to her that she has many successful strategies to stay sober. When her year of sobriety was juxtaposed against her last several weeks of returned urges, Dotty was able to see herself more clearly as a successful abstainer. After a brief consultation with the team, the following summary was given to Dotty to end the session.

Th: First of all, I want to tell you how impressed I am about your burning desire to do what is good for you. You take care of your body, you stopped drinking, you eat well. Not only that, but you also have the common sense to listen to good advice, you listen to your doctor, to your nurse, and you know when you need help. You know what you can do for yourself and when you need help.

Cl: Umm . . . yeah, I do.

Th: I think it's amazing that you are doing as well as you are doing, considering what you've been through.

Cl: Yeah, I lost my three children because of my drinking.

Th: Well, you lost a lot. Your close friends died because of their drinking, you lost your children. But you are a tough lady. You survived all that. And you are here today because you want to make sure that you don't go back to drinking and lose everything, like your friends did.

Cl: Yeah, I have. I want to hold on to what I have, though.
Th: Of course, you do. You are doing many good things to help yourself so that you can hang onto what you have. You go for a ride, go for a walk, eat right, think about your dead friends, and so on.
Cl: My sister-in-law died, too, because of her drinking. I don't want to be like that. My husband died of drinking, too, he is my son's father.
Th: You are doing many good things to make sure that it doesn't happen to you. You were surrounded by people who had problems with drinking.
Cl: Yeah, I sure did. That's what scares me the most.
Th: Of course, you are scared. But you also have enough sense to have found a man like Bill who is good to you, he doesn't drink. And you did the right thing by making sure that you don't drink. You also did the right thing by coming here today. This is your way of taking care of yourself because you know you are the only person who can take care of yourself. So, stay on track by continuing to do everything you have been doing during the past year. And call me whenever you feel like you need some help to stay on the right track.
Cl: Yeah, I will. I am glad I came.

8

Mr. Meeks's Miracle Day

"If you are going forward, it's hard to go backward."

— Former BFTC Client

"We can't do nothing that we couldn't do before."

— Former BFTC Client

MR. MEEKS WAS A 53-YEAR-OLD AFRICAN-AMERICAN male referred to the Brief Family Therapy Center by the state's Department of Social Services. At the time of the referral, the agency had served as a "payee" for Mr. Meeks for a period of nearly three years. As such, a social worker had been assigned by the agency to receive and manage the disbursement of state and federal assistance and disability payments made to Mr. Meeks. This arrangement had been made because, in the past, Mr. Meeks had used the money to purchase alcohol. In fact, money intended to last for an entire month had frequently been spent on alcohol within a period of a few days. Mr. Meeks's problems with alcohol were long-standing, spanning a period of 25 years. During this period, he had been in treatment in a number of both inpatient and residential settings. On each occasion, he either dropped out of treatment prematurely or quickly returned to his previous problematic use of alcohol after being discharged. Mr. Meeks had been homeless off and on over the course of his drinking career. At the time of his referral to BFTC, he had just returned to the home of his common-law wife and 8-year-old daughter.

SESSION ONE*

Prior to attending his first session at BFTC, Mr. Meeks scheduled and then failed to keep two appointments. Mr. Meeks finally managed to

---

*Therapist for this session was Stephan Langer, Ph.D.

attend his first session on his third scheduled appointment. Mr. Meeks
was introduced to the therapist and led to the consultation room. After
being seated, the session began with the therapist asking:

Therapist: So, how can I help?

Client: Well, to start out, well . . . how do I start now? (Pause) First,
   well, I have an alcohol problem, for one thing.

Th: Uh, huh.

Cl: Mine is an off and on type of situation and during that time, um
   . . . my wife and I, and the child, uh, sometimes have a little
   . . . well you know, conflicts on it. And uh, it just seems that,
   uh . . . I can't see what it is that I'm doing, and they won't seem
   to really come and tell me except to say that, "Hey you drink too
   much!" And, well, I keep saying, "What is it I do?"

Th: Hmm.

Cl: Because my memory isn't very good whenever I drink. My memory
   is completely bad. So I say to them, "Why don't you sit and tell
   me what it is I do." I say I know I talk a lot, but what do I be saying.

Th: Um hmm.

Cl: But then I can't seem to get, get it. What is it that I really do? Well
   . . . on occasions now we have had some violent altercations from
   it—some physical altercations from it. And, uh . . . I don't really
   know if . . . (pause). Well I know the drinking is a big problem in
   it. But what I can't seem to see, because *normally* I'm never violent at all, I just can never see myself as being a violent person that
   will . . .

Th: (interrupting) So how, how are you normally?

Cl: Normally I'm *this* way!

Th: *This* way?

Cl: (smiling and pointing to himself) This is me. This is really me!

Th: Tell me a little more about how *this* way is, because I don't know
   you very well yet.

Cl: Well, I like people. I'm very polite *this* way, and I seem to, uh . . .
   I'm always in a sympathetic mood with people that, uh, that's not
   as fortunate. And when I see a person that's not as fortunate as I
   am, I'll always try to help them.

Even in the initial comments made by Mr. Meeks, interesting information emerges that would likely be considered therapeutically significant. For example, certain of his statements might be construed as

preliminary evidence of the operation of various psychological defenses characteristic of all "alcoholics" (e.g., denial, projection, minimalization). Based on this view, the therapist might at some point choose to confront the client in order to break through these defenses. Other statements made by Mr. Meeks clearly indicate that he has experienced memory loss and blackouts as a result of his problematic drinking. Again, such data might be used in other treatment models to convince the patient that he is, in fact, an "alcoholic." However, in this case, the therapist chooses to focus on and amplify a comment that the client has made about being "normal." By requesting that Mr. Meeks describe how he is normally, the therapist elicits the first exception to the problem drinking. The impact of this question on Mr. Meeks is obvious in his nonverbal responses and in his subsequent dialogue.

Before returning to the dialogue, mention should be made regarding one additional statement made by Mr. Meeks. In his second statement, Mr. Meeks describes his "alcohol problem" as an "off and on type of situation." While it may not be immediately obvious, such a description implies that there are times when drinking is *not* a problem for this client. The solution-focused therapist would certainly want to take note of this so that a more detailed inquiry could be made at a later point in the session.

Therapist: How did you figure out to do that?

Client: (seriously) I just like, uh. . . . Well it was . . . say it started from high school. I was always the one that, um . . . I didn't drink, and I didn't smoke like my other buddies did, so . . .

Th: (incredulous) Really?! Uh, huh.

Cl: I more or less was the guy when you went to parties who would see that my buddies got home if they drank too much or if the girls drank too much. It was always me that would see that they would . . .

Th: (interrupting) Really?! Well, I'll be darned!

Cl: (continuing but smiling widely) . . . they would get, get where they were going. And that's the kinda role model I like to be.

Th: Uh, huh.

Cl: But . . . I never could see myself as being violent, but I can't remember if I started it, or if my . . .

Th: (interrupting) How long did this go on, that you were, that you were this role model and that's the way you would like to be?

Cl: Oh, all through high school, through the service, through my, uh, I had six months of active duty.

Th: Umm. Uh, huh.

Cl: And, uh, it carried through and, uh . . .

Th: Good.

Cl: (continuing) . . . even when I, after I started drinking and then
    quit, that was the kind of role model I was when I first met my
    wife.

The positive focus of the interview continues in this segment of the
transcript. The therapist begins with a question that seeks to attribute
the positive traits, attributes, and qualities described in an earlier comment by the client to conscious effort and goal-directed behavior. By
responding to the inquiry, the client tacitly accepts the implication that
is embedded in the question. When the conversation begins to drift
to a problem-focus (". . . but I can't remember if I started it, or if
my . . . "), as is typical of conversations in the initial stages of solution-
focused therapy, the therapist gently redirects the discussion to a solution-focus with another question. The dialogue becomes a sort of spontaneous solution-focused psychosocial history in which the client's
strengths, abilities, successes, resources, etc., in dealing with his problem are of primary interest and importance. In the final statement
included in this segment, the client makes mention of a previous success
in dealing with the drinking problem when he notes having quit at one
time. At some point, the solution-focused therapist would want to find
out in more detail what the client had done to be successful.

The conversation next began to focus on Mr. Meeks's family. Specifically, he told the therapist about his relationship with his wife and
child. The therapist learned that Mr. Meeks and his wife had recently
reconciled following a separation of two years. In particular, Mr. Meeks
noted having a desire to reestablish a closer relationship with his wife
and to become more involved with his daughter and her upbringing.
When queried, he indicated that he had made some recent progress in
these areas:

Client: Well it's a little shaky type of thing, because uh, due to our
    separation the child and I are not very close.

Therapist: Is that changing now?

Cl: Uh, very, very slowly . . . maybe a little too slow for me.

Th: Uh huh.

Cl: Very, very, very slow. Because uh . . .

Th: How can you tell that that is changing and that you're getting
    closer?

Cl: Well, uh, I bring her out and we play. I kinda, you know, throw the ball and do little things I never did with the kid.

Th: Yeah?

Cl: Never at all. In fact, through the entire eight years I never actually played with my kid.

Th: Except now?

Cl: Except now! You know, and now that I think about it . . . well, I have been doing a lot more things with her.

Th: Hmm!

Cl: And that's, I'd say that's been going on . . . maybe about a few weeks now.

This interchange continued in much the same fashion as the preceding interactions with an emphasis on the positive aspects of his family life and encouragement for the changes that he had already made. After considerable amplification, the therapist sought to clarify how, or if, this new topic area was related to the problem drinking by asking:

Th: I'm not sure how this, or if this, is related to your drinking, and to the violence you talked about earlier?

Cl: Well, I drank long before . . . (pause) that I can't understand. I really don't know . . . (pondering) if my family life does get bad when I drink . . . and I don't know, do I start these altercations or does she start them or is it because I've been drinking and can't remember . . . that I can't really get into because when I've been drinking I have very low memory of what I do.

Th: Uh huh.

Cl: Sometimes, I'll wake up after drinking a bottle and I can't remember where my shoes are or where I put my pants, where I put my wallet, or did I even come in with a wallet or not and then I'm told about the things I've done. I'm told about the little, uh, things I've said . . . I'm told about the little violent acts. A couple of times, I woke up in jail wondering what the hell am I doing there.

Th: Uh huh.

Cl: And then when I go the next day to see the district attorney they said, "well you act violently with your wife. You threatened to kill her or to beat her up or do different things." And I always feel that, hell, I don't remember that.

Th: Is all that something you'd like to change?

Cl: I've got to change!

Th: (curiously) Oh, you do?

Cl: Yes, because . . . by those years and years of drinking it's done something here (points to head).
Th: Uh huh.
Cl: It's done something bad . . .
Th: So what do you think you need to change about that?
Cl: Well, one, I need to work very hard not to drink.
Th: Oh!
Cl: Yes. Period. Very hard! Because that is . . . I know that is one of the major . . . that's the major problem.
Th: Oh, really?
Cl: Oh, yeah, I know that's a major problem because the fact that I can't remember when I drink . . . I cannot remember.

In the initial statements of this segment, Mr. Meeks states that at this point he is not entirely clear how, or if, his drinking and family problems are related. Note that the solution-focused therapist spends no time trying to convince him otherwise. Believing the connection to be obscured by "denial," some treatment professionals might have been tempted to intervene in order to "help" Mr. Meeks recognize the relationship between the two. However, at this point, such a move on the part of the therapist would have been uncooperative. Instead, in the solution-focused approach, the therapist accepts the client's present view and focuses the dialogue on what the client wants to change or be different. This focus serves to orient the client away from dialogue about the problem and toward a discussion of the goals he wishes to accomplish. Mr. Meeks indicates that the drinking is the "major problem" and that he wants to *do* something in order to bring about a change. Together, these clues suggest that a customer-type relationship is beginning to take form.

Soon after identifying alcohol as his major problem, Mr. Meeks indicated that he had not had a drink in over a week. Naturally, the therapist inquired about this exception including asking how Mr. Meeks had been able to be successful.

Therapist: Okay, so how long do you go . . . how long do you stay sober?
Client: Normally, I won't drink more than, maybe, if I do, maybe one day, maybe two at the most . . .
Th: How long has it been . . . ?
Cl: About a week now.
Th: (matter of fact) A week? How did you manage to do that?

Cl: I'm, like I said, I'm starting to, uh, I'm starting to pay attention, more or less, because, uh, there are things I can't remember. And also, now I notice when I'm like I am this week, the family is a little bit closer . . . and . . . .

Th: (as the client continues) Oh, really? I'll be darned!

Cl: I've been offered drinks and I didn't want them.

Th: Oh, you didn't even want it? Wow!

Cl: In fact, guys offered me drinks . . .

Th: You mean that someone offered you drinks today?

Cl: Yeah, in fact, as far as just a few blocks away from your office when I was on the bus.

Th: I'll be darned!

Cl: And I said, "No!" I really just don't want it. And I knew the person real well because we were old drinking buddies in the past.

Th: So, this was a friend? This just wasn't anybody that offered a drink to you then?

Cl: No, this was an old friend. Oh, gosh, I drank a lot with him and . . .

Th: How were you able to turn him down like that?

Cl: You know, with me being the alcoholic that I am, it was tough!

Th: I bet! How did you do that?

Cl: (shakes head from left to right)

The client literally does not "know" how he was able to turn down the offer by his drinking buddy and indicates this nonverbally by shaking his head. Chances are high that he has never thought about nor been asked to think about the absence of his problematic drinking. As is evident in the segment that follows, the client is much more able to talk about and predict the *presence* of his problematic drinking behavior. Such discussion has likely been the primary focus of most of Mr. Meeks's experiences in treatment. In this instance, however, the therapist quickly redirects the discussion toward a solution focus.

Th: I mean, wow, this sounds like a real challenge!

Cl: It was! And, it was a hell of a thing. I think that maybe if we would have ridden a little bit farther, I might have gave in.

Th: So, how did you manage to not give in until you, you know, until it was time to get off the bus?

Cl: I just felt that I had more important things to do.

Th: Oh, okay.

Cl: Yeah, I think this session was a heckuva lot more important than taking a drink. Because if I would have took just one drink then I would have gotten off the bus and gotten on another bus and headed back.'

Th: I'll be darned! So, you knew then that what you were already doing and what you already have going for you is more important.

Cl: Yeah, and also, my family is a hell of a lot more important than a drink and it seems that more than anything else my drinks are destroying the family.

Th: So, how do you know that you will be able to continue to turn down drinks? Because, as you already know, they are going to continue to be offered to you.

Cl: Well, I have quit . . . I did quit once . . .

Th: Right, yeah, you did say that.

Cl: For 12 years . . . it seemed like, uh . . .

Th: Oh, for 12 years? How did you manage to stay sober for 12 years? That's a long time!

As will be recalled from earlier discussion, the identification of exceptions to the problem drinking is, in itself, not enough. A vital part of using these exceptions to generate solutions is to help the client identify how the exceptions came about. In this regard, the therapist begins to inquire about how Mr. Meeks managed to not give in to his old drinking buddy on the bus. Initially, Mr. Meeks indicates that he does not know. The therapist has to persist for some time in an effort to help Mr. Meeks describe how the exception came about. Soon, however, Mr. Meeks connects this success to having managed to remain alcohol-free for 12 years. Following the above exchange, the therapist continued with this line of questioning and obtained a very detailed description about how the client had been able to be successful for 12 years. Mr. Meeks identified many factors that he believed had contributed to his long success (e.g., staying away from drinking buddies, being involved with family, being employed, helping others, etc.).

Up to this point, Mr. Meeks has indicated that drinking is his major problem. In addition, several exceptions to the problem drinking have been identified and discussed. However, while Mr. Meeks has identified drinking as a major problem, and while the exceptions elicited thus far are impressive and appear to be a strong foundation upon which to build a solution, one cannot, at this time, assume that the client's goal is to stop the problem drinking. Indeed, the client's goal may be something else entirely, and the drinking simply a means of obtaining that desired objective. Whatever the case, at this point, the therapist must be exceedingly careful to not come to a premature conclusion regarding the client's treatment goal(s), and must avoid the temptation to impose his own goals regarding the use/nonuse of alcohol on the client. For those who have seen the destructive effects of problem drinking on both individuals and families, this can be quite a challenge. However, in our experience, success in working *with* the problem drinker is contingent upon determining and working toward the client's goal.

To be sure, this is not to say that the interaction up to this point has been useless. Certainly, the positive focus of the interview has helped to create a cooperative working relationship between the client and the therapist. However, at this time, the therapist needs to determine with more certainty what the client wants to have happen as a result of coming into treatment. A question that has proven useful in determining what the client wants to accomplish in treatment — in other words, the client's goal — is the "miracle" question (see Chapter 5).

Therapist: Well, let me ask you another question that is related to this. Let's pretend for a moment that you went to bed tonight, you went to sleep, and a miracle happened . . .

Client: (laughs and begins smiling)

Th: (continues) and tomorrow morning you wake up and the problem that brought you here for therapy is resolved. How would you tell that this miracle had happened?

Cl: (smiling widely) Well, I think it would feel like today! Today is a "miracle day."

Th: Oh, okay.

Cl: It would really feel just like today. You know I'd be happy, happy with my wife and daughter, and I'd be doing things . . . more family things.

Th: Like what?

Cl: Like I said earlier, taking the kid out and playing a little pitch and catch . . . and being nice to my wife.

Th: Okay, what else?

In this brief segment, it appears that Mr. Meeks's goals for treatment revolve around his family life. Consistent with his earlier statements, Mr. Meeks indicates that changes for the better have already taken place. In the interaction that followed the therapist obtained a rich, behaviorally explicit description of how Mr. Meeks's family life was already different on this "miracle day" and how he wanted it to continue to be different. Then, most importantly, the therapist asked Mr.

Meeks to continue to describe the miracle in more and more explicit detail by asking the crucial question "what else?" For example, "What else will you notice that is different on your miracle day?" After identifying many things that were and would continue to be different (e.g., he would smile more, be more social, stay out of his "shell"), the therapist asked Mr. Meeks "what else?" one final time.

Th: Okay, anything else that would be different that would tell you that this miracle has happened?
Cl: Well, I'd be able to stay away from drinks like I have this last week!
Th: Oh, I see. How has that helped?
Cl: Well, my family and I are closer. We, you know, we are getting along better, and . . . now that I think about it . . . we haven't had no fights.
Th: Wow!

Unlike his earlier statements, Mr. Meeks now acknowledges that his drinking does impact his family life. What is perhaps most unique about this is that he has made this observation without any confrontational interventions by the therapist. Following this interchange, both Mr. Meeks and the therapist continued to discuss how changing his problem drinking had already affected and would continue to positively affect his home and family life. It soon became very clear to both the therapist and the treatment team (observing behind the one-way mirror) that Mr. Meeks's goal for treatment was, in fact, continuing to improve his home and family life. In this respect, controlling the problem drinking was merely a means to an end. Therefore, the earlier decision of the therapist to avoid prematurely making drinking the focus of treatment was a wise one.

At this point in the session, it was obvious to both the therapist and the team that a great deal of positive change had already taken place prior to this client coming in for treatment. For example, he had recently reconciled with his wife, he was making attempts to develop a closer relationship with both his wife and daughter, and he had stopped drinking for a period of one week. The discussion then turned to how Mr. Meeks could help all the various changes to continue:

Therapist: In some ways it sounds like the miracle has already started to happen.
Client: I hope so, I hope it don't change because it's hard, it's almost like . . . I have to pull away from something in order to do what I have been doing . . .

Th: How would you know that this miracle was going to continue, that how things are after this miracle was going to continue?

Cl: I'd have to wait, I really wouldn't . . .

Th: I mean, are there signs that you would be able to tell by?

Cl: I know that I just feel good. Now, other than that . . . I just felt like now is the time to get things out . . . I just feel great. So . . .

Th: So, I guess I'd want to make sure that you could hang on to that. And I was wondering, how you could tell that you were hanging on to that good feeling. Let's assume that this miracle has already happened. *How* would you know that this is lasting and that this was really the real thing that was going to stick around?

Cl: I would know it when I got home.

Th: Okay, how would you know?

Cl: I would know it because, normally the first thing I do is say "what's to eat?" and then I go to my easy chair and—"click"—turn on the T.V. and then, uh . . . I get bored, or my wife and I get into it, and then I decide to go out and find my buddies.

Th: So how are things going be different?

Cl: If I could go home and forget T.V. . . . (thinks) . . . not food! (laughs) Just forget the T.V. and walk in and give the wife a hug and a kiss, give the kid a hug and a kiss and ask them how was their day and whatnot. And when she is telling me about a few little problems she might have had on the job . . . (long pause) . . . if I could listen to my wife about her life I would know it was a miracle. (laughs)

As was the case with the exception and the miracle questions, here the therapist again asks questions that help Mr. Meeks specify his picture of the miracle in explicit detail. The description continued for several more minutes. In order to assess and reinforce Mr. Meeks's commitment to maintaining these positive changes, the therapist next employed a series of scaling questions.

Th: On a scale from 1 to 10, where a 10 is that you would do anything to hang onto the way things have been going and where 1 is that it doesn't really matter, what number would you give yourself?

Cl: A 10 because I want things to go, everyday, just like it went today. . . . Now I know there are going to be little conflicts . . . my wife and I aren't going to agree on everything . . . but, the way I am now, I can deal with it. If I took one drink, I would just say, "go to hell, who cares!" So, I've got to not get into the drinks too.

Th: Okay, on the same scale, because I think this is related, where 10 this time is that you have complete confidence that you will be able to continue with what you have already been doing, and 1 being that you have no confidence at all, about what number would you give it?

Cl: I think I would do a 5, because I couldn't be certain . . .

Th: Okay.

Cl: (continuing) . . . I'm half certain . . . but I would have to put that on about a 5. I couldn't give it a 10 and say that this is never going to happen. No way!

Th: Well, good, I'm glad you're being realistic. . . . Um, what would it take to get to 6 from a 5 on confidence?

Cl: Day by day! I'd have to work on that day by day in order to get to a 6. And, I'd say . . .

The client's last response likely reflects an idea that he learned in his previous treatment experiences. We neither agree or disagree with this "one day at a time" philosophy. Rather, the most important consideration is whether the client finds the idea useful in helping him achieve his goals. However, the therapist must help the client define such vague or clichéd responses in specific, concrete, and behaviorally explicit terms. This is accomplished in the next segment by returning to the scaling question.

Th: (interrupting) So, how would you know if you were at a 6 in confidence?

Cl: I would say that if I could be like I am today, even if I wake up feeling lousy. If I can go, just the way it happened today, about . . . five or six months . . . without drinking. Just without drinking, that would be one of the keys to getting it to a 6 . . .

Th: Okay, would there be signs along the way that would let you know that you are getting to a 6 . . . what sort of things?

Cl: Well, continuing to get more of a father-daughter relationship.

Th: And, how could you tell that that was happening?

Cl: Well, uh, if I don't blow up. Like I wouldn't get angry if she spilt water, or, uh . . . if she dropped a, uh . . .

Th: What would you do instead?

Cl: I would talk to her, like I would say, "Why don't we try eating at the table instead of in the living room?"

Th: Oh, I see. Like talking *with* her.

Cl: Yeah, instead of yelling and blowing up when she does these little things, little things I did when I was a kid, . . . but boy I heard it . . .

Th: So, anything else you can think of that will let you know that you are on the way to a 6?

Cl: Yeah, get along better with my wife . . . be a little more friendly with my wife.

Th: How would she be able to tell that you were being more friendly with her?

Cl: Well, tell her she looks nice every once in a while.

Th: Oh, Okay.

Cl: You know I never, uh, compliment her.

Th: (jokingly) Do you suppose she might faint the first time you do that?

Cl: (laughs) No, no, she has mentioned it, she said, "You never say I look nice," and I usually have said, you know, "Jesus Christ! I said that 12 years ago when I married you, why do I gotta keep saying that for?"

Th: (still laughing) If you haven't been telling her for 12 years then I would think that she might almost have a heart attack.

Cl: Well, in the past, I might have had a couple of belts and then I might say, "Whoa, hey, you look pretty cute today kid!" (client gives "thumbs up" signal and winks)

Th: So, how would this be different now?

Cl: I would be doing it sober now. Yeah.

Th: Okay, I see . . . (pause) . . . anything else that will let you know that you were heading up the scale to higher confidence.

Cl: Being a little more helpful around the house.

Th: Okay, like how?

Cl: Well, every once in a while, since I know she's, uh, working three days a week, I would help by vacuuming the rug or helping the kid read or do her homework, doing other little things.

Th: Oh, would that help?

Cl: Yeah, and if I stop doing little things that irritate her . . . like, uh, for example, walking in and I might pull off my T-shirt and there it goes (points to the ground).

Th: Oh, uh huh. So, what would you do instead?

Cl: Uh, well, she's a very clean person. So like when I take things off . . . put my shoes in the closet, put my clothes in the laundry.

Th: I see.

This last segment is a particularly clear example of how "scaling questions" can be used to help the client develop specific, concrete, and behaviorally explicit descriptions — in this instance, the client is able to describe what action he has to take in order to be more confident that he can continue to experience more "miracle" days. In this process, the therapist also uses questions that help the client make the descriptions in "small terms" and as the "presence rather than the absence of something," which, as will be recalled, are two qualities of well-formed goals outlined in Chapter 3. For example, with regard to the former, when the client indicates that in order to be at a 6 in confidence he must continue for a period of five or six months, the therapist quickly modifies the question to elicit interim signs of progress. With regard to the latter, whenever the client states his objective in negative terms (e.g., I wouldn't get angry with her), the therapist elicits a positive description of the desired behavior by asking what he will be doing *instead*.

The process of obtaining a rich, behaviorally explicit description regarding the confidence level of Mr. Meeks continued for a few more minutes. The therapist then asked the client about his willingness to continue with the changes he had already made as well as those he had identified as still needing to be made.

Th: Okay, we've talked about confidence . . . let me ask you another numbers-type question that is also related to this. This time a 10 is that you are very willing to continue with what you have already started doing, you know, the changes that you have already made . . . and that you are even willing to do the other things we have been talking about, and a 1 is that you are not willing at all, about what number would you give it?

Cl: (with certainty) A 10!

Th: A 10? Wow!

Cl: Yeah, because, like I said earlier . . . uh, I got to change. I owe it to my family.

Th: Uh, huh. And so . . .

Cl: (interrupting) And, uh, now that I think about it . . . I'd say that things have been better . . . so, uh, I'd say I'd give it a 10.

Following this brief interchange, the therapist asked if there was anything else the client wanted or needed to say before he took a break to consult with the team. Asking clients this question prior to taking the consultation break has become the standard method of closing the interview at the Brief Family Therapy Center. We have found the question useful because a handful of clients provide some crucial piece of information in response. However, in this instance, and as is most often the case, Mr. Meeks indicated that he had nothing else to add. At this point the therapist left the therapy room to join the team behind the one-way mirror.

The Team Meeting

Upon entering the room behind the mirror, the therapist was met with compliments and support by the team members. Together, the therapist and team then began to "brainstorm" possible compliments to include at the beginning of the intervention message that would be delivered to Mr. Meeks. This is the usual process that occurs behind the one-way mirror at BFTC. The following list was generated:

- good person
  -cares about others
  -history of being helpful to others
- honest
- open
- has his priorities in order
  -came to the session rather than blowing it off
  -knows what is important to him
- has a history of success
  -able to go without drinking for 12 years
- realistic
  -he is not overconfident
- made many changes already
  -spending time with daughter
  -trying to get closer with wife
  -stopped drinking for a week
  -turned down alcohol offered to him
- seems to know what he wants and needs to do
  -continue with changes already made
  -be closer with wife and daughter
  -stay away from booze
- willing
  -to continue with changes already made
  -to make more changes

In order to individualize the message to this particular client, various team members had made a point of listening for any idiosyncratic manners of speech that the client used during the session. The team members reported the following expressions:

- take it day by day
- stopping drinking is "hard work," a "heckuva thing"
- miracle day

Following this brainstorming session, some discussion took place regarding Mr. Meeks's goal for treatment. The questions facing the group were whether there was a goal for treatment and whether that goal met the criteria for a "well-formed goal." Team members were in agreement that Mr. Meeks wanted to improve his family life, especially with regard to being a "good" father. In other words, this was the goal that was most salient to him. Mr. Meeks had given a very rich and detailed description of what he wanted to have happen and had even made several changes in the desired direction. For this reason, the team agreed that the goal was framed in small rather than large terms.

We further agreed that continuing to remain free from problem drinking was one way for Mr. Meeks to achieve his goal. In this regard, he had already stopped his problem drinking for one week and had, at one time, been successful for 12 years. However, the team members and the therapist noted that stopping the problematic drinking did not fit the qualities of a "well-formed goal" as it was described as the absence rather than the presence of something. In addition, it was only one of the ways that Mr. Meeks could reach his goal. For this reason, the team determined that emphasis needed to be given to continuing with the positive changes he had made in his behavior toward his wife and child that came as a result of not using alcohol.

As changes had already taken place, the team members felt that the goals for treatment were obviously realistic and achievable within the context of Mr. Meeks's life. Finally, the team was convinced that Mr. Meeks recognized that achieving a better home and family life involved "hard work" and that he was, in fact, willing to work hard in order to obtain them. Based on all of these factors, the team determined that there was a well-formed goal for treatment.

Thereafter, the compliments and client expressions, generated just moments earlier, were evaluated in light of the goals for treatment. Only those compliments and expressions believed to be related to the goals for treatment were retained:

- honest
- open
- has his priorities in order
  -came to the session rather than blowing it off
  -knows what is important to him
- made many changes already
  -spending time with daughter
  -trying to get closer with wife

   -stopped drinking for a week
   -turned down alcohol offered to him
- seems to know what he wants and needs to do
   -continue with changes already made
   -be closer with wife and daughter
   -stay away from booze
- willing
   -to continue with changes already made
   -to make more changes

- client expressions
   -"little" things
   -stopping drinking is "hard work," a "heckuva thing"
   -miracle day

Following the discussion about goals, the team began to consider what type of homework task was appropriate. The team members and the therapist unanimously agreed that the relationship existing between the client and therapist was a "customer-type." Based on this view, the team determined that it would be appropriate to ask Mr. Meeks to "do" something. As Mr. Meeks had indicated during the session that he had already started making changes and, further, that he was willing to continue making these changes, the team decided to ask him to simply continue doing what he was already doing that was working. This was identified in Chapter 6 as a "do more of it" type of task. The rationale for asking him to do this would be that he obviously knew what he needed because he had already started making the changes.

Next, the discussion was summarized in a brief message comprised of the compliments, the bridging statement or rationale, and the homework task that would be read to Mr. Meeks. The entire team meeting took roughly ten minutes. As the therapist prepared to return to the consultation room, a team member suggested that the therapist start the message by shaking the client's hand in order to emphasize the team's view of his success.

The Intervention Message

The therapist returned to the room and, prior to sitting down, shook Mr. Meeks's hand.

Therapist: The team wanted me to make sure that I shook your hand.
     (sits down) There are a number of things that really impress us.

We are really impressed with all of these things that you are doing that you and I have talked about today. In fact, with all of these things you are doing to make things better, it is kind of hard to know exactly where to start . . .

Client: (client nods head affirmatively, smiles widely) Oh, uh huh.

Th: One thing that I can see, and that the team thinks is really helpful is your honesty. We all really appreciate your honesty and that you decided to come in here and be honest about things . . .

Cl: (strongly nodding head) Yeah!

Th: . . . and to be straight about what is going on. Also, it is impressive that you have a clear sense about what is important to you . . .

Cl: Especially when I'm not drinking!

Th: Yeah, just like you are doing now. And, it is clear to us that it is important to you that you are a good father, a good husband, and are good to yourself . . .

Cl: (client becomes tearful, continues to nod head)

Th: . . . and that you have a clear sense of these things. You are already doing many things that are serving to, Mr. Meeks, make a difference in your life. Like doing things to get closer with your daughter and your wife, helping out around the house, not drinking—even coming to counseling. This makes our job a lot easier!

Cl: (laughs) Yeah.

Th: Today was a kind of a "miracle day" in the way that we have been talking about and, um, we are really impressed that you are having a miracle day today.

Cl: (wipes eyes) It does seem like a miracle.

Th: Yeah, and from what you are telling us, you have been doing a lot of hard work that has led up to this.

Cl: Yeah, it's been hard.

Th: Altogether, this means to us that you know there is more hard work ahead of you and that you know you need to, Mr. Meeks, continue doing what you have been doing in order to have more days like today and repeat having more days like today.

Cl: (client continues to nod)

Th: The suggestion we have for you is that you, Mr. Meeks, continue doing what you are already doing in order to have more days like today and while you do that, Mr. Meeks, notice what more things you do to stay on the right track.

Together, the nodding of his head, the tears in his eyes, and the affirmative verbalizations suggested to the therapist and the team that the intervention message had been accepted by Mr. Meeks. After the message was delivered, the therapist and the client walked together to the reception area where a second appointment was scheduled.

SESSION TWO

Mr. Meeks returned on time for his second appointment one week later. His mood was bright as he presented to the receptionist and his general appearance had improved since his first appointment. As is typical of most second and subsequent sessions, the session began with the therapist asking Mr. Meeks:

Th: What's better?
Cl: Well, to start, my daughter and I, we've spent a lot of time together this week . . . you know, good time!
Th: Oh, really?
Cl: (continuing) . . . and I have been doing the little things around the house, even things that I said I'd never do like cooking dinner and washing the dishes.
Th: Wow!
Cl: Yeah, it just seems that my "miracle day" has continued most of this last week!
Th: Is that right?!

Together, Mr. Meeks and the therapist continued identifying many other positive changes that had taken place during the week. These changes included an overall improvement in the interaction between him and his wife as well as his continuation of no problematic drinking. Mr. Meeks's language and nonverbal behavior indicated how proud he was to be able to convey his accomplishments to the therapist. Each reported change was followed by a statement of encouragement and/or support by the therapist (e.g., "Wow!" "Is that right?" "That's great!" "Good going!"). This process was termed "cheerleading" in Chapter 7 and is vital in helping the client maintain the positive changes that have taken place between sessions (Kral & Kowalski, 1989).

When it appeared that Mr. Meeks had exhausted his list, the therapist began to amplify each of the reported changes by returning to the top of the list and asking for more information. One of the questions used in this process was the relationship-oriented type illustrated in the next excerpt:

Th: Now, let me just see if I've got it all straight for the week because you said a lot of things.

Cl: Okay.

Th: Over the week you spent more time with your daughter?

Cl: (nods affirmatively) Yeah, I spent a lot of time with her taking her out . . .

Th: Now, if your daughter were here, what would she tell me this last week she saw different about you?

Cl: (thinking) Um, I don't know . . . I think she would say that she enjoyed going to see the flowers at the arboretum . . . she might say she enjoyed going to the park and us playing together, and her and I walking, and playing down the street which we never did . . . we are kinda like pals, a little bit now.

Th: I bet that feels good!

Cl: Yeah, I'm really getting to know my kid . . . because I never really did anything like this before . . .

As when the client was listing all the changes that occurred between sessions, the therapist continues to "cheerlead" as each of the individual changes are amplified. Minutes later, a similar interchange took place about changes in Mr. Meeks's behavior around the house and in the relationship with his wife:

Th: You said you have been doing things around the house.

Cl: Yeah, I cooked dinner a couple of nights.

Th: You cooked dinner two nights?

Cl: Uh, two or three nights! Yes, three nights I cooked, let's see . . . (begins to count on fingers)

Th: Wow!

Cl: Wait a minute now, I cooked meatloaf, then we ate chicken with vegetables, and somethings else I did. . . . (Pause) Oh! We had chicken twice!

Th: (incredulous) So you cooked dinner three nights out of seven?!

Cl: (smiling broadly) Yeah!

Th: (laughing) And who did the dishes?

Cl: I did! Yeah. In fact, when the kid and I are alone we are there for breakfast and for lunch . . . and so, I washed the dishes for breakfast, and I washed the dishes for lunch!

Th: You mean you have been washing the dishes every day?!

Cl: Yeah. Well, that is, the days that she worked. . . .

Th: (puzzled) And these are all things that you . . .

Cl: (interrupting) That I wouldn't normally do!

Th: Oh! That you wouldn't do . . . and so you set them as goals?

Cl: Yeah, I kinda set those as goals, to do things around the house. . . .
Oh, I forgot! I vacuumed!

Th: (leans forward) Yeah? Wow!

Cl: Little things, you know, they are not big things, just little things
that I would have never thought of before, and that I wouldn't do
. . . and I was thinking that maybe some of those little things
might help.

Th: If she were here, what would your wife say about all these
changes?

Cl: (smiling broadly) Oh, she's amazed! She is really amazed! She came
in and she didn't have to wash dishes and she looked at the carpet
and it had been vacuumed, and there wasn't a shirt thrown here or
a pair of socks over there. Yeah, in fact, she looked it over and
asked me, "What's the matter?" and she touched my head and
said, "Are you feeling well?" (begins to laugh)

Th: (laughs)

Cl: And, then . . . then I told her that the outfit she had on was a nice
outfit and she . . . (client models wife's expression of a frozen
stare and eyes wide open).

Th: And so if your wife were here she would really say this has been a
different week?

Cl: Yeah, for a change . . . now, we do get into our little "bickers" but I
figured out how not to argue.

Th: How did you figure out to do that?

Cl: Well, in the early morning when we first wake up is when we do
most of our bickering . . . and I found out that if I just give her a
nice smile and listen to her, and then go over and kid around with
her and give her a few kisses then we make up.

Th: And that made a difference?

Cl: Oh, yeah.

Th: Smart!

In this segment, the therapist provides support and encouragement,
in other words "cheerleads," the client's reports of change through verbal, nonverbal, and paralinguistic channels. Verbally, the therapist continues to use various expressions such as "Wow" and "Smart!" A variety

of nonverbal methods such as hand gestures, posture, and facial expressions complement these verbal expressions. And finally, the therapist uses vocal effects, or paralinguistic processes, to support and encourage the changes the client is reporting.

In addition to "cheerleading," another technique that the therapist makes use of in the preceding segment is "positive blame." As will be recalled from Chapter 5, this interviewing strategy involves "blaming" the client for the positive changes that have taken place. In this segment, the client is "blamed" for having figured out how not to argue with his wife and, as is often the case when affixing blame, asked to explain himself!

The "positive blaming" and "cheerleading" continued when Mr. Meeks's next added that there had been no problem drinking during the week.

Cl: I've also been staying away from alcohol.
Th: (incredulous) All week?
Cl: (nodding head) All week! Uh, huh.
Th: (positively) How have you managed to do that?
Cl: (matter of fact) I just wouldn't take it.
Th: You just wouldn't take it . . . but, how did you do that?

At this point in the interchange, two members of the team observing the session from behind the one-way mirror entered the consultation room.

TM1: (entering the room) All week?
TM2: (entering after TM1) You have abstained all week?
Cl: All week!
TM1: (shakes Mr. Meeks's hand)
Cl: In fact, I'm going into the second week now.
TM2: (shakes Mr. Meeks's hand) Good work!

The team members then quickly left the room and returned to their positions behind the mirror. This "cheerleading" from team members behind the mirror is not an uncommon occurrence at the Brief Family Therapy Center. Moreover, it is usually never a result of formal planning or the overall treatment strategy. Rather, when so moved, team members spontaneously provide this type of encouragement and support. The dialogue then resumed with the therapist still attempting to help Mr. Meeks identify what he had done in order to be successful with regard to drinking.

Therapist: It sure is, now, how did you do that?

Client: I think I kinda "program" myself in the morning and I say to myself, "You don't need it, you shouldn't have it, so don't take it!"

Th: Good for you.

Cl: And then, when I go out, I don't! I'll avoid passing places where I might be influenced by it . . .

Th: Ah, I see, where you might be tempted.

Cl: Right, I'll avoid those places . . . and I know for a fact that if the kid is with me I'm not going to touch a drink. So *she* even helps me.

Th: So you know that having your daughter with you helps you to overcome that temptation.

Cl: It sure does! Because when she is with me I have to keep on my toes.

Thus far, the primary focus of the session had been the identification and amplification of the many changes that have taken place in the week between the first and second session. In order to help the client maintain these new behaviors, the therapist has provided support and encouragement for the new behaviors through verbal, nonverbal, and paralinguistic means. However, while necessary, we have found that simply providing support and encouragement is not sufficient to insure the continuation of the new behaviors in the future. In addition, the therapist and client must work together to identify those factors which need to be present for the new behaviors to continue. To this end, the therapist and client begin to explore what needs to happen so that the changes will continue:

Th: So, now how are you going to keep all of these wonderful things up?

Cl: I've just got to keep working.

Th: Working on it like you have been?

Cl: Yeah, I've just got to keep working on it.

Th: And that will help you keep it up?

Cl: Right! Now, I can't guarantee even to myself that it will keep going on and on.

Th: Of course. Now, when you say you have to "work on it" what do you mean you will be doing?

Cl: Well, first, I have to stay away from the drinks!

Th: Uh, huh.

Cl: And then, I have to keep doing the little things with the kid, you know, like I said, and with my wife . . . and around the house.

Th: And how will you do that?

Cl: Well, if I keep my kid in mind and the happiness I'm having right now in mind then maybe I can do it. I've done it once before when I abstained from drinking for 12 years.

Th: You certainly have, and it sounds like you are doing that again.

Cl: Yeah.

In this last segment, the client outlined what he needed to do in order for the changes to continue. In the next excerpt the therapist uses a scaling question to establish how Mr. Meeks views the progress he has made. In doing so, the therapist not only provides a method for evaluating Mr. Meeks's present progress relative to the overall goal for treatment, but also a useful criterion against which progress in future sessions can be measured. In addition, the same scale can be used to determine the next small change to be made in working toward the overall treatment goal.

Th: Let me go back to your sort of overall reason for having come here to BFTC.

Cl: Uh huh.

Th: Say, on a scale from 0 to 10, a 0 is a time when either you made the phone call here, or when things were really hard, like when you were sending your daughter away, and telling your wife to get away from you that you just wanted to watch T.V., and 10 is when you are finished with therapy, you no longer need to come for therapy, where would you say you are on that scale today?

Cl: I'd say about a 5 . . . yeah, about a 5 because I'm not up to a 6 yet.

Th: About halfway then?

Cl: Yeah, I believe I'm about halfway because I'm doing things that I would never necessarily ever do . . .

Th: Good for you!

Cl: (thoughtfully) . . . about halfway. But still I'm not all the way there yet . . . because sometimes my heart isn't *really* in to it and so I say, "Yes" when it really is no. And if I'm not really into it, then eventually it'll be no good.

Th: Okay, can you tell me then what will be the next small step that will tell you that you are getting more of your heart into it . . . that you are moving from a 5 to a 6 on that scale?

In the dialogue that followed, Mr. Meeks described what he needed to do to feel that his "heart" was in the changes that he had been making and, consequently, to move from a 5 to a 6 on the scale. Given that he knew what he needed to do, the only remaining questions were whether he was willing to work toward maintaining the progress he had already made and even make the additional small changes he had identified. In order to assess this, the therapist asked Mr. Meeks another scaling question:

Th: Well, let me ask you a question that I asked the last time you were here . . . another numbers-type question.
Cl: Okay.
Th: On a scale where a 10 is that you are very willing to, Mr. Meeks, continue working as hard as you have been this last week, and where a 1 is that you are not willing at all, about what number would you give it?
Cl: Oh, I am willing to keep working.
Th: So, what number would you give it?
Cl: A 10!
Th: A 10? Great! Okay. I think I would like to take a break now? . . . but before I do, is there anything else you would like to say before I take a few minutes and talk with the team?
Cl: Uh . . . no, I don't think so.

With this last statement, the therapist left the therapy room to join the team behind the one-way mirror.

The Team Meeting

The format of the meeting behind the mirror was essentially the same as in the previous session. Therefore, upon entering the team room, the therapist was met with compliments and support by the team members. After this, the therapist and team began "brainstorming" possible compliments for the intervention message that would be delivered to Mr. Meeks. The following list was generated:

- stayed on track for the week
- made *many* additional changes during the week
  -daughter, wife, and in the home
- continues to get his priorities in order
- good sense of humor
  -doesn't take himself too seriously
- a man of action not just words
  -learns from experience

- wants to do the right thing
- starting to become a real family man
  -making these changes on his own
  -becoming a real "self-made" man
- has ideas how to maintain changes
  -remain alcohol-free
  -keep his daughter, wife in mind
  -keep his current happiness in mind
  -keep working at it
- realistic
  -not overconfident
  -knows there are going to be "ups" and "downs"
  -no grandiose goals
- willing to work
  -to maintain the changes
  -to make additional small changes

After this, a list of the client's idiosyncratic verbal expressions that might be useful in individualizing the intervention message was compiled:

- miracle day
- keep working on it
  -hard work
  -little things
- heart into it
- halfway there

The goal for treatment became the next focus of discussion. The team members agreed that Mr. Meeks's overall goal for treatment remained the improvement of his family life, especially with regard to being a "good" father and husband. The team further agreed that Mr. Meeks had worked on achieving that goal during the week as evidenced by the many positive changes he reported. In response to a scaling question, however, Mr. Meeks made it very clear that additional progress needed to be made. In his words, he was only "halfway" there. When asked, he indicated that the next step in reaching his overall goal for treatment was that he be able to "get his heart into it." Thereafter, Mr. Meeks had described what he needed to do in order to feel this way. For this reason, team members concluded that, in addition to maintaining the changes he had been making, the goal for treatment included his doing those things that helped him to feel that his heart was into the changes.

Next, team members evaluated the compliments and client expressions in light of the goals for treatment. As in the first session, only those compliments and expressions believed to be related to these goals were retained.

- stayed on track for the week
- continues to get his priorities in order
- a man of action not just words
  -learns from experience
- wants to do the right thing
- starting to become a real family man
  -making these changes on his own
  -becoming a real "self-made" man
- has ideas how to maintain changes
  -remain alcohol-free
  -keep his daughter, wife in mind
  -keep his current happiness in mind
  -keep working at it
- realistic
  -not overconfident
  -knows there are going to be "ups" and "downs"
- willing to work
  -to maintain the changes
  -to make additional small changes
- know that it is important to have his heart in it
  -knows how to do this

- client expressions
  -keep working on it
  -hard work
  -little things
  -heart into it
  -halfway there

Team members then considered what type of homework task was appropriate. It was obvious to all that Mr. Meeks needed to work to maintain the gains he had made up to this point, so, once again, the team members decided to ask him to continue doing what he was doing that was working. Thereafter, in order to help Mr. Meeks feel that his heart was into the changes he had been making, the team decided to ask him to do the very things that he said would make him feel that way. The rationale for both tasks would be that he knew what he needed to do and, because his behavior over the last week obviously indicated that he was a man of action, that he simply needed to "do it!"

The therapist summarized the discussion in a brief, written message which was then read back to the team. The last topic considered was the scheduling of the next appointment. As considerable progress had been made between the first and second sessions, the team decided to set the next appointment for two weeks. The entire team meeting took only five minutes.

The Intervention Message

Therapist: The team is very impressed with how you have stayed on track and improved at being a good father and a helpful husband . . .

Client: Well, thank you, I'm working on it!

Th: . . . and a good family man. You've certainly managed to get your priorities in order and to, Mr. Meeks, keep your priorities in order. Now you are building the kind of life and family that you have always wanted to have. And it is particularly impressive because you are making these changes on your own! That is really a sign of a self-made man.

Cl: (smiles broadly)

Th: It's clear to us that you have the desire and the willingness to do what you need to in order to change your life, Mr. Meeks, and to continue with the changes you are making in your life.

Cl: (nods head affirmatively)

Th: . . . and this is not easy, it is damn hard work!

Cl: (agreeing) Yeah!

Th: So, first, what we would like you to do is to continue to do all the "little" things you need to do in order to stay on the track you are on.

Cl: Uh, huh.

Th: And then, because you know how important it is to have your heart into what you are doing, we want you to keep track, this week, of all the things you do that help you have that feeling and that move you toward a 6 on the scale . . . or even a 7!

Cl: Okay, I'll do it. Wow!

Th: And then, we would like to see you in . . . two weeks.
Cl: Two weeks, okay.

SESSIONS THREE, FOUR, AND FIVE

Mr. Meeks returned for his third appointment as scheduled, reporting continued improvement in his family life. In addition, he proudly related that he had not experienced any problems with alcohol. As in the previous session, a large amount of time was devoted to discussing the many positive changes that had taken place between sessions. Each reported difference was met with support and encouragement from the therapist and team. When eventually asked to rate his progress on a scale from 1 to 10, Mr. Meeks indicated that the maintenance of the many positive changes over the preceding two-week period led him to conclude that he had moved from a 5 to at least a $6^{1}/_{2}$ or a 7 on the scale. As he expressed the same high degree of confidence in his ability to continue with the changes as he had in the second session, the therapist and team merely asked him to "continue and even do more of what he was already doing that was working!" An appointment was set for one month.

In one month, Mr. Meeks returned. The session was very similar to the third session. Mr. Meeks shared new changes that had occurred since the prior session, which were greeted by support and encouragement from the therapist and team. The month-long period of success had resulted in a rating of "8" on the progress scale. When the therapist suggested that it would be nice to have "one additional appointment" just to review the progress that had been made, Mr. Meeks concurred. Spontaneously, he then suggested that he believed the next appointment could be set for two or three months in the future.

Mr. Meeks returned in three months for his fifth session. Prior to the session, the therapist and team had reviewed the videotapes of the four preceding sessions. Changes in Mr. Meek's appearance alone were impressive. However, dramatic differences were also noted in how he spoke about his family and his "prior" drinking problem. Most of the time in the session was devoted to "catching up" on the progress that had been made between sessions and reminiscing about prior sessions. Mr. Meeks expressed pleasure and satisfaction with the changes he had made while in treatment at the Center. When asked to rate his progress, Mr. Meeks placed himself at an 8 on the scale. He added that he did not expect things to be perfect (e.g., a 10) and expressed his belief that an 8 represented an acceptable amount of progress for him. As in the previous

sessions, he expressed a high degree of confidence in his ability to maintain the changes that had been made. For this reason, the therapist,
team, and Mr. Meeks agreed that treatment could be discontinued with
the proviso that Mr. Meeks could return at any time in the future to
either report on his progress or to deal with any difficulties.

SESSION SIX

About a year following his fifth session, Mr. Meeks contacted BFTC and
scheduled an appointment. While there had been no further treatment
sessions at the Center, one of the BFTC staff had learned indirectly —
through contact with Mr. Meeks's social worker-payee — that his family
life had continued to improve and that there had been no subsequent
episodes of problem drinking in the 12 months following the fifth session. In the same manner, it had been learned that Mr. Meeks was once
again in charge of his finances. Other than this, little was known about
his progress following termination or about his reason for seeking an
appointment.

Mr. Meeks arrived on time for his scheduled appointment and, with
the team members in place, the therapist began the session.

Th: Well, nice to see you!
Cl: (quietly) Thank you.
Th: How have you been?
Cl: (sadly) Uh, well? . . . first . . . a confession.
Th: Oh, okay.
Cl: Uh, I went on a little trip last week . . . taking some relatives who
    had been visiting for a couple of weeks to the airport in Chicago
    and . . . well, I had some drinks.
Th: Uh, huh.
Cl: Well, I was seeing them off . . . and I kinda got a little bit under
    the weather . . . you know, feeling kinda sorry for myself, and
    then I drank a little too much.

Mr. Meeks makes a straightforward and honest admission of a drinking episode. It is not uncommon for those clients who experience problems following successful treatment to quickly contact the Center and
schedule a follow-up appointment. Nor is it uncommon for these clients
to make similarly straightforward and honest admissions of the problem. We believe this is a result of the strong relationship that develops
between the therapist and client because of the overall positive, non-
blaming orientation of the model.

The discussion continued for a few more minutes with Mr. Meeks presenting the details of the drinking episode. After it appeared that Mr. Meeks had completed his "confession," the therapist helped to orient the conversation toward a solution-focus by asking:

Th: So, let me ask you then . . . a couple of things. How did you, uh, know to (emphasis here) stop drinking, Mr. Meeks?

Cl: Just by merely knowing that I was doing the wrong thing.

Th: Uh, huh. And what told you that it was the "wrong thing"?

Cl: Well, I knew very soon that it was bad for me . . . and then I couldn't drive home to be with my family because I had been drinking . . . so I knew it was bad for them, too.

Th: I see. So, this sounds different from other times . . .

Cl: (interrupting) Well, the drinking wasn't very much different. (laughs)

Th: (laughing) Oh, right!

Cl: But before, I didn't very much care whether it affected me or anybody else. But now, I know that my drinking do affect me *and* somebody else beside me, and it kinda makes me (disgusted expression) you know . . . and so, I said to myself, "You've had enough, now, come on, stop." And then, I did.

Th: Wow! And so, you thought about you and your family?

Cl: Uh, huh.

Th: . . . and that is one thing that helped you stop when you did?

Cl: Yeah! Now that I know it affects my own and other people's lives . . . well . . . it is just not like it was . . . and that helped me.

The event that Mr. Meeks presented in the initial minutes of the session as a failure is discussed in this last segment as a success! This is accomplished by the therapist focusing on how Mr. Meeks managed to bring the problem drinking episode to a successful conclusion *on his own*. Some popular treatment models might have continued to explore the problematic drinking episode in more detail — perhaps in an attempt to determine the cause of the relapse. However, in our experience, we have found such dialogue almost always less helpful than identifying and amplifying the positive and healthy steps the client has taken to recover his progress. Moreover, in most cases, it appears that the explanations generated from such discussions have more to do with theoretical tenets of the treatment model than with the behavior they purport to explain.

Not surprisingly, perhaps, Mr. Meeks relates the success in recovering his progress to his new awareness about the way that drinking affects his

family. This confirms the assumption, made by the team in the previous
sessions, that Mr. Meeks's goal for treatment was to improve his family
life and that changing his problem drinking was simply a means to that
end. The conversation continued.

Th: It sure sounds like you have turned this around into a learning expe-
     rience! Did thinking about your family help in any other ways?
Cl: Well, I know that without their friendship and without their care
     . . . well, I would really, uh, I don't know what I'd do . . .
Th: Uh, huh.
Cl: . . . and, I don't want to lose that now.
Th: I see, and so knowing that your wife and daughter care about you
     helped as well?
Cl: Yeah, and you know, they been telling me that quite a bit lately.
Th: Really!
Cl: Yeah, and even when I told her about what I done, my wife said to
     me, "Cal, I care . . . and I love you."
Th: Hmm. Was that different?
Cl: Oh yes! because I called her from the motel and confessed . . .
     and, well, in the past I would've never told her . . . or even called
     her . . . I would just stay away for a while and then when I did
     come home. . . . (shakes head from left to right)
Th: So that was really different! How did you know that calling her
     was the right thing to do?
Cl: I just want to keep things going the way they have been going . . .
     and so I called.
Th: I see. So calling her . . . that was one of the things you did that
     helped you to stop as quickly as you did?
Cl: Yeah, then I didn't feel as guilty as I would have and then just kept
     on with those drinks for who knows how long.

Here the therapist and client jointly identify additional ways in
which thinking about his family helped to bring the problem drinking
episode to an end. In the process, the therapist employs compliments
and "positive blame" to reinforce and empower the client. In the next
segment, the therapist expands the scope of the discussion by asking Mr.
Meeks what else he did, in addition to keeping his family in mind, that
contributed to his success.

Th: I see. Okay, so what else helped you get back on track and stay on
     track since then?
Cl: I just did it . . . just stayed on my toes.

Th: What helped you just "do it," to "stay on your toes" like you say?

Cl: Well, instead of just staying down there in Chicago and drinking
. . . I called, like I said, my wife and told her and then . . . the
next morning I came right home and . . . you know, had a little
talk with the wife and said, "I'm sorry" and everything . . .

Th: Uh, huh.

Cl: . . . and then, well . . . (puzzled) I've just been acting like I have
been . . . you know, for the last year.

Th: Oh, I see, so you just returned to doing what you have been doing.

Cl: Yeah.

Th: What kinds of things have you . . . because, you know, I haven't
seen you in a long time . . . what exactly have you been doing?

In this segment, the therapist asks Mr. Meeks to describe what he did
in addition to keeping his family in mind that helped him to "get back
on track." When his answer is vague, "I just did it," the therapist follows
up with a question that demands a more behaviorally explicit answer. In
response, Mr. Meeks repeats his earlier report of the difference in how
he handled the problematic drinking episode and adds in a matter-of-
fact manner that he has "just been doing it!" The therapist, however,
continues with the earlier attempt to broaden the description of the
factors that contributed to his success. The intention of such questions,
of course, is to identify and amplify a variety of strategies that clients
might have employed to recover their previous level of functioning.

This segment was followed by a lengthy discussion of the other ways
by which Mr. Meeks had managed to stop the drinking episode and
return to his previous level of functioning. At no time did the therapist
and client discuss what Mr. Meeks needed to avoid or *not* do in order to
stay on track or prevent future problems. Rather, in keeping with the
philosophy of the solution-focused model, the focus of the discussion
remained proactive in nature. After much discussion, the therapist began to question Mr. Meeks about how all of these factors he had identified would help him in the future.

Th: So, how do you suppose that all of these things are going to help
you from here on?

Cl: Well, it will help me from here on because when I'm almost into
moods where I want to do something . . . well, "bad" I will think
back and ask myself, "what good is it going to do me?"

Th: I see . . . and how will that help?

Cl: Well, like this last little, uh, problem . . . I, well, I did it . . . but I
stopped . . .

Th: (while client is speaking) Yeah!
Cl: . . . and I know that when I think about these things and do them, then I will feel better about myself.
Th: (curiously) Is that right?
Cl: (nods head affirmatively)
Th: What else? How else will these . . .
Cl: I guess what I've learned is that if I stumble and fall, hey, I shouldn't just lay there and cry, I should just get up and start over.
Th: Right!
Cl: (pointing to self) And . . . and I can do it!
Th: (laughs) I think you ought to write a book!
Cl: (smiles broadly, laughs)

In this last segment, Mr. Meeks is asked to connect his present efforts to the future. Mr. Meeks identifies what will be helpful should he experience similar problems at some future time. Again, the emphasis is placed on what actions Mr. Meeks needs to take in order to insure success as opposed to what he needs to avoid in order to avoid failure. The segment ends with Mr. Meeks spontaneously asserting that he "can do it." Obviously, this statement indicates that Mr. Meeks has been empowered by the discussion that has taken place up to this point.

In the next segment, the therapist follows up on Mr. Meeks's expression of confidence with a scaling question.

Th: Okay, so let me ask you one of those number-type questions again.
Cl: Okay.
Th: Say on that scale from 1 to 10, where a 10 means that you have all the confidence in the world that you can do it, and a 1 means, . . . well, hardly any confidence at all . . . where would you say you are on that scale that you can do it, Mr. Meeks?
Cl: (smiles, without hesitation) A 10!
Th: A 10? Really?!
Cl: Yeah, a 10. Because I know what I got to do and I just got to keep doing it.
Th: Right! Okay, now, would your wife and daughter . . . would they agree that you are at a 10?
Cl: Oh, yes, I think so . . . you know because I called and . . . since I been home things have, well, I been doing the things I was, you know, doing before.
Th: Uh, huh. I see, and so that is what makes them as confident as you are?
Cl: Yeah, (thinking) . . . and that I stopped so fast.

In the foregoing interchange, Mr. Meeks expresses a high degree of confidence in his ability to do what he needs to do in order to maintain the progress he has made and deal with any future problems. In the dialogue that followed this segment, Mr. Meeks indicated that he was also very willing to do these things as he believed they would lead to the outcome he originally desired and had, in many ways, already achieved — a vastly improved family life. The therapist and Mr. Meeks then talked about many of the positive changes that had taken place in his family life in the 12-month period between sessions. From this discussion, it was very clear why Mr. Meeks had been so discouraged and, perhaps, frightened by the drinking episode — the number and scope of the reported changes was staggering. To begin, his family life had improved dramatically. He talked affectionately about his relationship with his wife and daughter. In particular, he noted finally feeling like a "real father" to his daughter. Perhaps most astonishing, however, was that Mr. Meeks had enrolled in and been attending a state-sponsored job retraining program.

After considerable discussion about the many positive changes that had taken place over the last year, the therapist asked Mr. Meeks if there was any additional information he wanted to share before he took a moment and consulted with the team. When Mr. Meeks declined, the therapist ended the interview and joined the team behind the one-way mirror.

The Team Meeting

The format of the meeting behind the mirror was largely the same as in all of the previous sessions. That a client experiences difficulty in maintaining treatment gains is no special cause for alarm. As in the previous sessions, the focus is on solutions. In this instance, however, the solution being sought is how the client can recover his previous level of functioning and then maintain that level. The ability to do this may be due to the fact that in solution-focused therapy, in contrast to other models, no assumptions are made about the reasons for clients failing to maintain treatment progress. For this reason, when the therapist entered the team room there was no discussion about the treatment having been ineffective. Neither were there any suggestions that the person had not had enough treatment or that treatment must of necessity begin anew. Rather, upon entering the team room, the therapist was met with compliments and support by the team members, which immediately led to brainstorming possible compliments for the intervention message that would be delivered to Mr. Meeks. To do otherwise—in other words, to focus on what had caused the episode—would be tantamount to conducting an full-scale investigation of the barn door while the horse remains on the loose.

Together, the therapist and team generated the following list of compliments:

- immediately called and made an appointment
  -honest and straightforward
  -didn't wait
  -took action to solve his problem
  -stopped on his own
- turned the episode into a learning experience
- has priorities in order
  -knows what is important to him
  -good husband and father
- has over 12 months of success
- family obviously cares about him
  -strong family support
- knows what he needs to do
  -has already been doing it
- confident
- willing

As in the previous sessions, the team also compiled a list of the client's idiosyncratic verbal expressions that might be useful in individualizing the intervention message. The following expressions were noted:

- confession
- wants to be "real" father
- think about things first
- feel better about self
- just "do it"

After generating the list of compliments, the therapist and team began to discuss the treatment goal for the session. As in the previous sessions, all agreed that Mr. Meeks's goal for treatment remained the improvement of his family life. For Mr. Meeks, the attainment of this goal depended, in part, on his remaining free from problem drinking. Despite having been frightened by the drinking episode, the therapist and team members agreed that Mr. Meeks seemed confident in this respect. This, however, was only one part of what was needed in order for Mr. Meeks to reach his goal of an improved family life. Equally, and perhaps even more important was that Mr. Meeks continue with all of the other positive changes in his behavior that had resulted in the many improvements in his family life.

Following this discussion, team members evaluated the compliments and client expressions in light of the treatment goals. As in all of the previous sessions, only those compliments and expressions believed to be related to these goals were retained.

- immediately called and made an appointment
  -honest and straightforward
  -didn't wait
  -took action to solve his problem
- has priorities in order
  -knows what is important to him
  -likes the changes that have occurred in his family life
  -good husband and father
- family obviously cares about him
- knows what he needs to do
  -has already started doing those things again
- has over 12 months of success
- confident that he can do what he needs to do
- willing to do what he needs to do

- client expressions
  -wants to be "real" father
  -think about things first
  -feel better about self
  -just "do it"
  -stay on his toes

Team members then considered what type of homework task was appropriate. All agreed that the relationship existing between the therapist and Mr. Meeks was still a "customer-type" and, therefore, that it was appropriate to ask him to "do" something. As Mr. Meeks was aware of what he needed to do, the therapist and team decided to simply ask him to do what he knew he needed to do. Given that Mr. Meeks had experienced some recent difficulty, however, various team members suggested that the rationale for complying with the assignment should make mention of the "hard work" that it was likely to involve.

The last topic considered was whether or not to schedule another appointment. On this point, the team was split. Half of the team strongly believed that another appointment should be scheduled in a few weeks to follow up on the results of the session. However, the other half of the team argued that Mr. Meeks appeared very confident and, based on this, expressed the belief that scheduling another appointment might convey the wrong message; namely, that the team did not have confidence in Mr. Meeks. As the team could not agree whether to schedule another follow up appointment, it was agreed that the therapist would ask Mr. Meeks what he thought would be best. The team meeting was adjourned and the therapist returned to the treatment room to deliver the intervention message.

The Intervention Message

Therapist: We are all very impressed . . .

Client: (smiles) Thank you.

Th: . . . at how quickly you have been able to turn things around and get them on the right track . . . going in the direction that you want them to be going . . .

Cl: (nods head affirmatively)

Th: All of us, myself and the team, appreciated your honesty. You came right in and told us . . . no B.S.!

Cl: I would only hurt myself and my family if I didn't do that.

Th: Right! And I guess that is one of the other things that impressed us . . . and that is that you know what you want and you have your priorities in order!

Cl: (nods head affirmatively and smiles)

Th: For that reason, we all agree that you have learned a great deal from your recent experiences. You are clearly a very thoughtful person, Mr. Meeks, and once again, we can tell why your family cares about you as much as they obviously do both as a husband and a father. You seem to have found the right ideas for you . . . and you know what you need to do in order to be the "real" father that you want to be and have the type of family that you have been having.

Cl: (continues to nod head)

Th: Now, we don't think it is going to be easy. As before, it will take hard work and you will have to "stay on your toes," so to speak. But we believe, as you do, that you can "do it" just as you have been doing it for over a year now! So, what we would like you to do is to continue to do those things you know you need to do and that have led you to be so successful for the last year.

Cl: All right.

Following the delivery of the intervention message, both the therapist and Mr. Meeks stood and exited the therapy room. As they walked toward the reception area, the therapist asked Mr. Meeks what his thoughts were about the need for another appointment. Mr. Meeks indicated that he felt another appointment was not necessary. After all, he knew what he needed to do and was already doing it!

FOLLOW-UP

A year has passed since Mr. Meeks was last seen at BFTC. In that period, there have been no further requests for treatment. In a recent telephone interview conducted as part of one of the Center's ongoing outcome studies, Mr. Meeks indicated that he continued to maintain the progress he had achieved while in treatment. In addition, it was learned that Mr. Meeks had returned to work after successfully completing the state-sponsored job retraining program. He further reported that he was closer than ever before with his wife and child.

9

Square Peg in a Round Hole*

"I never seem to learn from my lack of mistakes."

— Former BFTC Client

"My therapist is like a girlfriend that I can't get rid of!"

— Former BFTC Client

JANET IS THE DIRECTOR OF A RESIDENTIAL treatment program for substance-abusing men in the city. She is a very dedicated, caring, and compassionate person and has a solid reputation in the community for her commitment to excellence. The treatment community and the residents generally have high regard for her and the program she operates. The residents in her program are usually limited to a six-month stay, during which time each person is expected to develop a plan for moving on to an independent living situation or to the next phase in his rehabilitation (e.g., job training, etc.).

Because of our ability to see cases on an emergency basis, and our willingness to try "unconventional" approaches with multi-treatment failure cases, Janet frequently refers what her staff regards as "difficult" cases. Janet referred Bob for treatment, relating that he had had numerous treatments without much success. By referring Bob, she hoped to break the repeated cycle of treatment failures.

Bob is a 22-year-old, white, single man who has drifted for the last five years since graduating from high school. Bob was "kicked out" of his parents' home shortly after graduating because of a substance abuse problem. He came from a stable working-class family background and saw himself as being different from the typical picture of a substance

*Insoo Kim Berg was the therapist for this case and Steve de Shazer was the team member.

188

abuser he saw in various programs in which he had participated. His boyish looks combined with a flair for humor and intelligence, caused people to initially warm up to Bob easily. It was readily obvious that Bob had the potential to do better than being a "street bum." His ability to "pull at your heart strings" endeared him to others, that is, until others were "hit for money" by Bob. People quickly became angry at being "fooled" and "manipulated" into doing favors for Bob.

At the time of the referral, Bob was on probation for setting fire to an apartment building of a drug dealer who cheated him in a deal. One of the many probation conditions was that he enter psychotherapy. He reported numerous treatment episodes for psychiatric problems and carried with him some serious diagnoses as well as a history of several suicide attempts for which he had been hospitalized several times. He reported that he had been on numerous medications, none of which, he claimed, were helpful. His substance abuse started in high school; he claimed he had taken "everything under the sun," and had received treatment in both inpatient and outpatient settings. Because of his obvious charm and ability to warm up to people, it was clear that Bob had managed to gain special favors among the helpers, including Janet.

Bob was seen for three sessions, during which he clearly tried to repeat his previous relationships with therapists. He expressed his desire to be "normal" like everyone else, his desire to have a stable relationship with a woman, and expressed his anger at his parents for "kicking me out." He was very comfortable in a therapy setting and knew all the right things to say. He articulated his objections to the strong religious overtones of A.A., which were his grounds for refusing to attend meetings. He made it clear how he hated the "shrinks" and being on medication. His ability to express his philosophical objections to the helping profession was impressive.

Since leaving home, he had lived with a girlfriend for a while, at other times "crashed" with friends, had been in and out of various treatment programs, and had spent time at the Rescue Missions during the cold weather. He found jobs easily, but when he earned enough money to meet his immediate needs, or when he became bored with the menial jobs he had, he would just walk out. Bob was allowed to visit his parents on special occasions such as holidays or special family gatherings, but he was not allowed to stay overnight. Even though his real desire was to live with his parents and to "save money," he acknowledged that he must "clean up my act first" before it could happen.

The assessment of our relationship with Bob was that we were hosting a "visitor," and that his commitment to treatment was marginal. It seemed that he was still waiting for "my turn to have it all" without being willing to work hard. These sessions were mainly devoted to finding ways to understand his thinking, becoming familiar with his "language," and his world view. At the same time, we cooperated with him by investigating his goals for therapy, his participation in the program, and his view of how a solution to his difficulties could happen.

One day we received an urgent phone call from Janet requesting an appointment for herself and Bob. The phone call was precipitated by Bob's walking out of his most recent job as a mail clerk only three hours after starting work. His explanation to Janet was that there were attractive young women at work and he felt too embarrassed to stay on the job. This was the "last straw" for Janet who felt that Bob walked out of jobs "too many times" with such flimsy excuses. This was the shortest period Bob stayed on a job in the "five months, two weeks and three days" of his stay in Janet's program. In view of the limited remaining time to bring about real changes with Bob, Janet became quite concerned that his stay in her program would be one more in his long strings of failures.

We had a number of options as to how to respond to Janet's request for service. Her phone call signaled to us that Janet was interested in negotiating a different type of help from us. Unlike her usual position of referring her client to an outside treatment facility when it was appropriate, she was requesting help for herself as a program director concerned about her client. We could meet with her alone and respond to her request for direct service. Our other option was to meet with both Janet and Bob to assess and intervene in their relationship directly.

We decided on the second option and asked to see them together as if they were a family unit. Our clinical hunch was right. As you will see in the following case narrative, Janet and Bob acted as if they were mother and son, with Janet being supportive and encouraging and at times nagging Bob into being productive in the program.

Fairly early in the session, Janet and Bob showed us what their relationship pattern was. Janet immediately worked very hard to soothe and convince Bob that staying in her program should be viewed *not* as a "penance" as Bob expressed, but rather, he should see it as a positive opportunity for him. Janet thought that Bob must do a "wonderful job" in interviewing for jobs, because he was able to get so many jobs. However, "something must happen after he starts working" because he usually quit after a week or two. Both agreed that the longest Bob stayed on any job was a month, and the three hours as a mail clerk was the shortest on a job. Janet also thought that Bob should get a job first, in order to gain some discipline and learn work habits before going to school as Bob thought he wanted to do. The initial therapeutic task was to assess what each person was willing to do to solve the problem.

The therapist began the session by asking Janet what prompted her to call for an appointment the day before the session. The therapist was curious about her perception of what was different about Bob's losing a job this time.

Therapist: What is different about Bob this time?

Bob: Nothing.

Janet: (laughing) I think there is. (to Bob) Maybe you are getting healthier. Even when you are drinking, there is more clarity. So, when you are straight, you are more clear about what the problems and issues are. I am hoping. (to the therapist) I see a lot of hope in Bob.

Therapist: Do you have as much hope for yourself as Janet does, Bob?

Bob: For me?

Therapist: Yes, for you. Do you have as much hope for yourself as Janet does for you?

Bob: No.

Therapist: So, she has more hope for you than you do for yourself? Where does she get the idea that you can do all this?

Bob: Probably because she hasn't been with me long enough.

Therapist: You mean five months and two weeks is not long enough?

Bob: My parents were with me for 17 years and they have no hope. I remember what my dad told me when I first tried to kill myself. He said, "You will never amount to anything and will never make as much money as I do. I will just have to be happy with your being a busboy."

Therapist: So, are you saying your parents are right and Janet is wrong? Who is right between the two; your parents who say there is no hope for you or Janet who says there is hope for you. Who is right?

Bob: I have no idea, Insoo, probably Janet, probably.

Therapist: Who do you want to be right, Janet or your parents?

Bob: It all depends. It depends on what I can get out of it.

Therapist: What do you mean?

Bob: It depends on what will make me happy. Will I be happy being a busboy and that's enough for me? Or do I want to go on and try to make something of myself.

Therapist: So, what do you think is good for you? Janet has an idea of what is good for you. What is your idea of what is good for you?

Bob: Umm . . . my idea is, at my age of 22, what Janet says will be good for me. But on paper. What she wrote down, it sounds good on paper.

Therapist: Okay . . . what about in reality? What is good for you in reality?

Bob: Yeah, that will be good for me, in reality, too.

The therapist decided to ignore Janet's reassuring stance with Bob and decided to focus on what needs to happen in the session in order for it to be productive. It was becoming clear that Janet was repeating the same patterns that many others had tried previously with Bob, without success. Not only was Bob engaged in a "visitor-type" relationship with us, but it was clear that he had had a similar relationship with Janet's program for over five months. He had been a passive participant with various treatment efforts. The therapist decided to shift the focus and start to assess his motivation for change that everyone wanted him to make, including us. The scaling questions would provide an accurate gauge for his willingness to take steps to change.

Therapist: Bob, let's say 10 means you believe that you have every chance of making it, that is, you will do whatever it takes to make something of yourself, and feel like you are a success. 10 means you have every chance of doing it and 1 means the opposite. Where would you put yourself today, between 1 and 10?

Bob: Today?

Therapist: Yeah, today.

Bob: I would say about 2.

Therapist: How about you, Janet?

Janet: I would say about 4½ today. There is a hope that it could be at 6, even 7 on some days, but not today.

Therapist: Bob, let's say that 10 means you will do anything to be at 6 or 7, where Janet says you are at sometimes, and 1 means ah . . . I will just sit and say I could take it or leave it.

Bob: I think that if I would do anything and still end up at 6 or 7, it sucks, man.

Janet: This is just today, Bob. (putting her arm around Bob)

Bob: Today, I will have to be wishy-washy and say I'm at 5.

Therapist: I appreciate your being honest, Bob. What about you, Janet; his willingness, motivation and wanting it badly, where would you put him today?

Janet: I guess I would say between 4 and 5. There is a willingness to want it.

Therapist: Well, I'm talking about his willingness to *do* it, to put up with the hassles, to stick with it even though he doesn't like it at times.

Janet: I think there is willingness. There is willingness to go out and get a job but there is no willingness to stick with it. So, I guess I'll have to say his willingness to stick with it is about 5. He needs to find tools that will enable him to stay on the job. But I think it is really hard for him.

The discussion then centered on Janet elaborating further about what a wonderful interview Bob must give to his potential employer, because he gets jobs easily, but how he also must stick with the job in order to learn the discipline of going to work on time, day after day. Janet further thought that after first learning the necessary discipline on the job, it would be best for Bob to return to school to increase his options for better jobs and to earn more money than the minimum wages he makes now. Bob flatly stated that he had no interest in returning to school. The therapist decided to focus on the disparity and inconsistency between Bob's perception of himself and others' perceptions of him.

Therapist: (to Janet) So, sounds like you see a lot more potential in Bob than he sees in himself.

Janet: I think I do.

Bob: Yeah, she does.

Therapist: Do other people tend to see more potential in you than you see in yourself?

Bob: Yeah, I always got that. In school, my report cards would say, Bob should live up to his potential and then I will get Cs and Bs. That kind of crap. The school psychologists, too, they thought I was crazy because I was always making jokes and stuff.

Therapist: So, everybody saw more in you than you saw in yourself. So, who is right? You or them?

Bob: I don't know, Insoo, I guess I will have to say, because it's so many against one, I will have to say they are right.

Therapist: Well, never mind the numbers. Are they right? Or are they seeing things that are not there? Are they deluding themselves, or are you deluding yourself? Who is right here? What is real here?

Bob: I think we both are deluding ourselves, Insoo.
Therapist: So, what's real here?
Bob: What's real is I have good days with it, and I have bad days with it.
Therapist: Are you conning them to think that you have a lot more potential than you really have, or are they conning you to make you believe that you have lot more potential than you really have? What's the deal here?
Bob: There is no way that I can con Janet because she has a lot more insight into people than others.

Strong words like "conning" were used deliberately to join Bob's "street language" and to make a point about how Bob has tried to convince other — and others have tried to convince Bob — of his potential. The pattern was becoming clear that the more others encouraged Bob, the easier it was for Bob to ignore them, which led to the others becoming frustrated with Bob and giving up. By making this pattern more explicit, it would be difficult for Janet and Bob to continue this pattern. Bob's view of himself needed to be challenged in a way that was easy for him to accept. The last remark about his inability to con Janet because of her expertise about people is viewed as positive.

Therapist: Are you conning yourself into believing that you don't have as much potential as you really do?
Bob: I think so.
Therapist: You do?
Bob: Yeah.

Bob is positioning himself as having to admit that others are right about him, that he has more potential that he is not using.

Therapist: So, you think it's more accurate to say that you are trying to con yourself into believing that you don't have as much potential as you really have, rather than trying to con other people.
Bob: Yeah, I think so.
Therapist: So, you do have a lot more potential than you believe yourself to have.
Bob: My potential is, I'm bright, I'm funny, um . . .
Therapist: How do you know this?
Bob: I am sure of this.

As we expected, it was much easier for Bob to accept that he was conning himself than to acknowledge that he was conning others. Repeated affirmation of this point makes it easier for the client to start to believe this himself. We find that simply asking "How do you know this?" is a powerful question that impacts the client in a way that is very empowering. In order to answer this question, the client must be able to provide some external evidence that tells him that he *knows*. Once Bob admitted that he had potential that he was hiding from everyone, he needed to be helped to articulate it with evidence. The next task for the therapist is to challenge Bob to channel this potential into productive use.

Therapist: So, what stops you from using this potential?
Bob: Umm . . . I think what stops me is the goal of what I want to achieve from that.
Therapist: You mean, you don't know what to do with this potential?
Bob: No. I don't know what the heck to do with it.
Therapist: So, what do you believe your real potential is good for?
Bob: Being comic relief. (laughter)

These questions opened up directions for the client to follow. As the therapist pursued the client's idea of what he wants to do with his potential, his relationship with the therapist was transforming into a complainant-type, that is, Bob now has a complaint of not knowing what to do with his potential.

Further exploration of what he is willing to do with his potential, whether to be a comedian, a disk jockey, have a T.V. show of his own, or whether to become a famous musician, led to his conclusion that they are just "pipe dreams."

Therapist: How badly do you want this? Where would you put your desire to do all this?
Bob: To use your number, I would say I'm at 3.
Therapist: Janet, what number would you say his desire is at to use his talent?
Janet: I would put it at high. He plays for friends, for the Serenity Club, for a funeral a couple of weeks ago, and he is trying to get hooked up with the church to play at mass. His desire is very high.
Therapist: So, what do you think it will take for Bob to translate his

desire into doing what he has to do? What do you think it will take
for him to do that?

Janet: I feel he will have to go to school. Maybe not. Maybe he'll just
have to get some experience. Ultimately, he will have to go to
school, though. He has to get through a crisis day successfully.

Therapist: How does that sound to you, Bob? Do you agree with that?

Bob: Yeah, I agree with that.

Therapist: So, how badly do you want to do what needs to be done?

Bob: Pretty bad. (pause) But then, we are talking desire or my actually
doing it? I'm not doing shit.

Therapist: So, do you want to do some "shit," to get ahead with your
life?

Bob: Yeah, I would. But, I think this is all superficial. We are not
talking about why I'm not doing it.

Bob's goals of what he wants to do with his potential have become a
bit more clear. The next task is to negotiate with Bob on how willing he
is to go through the difficult process of making the effort to succeed.
Bob's last comment came as a surprise to the therapist. The therapist
expected a great deal of insight into what interfered with Bob being
productive and was ready to discuss Bob's "real" reasons for not doing
what had to be done. However, what followed was not only a surprise,
but could have easily distracted the therapist, resulting in an analysis of
his prejudice and attitude toward the African-American men in the
program. Bob was signaling one more time he needed help with justify-
ing why he was not doing what he needed to do.

Therapist: I don't understand.

Bob: It's because where I'm living. Another group home. I don't belong
there. Man, everyone there is all into this stuff of "Yeah, I'm a
man, I'm a man" stuff. The macho stuff, everybody says "fuck
this, fuck that," "dog this, dog that," and man, the music sucks. It's
a culture shock. I can't stand their music. I tried to be macho and
didn't take a shower for a week. (laughs) I'm not talking about the
blacks I live with. The culture shock. "Motherfuck this, or motherfuck that," which I can't stand! (he looks disgusted)

Therapist: So, what will help you? What do you want to do?

Bob: I don't know.

Again it would have been easy to become distracted by Bob's attempt
to find excuses for not being able to do what he needed to do. The

therapist shifted the focus back to Bob's willingness to take steps to achieve his goal. One of the most effective methods of refocusing client initiative is to phrase the questions in a positive, affirmative manner.

Therapist: What will be good for you?
Bob: I could move out, just like that (snapping his fingers), but I'll be moving to a Rescue Mission and busing tables. That will be no change.
Therapist: So, what will be *good* for you?
Bob: What will be *good* for me?
Therapist: Yeah, what will be *good* for you?
Bob: I should move out of there. That will be good for me.
Therapist: So, what do you have to do so that you will do what is good for you?
Bob: What I have to do is, to work my balls off, save some money, and move out with someone to share the apartment with, it will take a lot of starting from the bottom, which is why I have a problem sticking with the jobs.
Therapist: What, you want to start from the middle?
Bob: Yeah, I do.
Therapist: So, what do you have to do so that you start at the bottom and stick with it until you move up to the middle? What do you have to do?
Bob: I have to punch out of work and do whatever turns me on.
Therapist: When you punch out of work, you mean. Okay, so, you know what you have to do. What happens if you decide *not* to do that?
Bob: Nothing.
Therapist: What do you mean, nothing?
Bob: I'll still be at Janet's program. I'll still be living there.

Bob tries one more time to test Janet's commitment to him and see if she is committed enough not to let him off the hook.

Janet: But you know, you can't do that. I can't keep you there indefinitely.
Bob: I know.
Therapist: You mean, Janet, Bob cannot stay there indefinitely?
Janet: No, we have to have a plan. I would hate to have him just move to another shelter or to a Rescue Mission again. I don't see how

that is going to help. He moved out once for a short period. Nothing great happened.

Therapist: Is it possible that you may be on the street for the next 25 or 30 years?

Bob: That's a possibility. It all depends on how I screw things up. It's a possibility.

Therapist: You have seen what other guys have done. Do you want that?

Bob: No.

Therapist: Are you *sure?*

Bob: Yeah, I'm sure. *No. I don't want that.*

Therapist: What do you want instead?

Bob: I want to be like everybody else . . . to be normal . . . have a place of my own, have a job, play my music, maybe have a woman.

At this point, the therapist took some time to consult with the team. We saw Janet's concern for Bob as a strength, but it also could potentially interfere with Bob's need to *do* what he needed to do, that is, to start with an entry-level job and stick with it long enough to develop a sense of competency and a feeling of success and move up to the middle position, like "everybody else." Janet needed to "back off" and allow Bob to agonize over his choices about how he wanted to use his talent. Janet was making a common mistake of seeing Bob as deficient in his ability to figure out what is good for him. Her solution was to present a program — stick with the minimum wage level jobs for a while, in order to learn the discipline of a job, then go to school, get a real job, save money, and so on. What Bob needed from her, instead, was help in clarifying what he was willing and interested in doing with his life. The therapist kept the focus on "What is good for you to do?" and "What do you have to do so that you can do what is good for you?"

His dream of finding a "cushy" job without working hard at it was unrealistic and, at some level, Bob was aware of this. We recognized that Bob was indeed a bright, articulate young man. We also realized that it was easy for helpers to give him encouragement and "pep talks," which clearly had not worked in the past. It also became clear that except for his vague dreams of "making it" in the entertainment world, Bob really did not know what he wanted to do. This certainly is a difficult question for any young person to answer without guidance. We believe that such decisions are commonly made through trial and error, through having had many small successes that teach a person about his interests as well as his talents. Bob had not stayed at a job long enough to figure out what he liked and did not like about various aspects of different jobs.

Because Janet is one of our professional colleagues who has earned our high regards for integrity and dedication to her work, she deserved a straightforward and helpful recommendation that would enhance her chance of success with Bob. At the same time Janet needed to "back off" from hovering over Bob in a maternal fashion. The following message was given to both of them at the end of the consultation break.

"Janet, the team's impression is that Bob is convinced that you are on his side. Even though you may have to insist that he take some steps in order to stay in the program, you are doing that out of respect for Bob's ability to do something about his life, not because you are being hard on him. So, when the time comes, either he takes steps to move out of your program to something better for himself, or he ends up in the Rescue Mission. We think that your insisting that he take positive steps is your way of respecting his ability and we also agree with your desire not to treat him like a little boy and not to coddle him, even though it may seem harsh to you. The team is impressed by your desire to do what is good for him.

"Bob, the team says you seem to believe your own con. You forget this is just a con job you are doing to yourself. At times, you forget because you've been doing it so long that you have come to believe your own con. The other, more unfortunate point, is that people have been trying to force you to fit your square peg into a round hole for a long time. Everyone has been trying to do that, including yourself.

"Since you know what you have to do, we suggest that you take some steps. The only way that we know you can stop believing in your own con is to do what you have to do. Also, your not trying to force yourself into a round hole is also doing what you have to do. So, we would like you to take some steps. Since you know what you have to do, we are not going to insult your intelligence by telling you what to do. You just have to *do* it. I want to see you again, Bob.

"Janet, we would like to keep you on call, just to get an idea from you about how well Bob is doing. Since Bob knows, and since he is convinced that you are on his side, that you are rooting for him, that you want him to make it in life, you may want to stop talking to him entirely about all this.

"Lastly for you, Bob, the team thinks you have a 50–50 chance of taking steps, the steps you know you have to take. Now, I'm not sure if I agree with that."

At this point the therapist was ready to end the session when Bob interrupted,

Bob: Wait a minute. Why would the team offer that kind of input? The 50–50 thing. Maybe they think, I will say, "I will show you?"
Therapist: I'm not sure, Bob. They just wanted to give their honest opinion.

The session ended at this point. The message delivered following the consultation break can be viewed as the summary of what transpired during the session. The interview started with many indications that Janet was more invested and was working harder than Bob was to insure Bob's success in life. Like numerous "helpers" before her, Janet had many good ideas on the best way Bob should approach the goals she set out for him. If it continued much longer, Janet's relationship with Bob was likely to end as many others had before her, including Bob's relationship with his parents. They all seemed to become angry and exasperated with him and then label him as hopeless, hostile, or as having not "hit bottom" yet. Many well-meaning people such as Janet are often misunderstood and are described as "enablers" or "codependents" who need serious treatment in order to detach.

We decided to try the simplest, easiest and least intrusive approach first. First, the dyad was complimented separately, each for their good intentions that were somehow misdirected.

Janet was reassured that her hard work with Bob had been accomplished, that is, he was convinced of her positive regard, her support and unconditional confidence in his ability to succeed. The second step in the message was the rationale for her need to detach and pull back from her intense investment in Bob's success. Detachment was labeled as respect and confidence for Bob's ability, thus, her continued hovering over him would be viewed as a lack of confidence and respect. This view allowed Janet a graceful way to detach.

Bob was also given a rationale of having confused himself by believing in his own con job, in addition to having failed to fit into a round hole. The team also refused to follow the previously failed attempt of showing him what he needed to do. Instead of seeing Bob as ignorant of what he needed to do, which he was able to easily excuse himself from, the team held him responsible for his own failure because he refused to do what he knew how to do.

It was clear from the beginning of the session that Janet was in a customer-type relationship, while Bob was a visitor. However, the relationship with Bob transformed into that of a customer and, therefore, both Janet and Bob were given a behavioral task. It was suggested that Janet be respectful of Bob's ability and discontinue her reminders to Bob. On the other hand, it was suggested that Bob *take some steps* in the direction of what was *good* for him. Notice that "what is *good*" for him was left vaguely defined.

Even though Bob set up an appointment for the following week, he canceled twice, saying he was working late. At one point, he requested a statement from the therapist indicating his participation in treatment for substance abuse. Reportedly the purpose of such a written statement was that he needed it to apply for a sheltered work program.

The follow-up information on Bob came from Janet when we met her at a meeting on other issues related to treatment service delivery. She reported that Bob moved out when his six-month stay was up and had been working since, at first, with a vocational rehabilitation program, and then in a sheltered training program. Bob frequently came around to visit Janet. The last such visit from Bob occurred about nine months after our session. It seemed that Bob had invited Janet out to lunch, which in itself was not unusual. What was unusual was that instead of asking Janet to pay for the lunch, Bob took the check and insisted on paying for Janet's lunch as well. She reported that she "nearly fell over" at the offer, which was a drastic turnaround for Bob. Besides this, she reported that Bob was doing well, he looked healthier, and he was working while currently sharing an apartment with another man. He occasionally sang at church services and played music with a group. Recently, he began to speak to high school students about the dangers of drugs and alcohol. It seems that Bob had gone far beyond taking those "first steps" in his progress towards living a more purposeful life and reaching his goal of being "normal."

Epilogue

IN MANY WAYS, WRITING A BOOK IS AN exercise in compromise. As we finish this book, we realize that we have managed to say a great deal about the use of the solution-focused model in the treatment of the problem drinker. At the same time, we are aware of many things that we have not been able to include.

At the beginning of the book, we indicated that our objective was to write a practical, step-by-step, "how to" book describing the process of solution-focused treatment of problem drinking. In particular, we wanted to detail the concepts and techniques we have found useful in the treatment of this challenging population. The "how to" described in this book flows from the basic belief we hold about our work with clients. Of course, we do not feel that our model is *the* final statement on the treatment of problem drinking. Nor is it the last word we wish to say on the application of this model to problem drinking. Rather, our hope is that the concepts and techniques presented herein will serve to introduce professionals who are confronted with problem drinking clients to a model designed to empower their clients.

The model of solution-focused therapy is an evolving one. Even during the writing and compilation of this book, it continued to change and adapt to meet the needs of individual clients with whom we were working. Initially, we attempted to incorporate these changes into the book. At some point, however, we had to stop this process and merely write about the model. As we continue to listen to our clients, the model will continue to grow, change, and evolve. In our travels, we have become aware of many professionals who are adapting the model to work in different cultures and in combination with different treatment models. This reaffirms our basic belief that there are many paths to solutions and that the solution-focused model is but one of these.

References

Aiken, L. S., LoSciuto, L. A., & Ausetts, M. A. (1984). Paraprofessional versus professional drug counselors: The progress of clients in treatment. *International Journal of Addiction, 19*, 383–401.

Alcoholics Anonymous (1939). *The story of how more than one hundred men have recovered from alcoholism*. New York: Works Publishing Company.

Alcoholics Anonymous (1976). *The story of how many thousands of men and women have recovered from alcoholism*. New York: Alcoholics Anonymous World Services.

Alcoholics Anonymous (1987). *Alcoholics Anonymous surveys its membership: A demographic report*. New York: Alcoholics Anonymous World Services.

Amatea, E. S. (1989). *Brief strategic intervention for school behavior problems*. San Francisco: Jossey-Bass.

Andersen, T. (1990). The reflecting team: Dialogue and metadialogue in clinical work. *Family Process, 26*(4), 415–428.

Anderson, D. (1987). If he keeps this up, he'll die . . . soon. *Family Therapy Networker, 11*(4), 38–41.

Anderson, H., & Goolishian, H. (1988). A view of human systems as linguistic systems: Preliminary and evolving ideas about the implications for clinical theory. *Family Process, 27*(4), 371–393.

Annis, H. M. (1982). *Inventory of Drinking Situations (IDS-100)*. Toronto: Addiction Research Foundation of Ontario.

Annis, H. M. (1986). A relapse prevention model for treatment of alcoholics. In W. R. Miller & N. Heather (Eds.), *Treating addictive behaviors: Processes of change*. New York: Plenum.

Annis, H. M., & Davis, C. S. (1989). Relapse prevention. In R. K. Hester & W. R. Miller (Eds.), *Handbook of alcoholism treatment approaches*. New York: Pergamon Press.

Annis, H. M., Graham, J. M., & Davis, C. S. (1987). *Inventory of Drinking Situations (IDS) user's guide*. Toronto: Addiction Research Foundation of Ontario.

Armor, D. J., Polich, J. M., & Stambul, H. B. (1978). *Alcoholism and treatment*. New York: Wiley.

Bailey, M. B., & Stewart, J. (1966). Normal drinking by persons reporting previous problem drinking. *Quarterly Journal of Studies on Alcohol, 27*, 30–41.

Barcha, R., Stewart, M. A., & Guze, S. B. (1968). The prevalence of alcoholism among general hospital ward patients. *American Journal of Psychiatry, 125*, 681–684.

Beattie, M. (1986). *Denial*. Center City, MN: Hazelden.

Beattie, M. (1987). *Codependent no more*. Center City, MN: Hazelden.

Beattie, M. (1989). *Beyond codependency and getting better all the time*. San Francisco: Harper/Hazelden.

Beers, C. (1908/1940). *A mind that found itself: An autobiography*. New York: Doubleday.

Berg, I. K. (1988a). Couple therapy with one person or two. In E. Nunnally & K. Chilman (Eds.), *The families in trouble* (Vol. 3, pp. 30–54). Newbury Park, CA: Sage Publications.

Berg, I. K. (October, 1988b). Alternative treatment of addiction (6 tapes). Presentation to the Milton H. Erickson Foundation of Colorado. Boulder, CO.

Berg, I. K. (1989). Of visitors, complainants, and customers: Is there really such thing as resistance? *Family Therapy Networker, 13*(1), 21.

Berg, I. K. (1991). *Family preservation: A brief therapy workbook*. London: BT Press.

Berg, I. K., & Gilkey, J. (in press). Different and same: Family therapy with Asian-American families. *Journal of Marital and Family Therapy*.

Berg, I. K., & Gallagher, D. (1991). Solution focused brief treatment with adolescent substance abusers. In T. Todd & M. Selekman (Eds.), *Family therapy approaches with adolescent substance abusers*. Boston: Allyn & Bacon.

Black, C. (1987). *It will never happen to me*. New York: Ballantine.

Bloom, B. L. (1981). Focused single-session therapy: Initial development and evaluation. In S. H. Budman (Ed.), *Forms of brief therapy*. New York: Guilford.

Boscolo, L., Cecchin, G., Hoffman, L., & Penn, P. (1987). *Milan systemic family therapy: Conversations in theory and practice*. New York: Basic Books.

Bratter, T. E., & Forrest, G. G. (1985). *Alcoholism and substance abuse: Strategies for clinical intervention*. New York: Free Press.

Budman, S. H., & Gurman, A. S. (1988). *Theory and practice of brief therapy*. New York: Guilford.

Cartwright, A. (1981). Are different therapeutic perspectives important in the treatment of alcoholism? *British Journal of Addictions, 76*, 347–361.

Cox, F. M., Chilman, C. S., & Nunnally, E. W. (1989). *Mental illness, delinquency, addictions and neglect*. Newbury Park, CA: Sage Publications.

Cummings, N. A. (1977). Prolonged (ideal) versus short-term (realistic) psychotherapy. *Professional Psychology, 8*, 491–505.

Cummings, N. A. (1986). The dismantling of our health system. *American Psychologist, 41*(4), 426–431.

Cummings, N. A. (1988). Emergence of the mental health complex: Adaptive and maladaptive responses. *Professional Psychology, 19*(3), 308–315.

Cummings, N. A., Dorken, H., Pallack, M., & Henke, C. (1990). *The impact of psychological intervention on healthcare utilization and costs.* San Francisco: Biodyne Corporation.

Cummings, N. A., & VandenBos, G. (1979). The general practice of psychology. *Professional Psychology, 10,* 430–440.

DeAngelis, T. (1987). Short-term therapy is "magical" choice for many patients. *APA Monitor, 18*(8), 34.

de Shazer, S. (1982). *Patterns of brief family therapy.* New York: Guilford.

de Shazer, S. (1985). *Keys to solution in brief therapy.* New York: W. W. Norton.

de Shazer, S. (1986). An indirect approach to brief therapy. In S. de Shazer & R. Kral (Eds.), *Indirect approaches in therapy.* Rockville, MD: Aspen.

de Shazer, S. (1988). *Clues: Investigating solutions in brief therapy.* New York: W. W. Norton.

de Shazer, S. (1991). *Putting difference to work.* New York: W. W. Norton.

de Shazer, S., & Berg, I. K. (in press). Doing therapy: A post-structural revision. *Journal of Marital and Family Therapy.*

de Shazer, S., Berg, I. K., Lipchik, E., Nunnally, E., Molnar, A., Gingerich, W., & Weiner-Davis, M. (1986). Brief therapy: Focused solution development. *Family Process, 25*(2), 201–211.

Dolan, Y. (1991). *Resolving sexual abuse.* New York: W. W. Norton.

Efran, J. S., Lukens, M. D., & Lukens, R. J. (1988). Cultivating simple-mindedness: An antidote for complexity. *The Family Therapy Networker, 12*(2), 17–18.

Efran, J. S., Lukens, M. D., & Lukens, R. J. (1990). *Language, structure, and change.* New York: W. W. Norton.

Erickson, M. H. (1959). Further clinical techniques of hypnosis: Utilization techniques. *American Journal of Clinical Hypnosis, 2*(1), 3–21.

Erickson, M. H. (1965). The use of symptoms as an integral part of hypnotherapy. *American Journal of Hypnosis, 8,* 57–65.

Erickson, M. H., & Rossi, E. L. (1973). From a taped dialogue. In E. Rossi (Ed.), *The collected papers of Milton H. Erickson* (vol. 4). New York: Irvington.

Erickson, M. H., & Rossi, E. L. (1979). *Hypnotherapy: An exploratory casebook.* New York: Irvington.

Fingarette, H. (1988). *Heavy drinking: The myth of alcoholism as a disease.* Los Angeles: The University of California Press.

Fisch, R., Weakland, J. H., & Segal, L. (1982). *The tactics of change.* San Francisco: Jossey-Bass.

Forman, R. (1987). Circle of care: Confronting the alcoholic's denial. *The Family Therapy Networker, 11*(4), 35–41.

Frank, R. G., & Kamlet, M. S. (1985). Direct costs and expenditures for mental health care in the United States in 1980. *Hospital and Community Psychiatry, 36*(2), 165–168.

Garfield, S. L. (1971). Research on client variables in psychotherapy. In A. E. Bergin & S. L. Garfield (Eds.), *Handbook of psychotherapy and behavior change.* New York: Wiley.

Garfield, S. L. (1986). Research on client variables in psychotherapy. In S. L. Garfield & A. E. Bergin (Eds.), *Handbook of psychotherapy and behavior change*. New York: Wiley.

Garfield, S. L. (1989). *The practice of brief psychotherapy*. New York: Pergamon Press.

Garfield, S. L., & Bergin, A. E. (1986). *Handbook of psychotherapy and behavior change*. New York: Wiley.

Garfield, S. L., & Kurtz, M. (1952). Evaluation of treatment and related procedures in 1216 cases referred to a mental hygiene clinic. *Psychiatric Quarterly, 26*, 414–424.

Goodwin, D. W., Crane, J. B., & Guze, S. B. (1971). Felons who drink: An eight year follow-up. *Quarterly Journal of Studies on Alcohol, 32*, 136–147.

Gordon, D., & Myers-Anderson, M. (1981). *Phoenix: Therapeutic patterns of Milton H. Erickson*. Cupertino, CA: Meta Publications.

Gottheil, E. et al. (1982). Follow-up of abstinent and non-abstinent alcoholics. *American Journal of Psychiatry, 139*, 564.

Haley, J. (1967). *Advanced techniques of hypnosis and therapy: Selected papers of Milton Erickson*. Cupertino, CA: Meta Publications.

Haley, J. (1987). *Problem solving therapy (2nd ed.)*. San Francisco: Jossey-Bass.

Heather, N., & Robinson, I. (1985). *Controlled drinking*. London: Methuen.

Helzer, J. E., Robins, L. N., Taylor, J. R., Carey, K., Miller, R. H., Combs-Orme, T., & Farmer, A. (1985). The extent of long-term drinking among alcoholics discharged from medical and psychiatric facilities. *New England Journal of Medicine, 312*, 1678–1682.

Hester, R., & Miller, W. (1989). *Handbook of alcoholism treatment approaches: Effective alternatives*. New York: Pergamon Press.

Holden, C. (1986). Alcohol consumption down, research up [Letter to the editor]. *Science, 198*, 773.

Holden, C. (1987). Is alcoholism treatment effective? *Science, 236*, 20–22.

Horney, K. (1937). *The neurotic personality of our time*. New York: W. W. Norton.

Howard, K. I., Kopta, S. M., Krause, M. S., & Orlinsky, D. E. (1986). The dose-effect relationship in psychotherapy. *American Psychologist, 41*, 159–164.

Institute of Medicine (1990). *Broadening the base of treatment for alcohol problems*. Washington, DC: United States Government Printing Office.

Johnson, V. (1973). *I'll quit tomorrow*. New York: Harper & Row.

Johnson, V. (1986). *Intervention: How to help someone who doesn't want help*. Minneapolis, MN: Johnson Institute Books.

Joint Commission on Mental Illness and Health (1961). *Action for mental health*. New York: Basic Books.

Kamerow, D. B., Pincus, H. A., & Macdonald, D. I. (1986). Alcohol abuse, other drug abuse and mental disorders in medical practice. *Journal of the American Medical Association, 255*(15), 2054–2057.

Kendall, R. E., & Stanton, M. D. (1966). The fate of untreated alcoholics. *Quarterly Journal of Studies on Alcohol, 27*, 30–41.

Kiser, D. J. (1988). A Follow-up Study Conducted at The Brief Family Therapy Center of Milwaukee, Wisconsin (unpublished).

Kiser, D. J. (1990). Brief therapy on the couch. [Letter to the editor]. *Family Therapy Networker, 14*(4), 7.

Kiser, D. J., & Nunnally, E. (1988). The relationship between treatment length and goal achievement in solution-focused therapy. (Unpublished study conducted at BFTC, Milwaukee, WI)

Kissin, B., Rosenblatt, S. M., & Machover, K. (1968). Prognostic factors in alcoholism. *American Psychiatric Association Research Reports, 24*, 22–43.

Kogan, L. S. (1957a). The short-term case in a family agency. Part I. The study plan. *Social Casework, 38*, 231–238.

Kogan, L. S. (1957b). The short-term case in a family agency. Part II. Results of study. *Social Casework, 38*, 296–302.

Kogan, L. S. (1957c). The short-term case in a family agency. Part III. Further results and conclusions. *Social Casework, 38*, 366–374.

Koss, M., & Butcher, J. N. (1986). Research on brief psychotherapy. In S. L. Garfield & A. E. Bergin (Eds.), *Handbook of psychotherapy and behavior change.* New York: Wiley.

Kral, R. (1986). Indirect therapy in the schools. In S. de Shazer & R. Kral (Eds.), *Indirect approaches in therapy.* Rockville, MD: Aspen Publishers.

Kral, R. (1988). *Strategies that work.* Milwaukee, WI: Author.

Kral, R., & Kowalski, K. (1989). After the miracle: The second stage in solution focused brief therapy. *Journal of Strategic and Systemic Therapies, 8*(2 & 3), 73–76.

Kral, R., & Schaffer, J. (1989). *Creating relationships in adoption.* Milwaukee, WI: Milwaukee County Social Services.

Lawson, G. (1982). Relation of counselor traits to evaluation of the counseling relationship by alcoholics. *Journal of Studies on Alcohol, 43*, 834–838.

Madanes, C. (1984a). *Behind the one-way mirror: Advances in the practice of strategic therapy.* San Francisco: Jossey-Bass.

Madanes, C. (1984b). *Strategic family therapy.* San Francisco: Jossey-Bass.

Marlatt, G. A. (1980). Determinants of relapse and skill training interventions. In G. A. Marlatt & J. R. Gordon (Eds.), *Relapse prevention: Maintenance strategies in the treatment of addictive behaviors.* New York: Guilford.

Marlatt, G. A., & George, W. H. (1984). Relapse prevention: Introduction and overview of the model. *British Journal of Addiction, 79*, 261–273.

Marlatt, G. A., & Gordon, J. R. (1980). Determinants of relapse: Implications for the maintenance of behavior change. In P. O. Davidson & S. M. Davidson (Eds.), *Behavioral medicine: Changing health lifestyles.* New York: Brunner/Mazel.

Marlatt, G. A., & Gordon, J. (Eds.) (1985). *Relapse prevention.* New York: Guilford.

Maslow, A. (1976). *The farther reaches of human nature.* New York: Penguin.

Mead, G. H. (1934). *Mind, self and society.* Chicago, IL: University of Chicago Press.

Metzger, L. (1988). *From denial to recovery.* San Francisco: Jossey-Bass.

Miller, W. (1985). Motivation for treatment: A review with special emphasis on alcoholism. *Psychological Bulletin, 98*(1), 84–107.

Miller, S. (in press). The symptoms of solution. *The Journal of Strategic and Systemic Therapies.*

Miller, W., & Hester, R. (1986). Inpatient alcoholism treatment: Who benefits? *American Psychologist, 41*(7), 794–805.

Miller, S. D., & Berg, I. K. (1991). Working with the problem drinker: A solution-focused approach. *Arizona Counseling Journal, 16*.

Molnar, A., & de Shazer, S. (1987). Solution-focused therapy: Toward the iden-
    tification of therapeutic tasks. *Journal of Marital and Family Therapy,*
    13(4), 359–363.
Molnar, A., & Lindquist, B. (1990). *Changing problem behavior in schools.* San
    Francisco: Jossey-Bass.
Mosher, V., Davis, J., Mulligan, D., & Iber, F. (1975). Comparison of outcome
    in a 9-day and 30-day alcoholism treatment program. *Journal of Studies on*
    Alcohol, 36(9), 1277–1280.
Noonan, R. J. (1973). A follow-up of psychotherapy dropouts. *Journal of Com-*
    munity Psychology, 1, 43–45.
Norton, R. (1982). *Communicator style: Theory, application and measures.*
    Beverly Hills, CA: Sage Publications.
O'Hanlon, W. H., & Hexum, A. L. (1990). *An uncommon casebook: The complete*
    clinical work of Milton H. Erickson, M.D. New York: W. W. Norton.
O'Hanlon, W., & Wilk, J. (1987). *Shifting contexts: The generation of effective*
    psychotherapy. New York: Guilford.
Papp, P. (1980). The Greek chorus and other techniques of paradoxical therapy.
    Family Process, 19(1), 45–57.
Peele, S. (1986). The implication and limitations of genetic models of alcohol-
    ism and other addictions. *Journal of Studies on Alcohol, 47,* 63–73.
Peele, S. (1989). *The diseasing of America.* Lexington, MA: Lexington Books.
Penn, P. (1985). Feed-forward: Future questions, future maps. *Family Process,*
    24(3), 299–310.
Polich, J. M., Armor, D. J., & Braiker, H. B. (1981). *The course of alcoholism:*
    Four years after treatment. New York: Wiley.
Rabkin, R. (1983). *Strategic psychotherapy.* New York: Meridian.
Reps, P. (Ed.) (1957). *Zen flesh, Zen bones: A collection of Zen and pre-Zen*
    writing. Rutland, VT: Charles E. Tuttle Co.
Rosen, S. (Ed.) (1982). *My voice will go with you.* New York: W. W. Norton.
Rossi, E. L. (1973). Psychological shocks and creative moments in psychother-
    apy. *American Journal of Clinical Hypnosis, 16*(1), 9–22.
Rossi, E. (1980). *The collected works of Milton H. Erickson. Vol. IV: Innova-*
    tive hypnotherapy. New York: Irvington.
Rush, B. R., & Ogborne, A. C. (1986). Acceptability of non-abstinence treat-
    ment goals among alcoholism treatment programs. *Journal of Studies on*
    Alcohol, 47, 146–149.
Sanchez-Craig, M., Annis, H. M., Bornet, A. R., & McDonald, K. R. (1984).
    Random assignment to abstinence and controlled drinking: Evaluation of
    cognitive-behavioral program to problem drinkers. *Journal of Consulting*
    and Clinical Psychology, 52: 390–403, 1984.
Selvini Palazzoli, M., Boscolo, L., Cecchin, G., & Prata, G. (1980). Hypothe-
    sizing-circularity-neutrality: Three guidelines for the conductor of the ses-
    sion. *Family Process, 19*(1), 3–12.
Shulman, M. E. (1988). Cost containment in clinical psychology: Critique of
    Biodyne and the HMO's. *Professional Psychology, 19*(3), 298–307.
Smart, R. G. (1975/1976). Spontaneous recovery in alcoholics: A review and
    analysis of the available research. *Drug and Alcohol Dependence, 1,* 277–
    285.
Smith, M. L., Glass, G. V., & Miller, T. I. (1980). *The benefits of psychother-*
    apy. Baltimore, MD: Johns Hopkins University Press.

Spiegel, H., & Linn, L. (1969). The "ripple effect" following adjunct hypnosis in analytic psychotherapy. *American Journal of Psychiatry, 126*, 53-58.

Sullivan, H. S. (1952). *The interpersonal theory of psychiatry.* New York: W. W. Norton.

Sullivan, H. S. (1954). *The psychiatric interview.* New York: W. W. Norton.

Super, D. E. (1980). From vocational guidance to counseling psychology. In J. M. Whiteley (Ed.), *The history of counseling psychology.* Monterey, CA: Brooks/Cole.

Talmon, M. (1990). *Single session therapy: Maximizing the effect of the first (and often only) therapeutic encounter.* San Francisco: Jossey-Bass.

Tomm, K. (1987a). Interventive interviewing. Part I. Strategizing as a fourth guideline for the therapist. *Family Process, 26*(1), 3-13.

Tomm, K. (1987b). Interventive interviewing. Part II. Reflexive questioning as means for the therapist to enable self-healing. *Family Process, 26*(2), 167-183.

Treadway, D. (1987). The ties that bind. *Family Therapy Networker,* July-August, 18.

Tzu, Lao (1963). *Tao te ching* (D. C. Lau, Trans.). New York: Penguin.

Vaillant, G. E. (1983). *The natural history of alcoholism: Causes, patterns, and path to recovery.* Cambridge, MA: Harvard University Press.

Vaillant, G. E., & Milofsky, E. S. (1982). The etiology of alcoholism: A prospective viewpoint. *American Psychologist, 37*, 494-503.

Wallerstein, R. S. (1986). *Forty-two lives in treatment: A study of psychoanalysis and psychotherapy.* New York: Guilford.

Wallerstein, R. S. (1989). The psychotherapy research project of the Menninger Foundation: An overview. *Journal of Consulting and Clinical Psychology, 57*(2), 195-205.

Watzlawick, P. (1976). *How real is real?* New York: Random House.

Watzlawick, P. (Ed.) (1984). *The invented reality.* New York: W. W. Norton.

Watzlawick, P., Weakland, J., & Fisch, R. (1974). *Change: Principles of problem formation and problem resolution.* New York: W. W. Norton.

Weakland, J. (1991, June). MRI brief therapy—conversational and strategic. Presentation at the Conference on Therapeutic Conversations, Tulsa, Oklahoma.

Weeks, G. (Ed.) (1991). *Promoting change through paradoxical therapy* (rev. ed.). New York: Brunner/Mazel.

Weiner-Davis, M., de Shazer, S., & Gingerich, W. J. (1987). Building on pretreatment changes to construct the therapeutic solution: An exploratory study. *Journal of Marital and Family Therapy, 13*(4), 359-363.

Weisner, C. M., & Room, R. (1984). Financing and ideology in alcohol treatment. *Social Problems, 32*, 167-184.

Whiteley, J. M. (Ed.) (1980). *The history of counseling psychology.* Monterey, CA: Brooks/Cole.

Winnokur, J. (1989). *Zen to go.* New York: New American Library.

Zeig, J. K. (Ed.) (1980). *A teaching seminar with Milton H. Erickson, M. D.* New York: Brunner/Mazel.

Zeig, J. K. (Ed.) (1985). *Ericksonian psychotherapy. Volume I: Structures.* New York: Brunner/Mazel.

Zweben, A., Perlman, S., & Li, S. (1988). A comparison of brief advice and conjoint therapy in the treatment of alcohol abuse: The results of marital systems study. *British Journal of Addiction,* February.

Index